C000130737

DONALD MICHIE
on Machine Intelligence, Biology and More

Compiled and edited by
ASHWIN SRINIVASAN

With contributions to the Foreword by
I. J. GOOD
J. D. BIGGERS
C. A. SAMMUT
S. H. MUGGLETON

OXFORD
UNIVERSITY PRESS

OXFORD

UNIVERSITY PRESS

Great Clarendon Street, Oxford ox2 6DP

Oxford University Press is a department of the University of Oxford.
It furthers the University's objective of excellence in research, scholarship,
and education by publishing worldwide in
Oxford New York

Athens Auckland Bangkok Bogotá Buenos Aires Cape Town
Chennai Dar es Salaam Delhi Florence Hong Kong Istanbul Karachi
Kolkata Kuala Lumpur Madrid Melbourne Mexico City Mumbai Nairobi
Paris São Paulo Shanghai Singapore Taipei Tokyo Toronto Warsaw
with associated companies in Berlin Ibadan

Oxford is a registered trade mark of Oxford University Press
in the UK and in certain other countries

Published in the United States
by Oxford University Press Inc., New York

© Ashwin Srinivasan, 2009

The moral rights of the author have been asserted

All ⟨…⟩ ⟨…⟩ be reproduced,
stored ⟨…⟩ ⟨…⟩ transmitted, in any form or by any means,
wit⟨…⟩
or as ex⟨…⟩ ⟨…⟩ under terms agreed with the appropriate
repr⟨…⟩ ⟨…⟩ on
outsi⟨…⟩ ⟨…⟩ nt,

LANCASHIRE
COUNTY LIBRARY

1137000102	
Askews	
Cℓℓ 1/10	

Library of Congress Cataloging-in-Publication Data

Michie, Donald.
On machine intelligence, biology, and more / Donald Michie;
compiled and edited by Ashwin Srinivasan; with contributions to
the foreword by I.J. Good ... [et al.].
p. cm.
Includes bibliographical references and index.
ISBN 978–0–19–957304–2 (hardback : alk. paper)
1. Artificial intelligence. 2. Biology. I. Srinivasan, Ashwin. II. Title.
Q335.M483 2009
006.3–dc22 2009028487

Typeset by SPI Publisher Services, Pondicherry, India
Printed in Great Britain
on acid-free paper by
Clays Ltd, St Ives plc.

ISBN 978–0–19–957304–2

1 3 5 7 9 10 8 6 4 2

For DM

To strive, to seek, to find, and not to yield.

Editor's Note

'What is the greatest miracle of all?' asks a demi-god, in the Indian epic the *Mahabharata*. Yudhishthira, Prince of Righteousness and future King of the World, replies: 'Every day people are born and people die. Yet we wake up thinking we are immortal.' And so it was that I, along with many others I'm sure, expected Donald Michie to be alive today. Yet there is a kind of immortality, reserved for those who see beyond the present and have the energy to chart a path to new horizons. Many of us, who had the privilege of being part, even as deckhands, on Donald Michie's team will long tell his stories and continue to be guided by answers to 'What would DM have done?'

What then of this particular book? I would like to think of it as telling a story of the many facets of Donald Michie's extraordinary life. But how does one tell the story of a would-be classicist, cryptographer, biologist, computer scientist, and humanist? I have chosen to do it through his essays and interviews, that are, whenever possible, of a non-technical nature. There are other ways of course. Some would have picked seminal papers. Others, with more courage, would have written a biographical account. I wanted a readable story that would bring out not just his insights, but also some of his own humorous style. In cases where I could not find non-technical descriptions, I have resorted to an edited version of a technical paper. In all cases, I have selected material already published, but which I found unusual, in the hope of being able to interest more than just his friends and colleagues. But the combination of tributes in the Foreword and the introductory notes in each section will give readers a glimpse of some of the other ways in which this book could have been written.

It is inevitable that a collection like this will not be to everyone's taste. Some may feel that by leaving out many of his technical papers, I could not possibly bring out the true nature of Donald Michie's contributions. Others will find their special favourites missing. I myself am keenly aware that I do not have anything here that captures his great love of poetry. There is also nothing here that brings out the nature of a man who loved playing the villain in family Christmas pantomimes, a humanist deeply concerned about the state of the planet, an enthusiastic pasta maker, a squash player who practised with the best professional in the land just to be able to beat his brother (only to find, much to his consternation, that he could for a long time beat all others but him!), an optimist who learned to treat triumph and disaster the same, or a famous scientist who really believed young researchers to be his colleagues. These are stories that will just have to be told, not written.

A. S.

Contents

Foreword

Donald and Bletchley*

Irving John (Jack) Good

Department of Statistics, Virginia Tech

Donald Michie was my best friend from 1943 when we both worked on cryptanalysis against enemy ciphers at Bletchley Park (BP) in World War (WW) II, exchanging confidences as if each were the father confessor of the other.

To be more specific regarding how we met, let's go back a few years. (Not so far back as to invoke the 'flybutter' effect, the butterfly effect with causes reversed in time so to speak.)

There was a non-secret enciphering machine, the Enigma, invented in the 1930s by Scherbius, and used commercially by banks. The German military, in WW II, used an Enigma which had an additional plugboard, or Steckerboard, which gave it enormously greater security. The original cryptanalytic break into the German military use of the Enigma was made by a Polish mathematician

---

* In September 2008, Jack Good, then 91, fell and injured himself. He subsequently suffered a heart attack and several strokes that left him precariously unwell and unable to resume active work (he died on 5 April 2009). This document—a slightly edited version of almost certainly the last thing he wrote—is unfinished, as will be apparent from those familiar with Good's attention to perfection in his writings. That we have this write-up at all is largely due to the efforts of Leslie Pendleton.

named Marian Rejewski in the 1930s. He was helped by information from Colonel Bertrand of the French Secret Service.

In addition, the German military used at least two kinds of teleprinter machines, the Z42 (Tunny) and the T52 (Sturgeon). Both kinds of machine, Tunny and Sturgeon, contained rotatable wheels. If the wheels had not rotated the machines would have merely produced simple substitutions. The wheels in the Enigmas were each wired from one face to the other face, while in the teleprinter machines each wheel had notches, representing 'dots and crosses' or 'zeros and ones,' round the circumference. In the enigma a 'plain language' letter would be represented by an electric current entering the machine, going through three (or sometimes four) wheels, then in and back through an *Umkherwaltz*, the letter (or its representation) being always changed to a different letter. The total effect was to convert the input letter into a different letter of the alphabet. A 'plain language' message would thus be converted into an enciphered message of the same length. The teleprinter machines had this property, but by a completely different method.

One of the teleprinter machines, the SZ42, was called Fish or Tunny by us. It had twelve wheels, five of them were called chi wheels, χ_1, χ_2, χ_3, χ_4, and χ_5. Another five were called psi wheels, Ψ_1, Ψ_2, Ψ_3, Ψ_4, and Ψ_5, and two were called 'motor wheels', μ_{37} and μ_{61}. The 'length' of a wheel (the number of notches on its circumference) depended on which wheel. The lengths of the chi wheels were 41, 31, 29, 26, and 23. The total number of positions of the set of five chi wheels was $41 \cdot 31 \cdot 29 \cdot 26 \cdot 23$ of course. Each chi wheel moved one notch place for each encipherment of a letter.

The χ wheels, in given position, produce a 'pentabit' such as .xx.x or 01101. The psi or Ψ wheels all moved together but not regularly, their motion being governed by the two wheels μ_{37} and μ_{61} (lengths 37 and 61). The psi wheels produced a pentabit, say x.xx. or 10110. The 'binary' sum of the two pentabits (which in this case is 11011) is the 'key letter'. This is added modulo 2 to the 'plain language' letter (pentabit) to obtain the cipher letter for that position of the wheels of given patterns. The original break into Fish was largely due to Brigadier Tiltman and more so by W. T. Tutte, sight unseen. Because the patterns and settings of the wheels changed periodically, there was more than enough work for us (the mainly neo-Bayesian cryptanalysts). Finding the patterns was called 'wheel breaking', whereas finding their angular positions at the beginning of a message was called 'wheel setting'.

The cryptanalysis was performed at Bletchley Park (BP), also known as Room 47 Foreign Office, or Station X. When I joined BP I was at first in 'Hut 8', where the cryptanalysis of the German Naval Enigma was done. I worked in the more mathematical section consisting of the following people: Alan M. Turing (Head), G. H. O. D. Alexander (Deputy Assistant of Hut 8 and later Head), Joan Clarke, Harry Golombek, Peter Hilton, Tony Kendrick, Peter Twinn, and Leslie Yoxall. (Rolf Noskwith and Shaun Wylie were in the 'crib' section.)

Donald's cryptanalytic work during the war was entirely on Fish as far as I know; certainly he never worked on the Enigma. He began work in Major Tester's section, working on Fish by hand methods, in company with about eight other people including Roy Jenkins (later a Chancellor of the Exchequer in the UK, and biographer of Winston Churchill), Peter Benenson (founder of Amnesty International), Peter J. Hilton (later a distinguished mathematician), and Peter Ericson. Peter Hilton taught Donald elementary algebra. The famous Alan Turing and M. H. A. (Max) Newman FRS also worked in that section for a short time. Donald and Turing became friends and that was the origin of Donald's interest in artificial intelligence (AI). I had also had discussions of AI with Turing, which might have been the origin of Turing and my interest in the topic. Peter Hilton became friends with Donald and me.

Newman felt that much of the work in the 'Testery' would be capable of mechanization. He suggested this to Major Travis, the head of BP. Travis put Newman in charge of a new section or department, the Newmanry, to investigate this possibility. Donald joined the Newmanry in April 1943 and was the first cryptanalyst, apart of course from Newman himself. I arrived a few weeks later from Hut 8. This move occurred because the need for cryptanalysts had decreased in Hut 8. This in its turn was because the supply of large cryptanalytic machines ('Bombes'), used for attacking the enigma, had increased greatly, and also because the work of the cryptanalysts had become more routine.

The first person I met at the Newmanry was Donald. I put out my hand and said 'I am Good.' Later, after the war, when Donald invited me to give a lecture at Syracuse University, New York, he was the chairman and he introduced me by saying that I had been getting better ever since! This was typical of his humour and friendship.

When I arrived in the Newmanry, the first electronic machine in the department was nearly completed. It was called (Heath) Robinson. It was about the size of a door with a thickness of one foot. When it became slightly operational it was very unreliable. Donald and I, by research in the evenings, managed to set the wheels of a few messages and this led to the building of a better Robinson. This in turn led to the building of a much larger and faster machine, the famous Colossus which was the first large electronic computing machine, though special purpose. The head engineer was Tom Flowers. Four books have been written about Colossus, the most readable being the one edited by Jack Copeland.

Donald, with a little help from me, showed that a 'rectangle' (in Bill Tutte's sense; see his chapter in the book edited by Copeland) could be constructed on a Colossus. The rectangle was essential for 'breaking' the wheel patterns. The construction of the rectangle was much faster by Colossus than by hand (and supported Newman's belief in the potential value of machine methods in the breaking of Fish). Donald's idea led to an 'attachment' for Colossus II, and successive improved attachments to later Colossi. Eventually the improvement would have led to the '(crude) convergence' of rectangles by the Colossi, but the war ended just before this convergence could be done on a Colossus.

At the Newmanry, Donald showed a lot of initiative. He proposed that the Department should be divided, though not completely, into two subsections, one for aids to wheel breaking, and one for wheel setting. He also proposed that there should be a 'Mr. X' who would act as a permanent liaison between the Newmanry and Testery. Peter Hilton was Mr. X. Donald told me that to get his suggestions implemented he would convince Newman that they were Newman's. I was in the wheel-setting section, but was responsible for four significance tests related to 'rectangles', both Bayesian (neo-Bayesian) and 'frequentist'. I was also responsible for most of the statistics actually used in the wheel-setting section.

Donald, before he entered BP, won a scholarship to Balliol College, Oxford, where he studied classics perhaps for about a year. He was the 'curator of the book of bawdy verse' there. His wartime experience made him wish to become a mathematician instead of a classicist. He asked the advice of [the mathematicians]

Henry Whitehead and Shaun Wylie. Whitehead supported him, saying he should 'go for it if his belly was on fire for it', but Wylie gave the opposite advice on the grounds that Donald was too old to start. As a result of his work in the Newmanry, Donald became interested in quantitative methods because he wanted to be directly useful to society. (Although the classics are educational for understanding human nature, he thought they are not as useful as engineering mathematics.)

At the end of the war with Hitler, Newman became a professor at the University of Manchester and gave me an Associate Professorship in his department. Before leaving BP he had suggested that I edit a history of the Newmanry. I co-opted Donald, possibly at Newman's suggestion, and Donald and I co-opted Geoffrey Timms. Thus the book was written by the three of us. We could have it have 1,500 pages double-spaced, but we decided to limit it to 500 pages. It was called 'General Report on Tunny'. I wrote my part very quickly. I knew by heart every useful routine (or run). I even knew the page numbers of most of them in the five research logbooks called R1, R2, R3, R4, and R5. I was able to finish my parts of the history in about six weeks. I wanted to finish quickly to start my job at Manchester. The book was completed in a few months by Donald (mainly) and by Geoffrey. I was responsible for the 'Conclusions' and algebraic parts, Geoffrey for the account of the functions of the various machines, and Donald for the rest.

Donald and I departed for our two universities, but Geoffrey stayed on at BP, at least until 1962. I moved to Manchester for a couple of years but returned to GCHQ, where I expected to be useful in the 'Cold War'. Later I worked at the Admiralty Research Laboratory, Trinity College, Oxford, and Virginia Tech, Blacksburg, VA. Donald moved from classics to artificial intelligence. Sadly, Geoffrey died of a heart attack when running to catch a bus.

Donald several times invited me to his homes in Edinburgh and elsewhere (usually overnight), and also to his parent's home in London where I met his parents, two brothers, and sister. Donald's first wife resembled Betty Jo Perske, famously known as Lauren Bacall, Humphrey Bogart's fourth wife. There was a Bogart 'cult' at that time. I asked Donald whether this marriage occurred because Donald identified himself with Bogart, and Donald admitted this was true.

Donald's marriage to Anne McLaren, the famous biologist and Fellow of the Royal Society, was a real love affair. She was a communist although very wealthy. I don't think Donald was a communist in spite of what was stated in an obituary by his first son. Donald always respected intelligence, and this must have been a reason for his love for Anne McLaren and for his last wife, Jean Hayes. They were both physically attractive; indeed Jean had been a model in Paris when she was younger.

We both regarded our contributions to the war effort as of great value and hard acts to follow. That increased our bond of friendship, which was already very close.

* * *

Donald's Contributions to Genetics and Reproductive Biology

John D. Biggers

Department of Cell Biology, Harvard Medical School

My close association with Donald Michie began in the summer of 1955 when we came to occupy adjacent laboratories in the Royal Veterinary College, London, although I had met him for the first time the year before. An early recollection is Donald showing me a book he kept in his office on 'fancy' mice. Fancy mice, which he kept as a boy, are bred as pets and they are often exhibited at shows. Thus, it may not be surprising that Donald chose to study mouse genetics in fulfilment of his Doctor of Philosophy degree at Oxford University. His first paper, published in *Nature* in 1952, was entitled: 'A New Linkage in the House

Mouse: Vestigial and Rex'. Probability theory, for which Donald had a natural aptitude, is clearly demonstrated in this paper. There can be no doubt that this interest was acquired and honed by his wartime work at Bletchley, where he was involved in developing the computer which broke the German code. He had a close association with I. J. Good, a leading expert on probability and statistics, whom he often mentioned in conversations I had with him at a later time. Four more papers were published subsequently on the vestigial tail mutant.

In 1953, Donald published a paper, also in *Nature*, entitled 'Affinity: A New Genetic Phenomenon in the House Mouse: Evidence from Distant Crosses'. In this paper, Donald described a form of non-random segregation of chromosomes in mice. The phenomenon was discovered by statistical analysis of data which had been published several years before from studies of interspecific crosses between the European laboratory mouse and the Japanese waltzer mouse. Donald discussed his results with Sir Ronald Fisher, a major figure in statistics and genetics, who was obviously so impressed with the phenomenon that he suggested that it be called 'affinity'.

Two years later, 1955, Donald wrote a much longer paper on affinity which was published in the *Proceedings of the Royal Society of London* entitled 'Affinity'. This paper reveals two characteristics of Donald's approach to problems—the use of data published by others, and the application of a rigorous statistical analysis of the data to produce a new interpretation. The discovery of affinity, or quasi-linkage as it is now called, in mice over 50 years ago, still continues to attract interest.

In 1952 Donald began an active and fruitful period of research with Anne McLaren, who was soon to become his wife. The collaboration took place first at University College, London, and later at the Royal Veterinary College, London. It is very difficult to separate their individual contributions as they worked as a close-knit husband and wife team, sharing the same office and laboratory.

An early interest of Donald and Anne was the possibility that maternal influences during pregnancy could permanently affect the characteristics of offspring, the so-called maternal effects. A well-known example is the fact that horses and asses have six and five lumbar vertebrae, respectively.

Crosses between he-asses and mares (mules) tend to have six lumbar verte-brae, whereas crosses between she-asses and stallions (hinnys) tend to have five lumbar vertebrae. There are three mechanisms that may lead to these differences: (1) via sex chromosomes—a mule has a horse X-chromosome whereas a hinny has an ass X-chromosome (this phenomenon is known as sex-linkage and is only manifest in the male offspring), (2) via the egg cyto-plasm—a mule starts as a horse ovum and a hinny starts as an ass ovum, and (3) via uterine effects—a mule develops in a she-ass uterus and a hinny develops in a horse uterus. All of the three may have potential maternal effects. Donald and Anne decided to test these alternative possibilities by exploiting the fact that lumbar vertebrae number varies between different inbred strains of mice. Others had shown that the C3H/Bi and C57BL mouse strains had 5 and 6 lumbar vertebrae, respectively. Reciprocal crosses between these two strains result in offspring whose number of lumbar vertebrae tend towards the number in the gestating mother. One can distinguish between an egg cytoplasmic mechanism and a uterine mechanism using embryo transfer experiments and eliminating the possibility of sex linkage by only studying the females. Their work led to the publication of four papers between 1954 and 1958. The final conclusion was that the difference in the number of vertebrae between strains originates in the uterus. The work was subsequently summarized in a letter to *Nature* ('An Effect of the Uterine Environment upon Skeletal Morphology in the Mouse.')

Although the transfer of embryos from one mother to another had been done by others, the technique in mice was not particularly reliable. In order to do their work on the lumbar vertebrae number, Donald and Anne set about optimizing the technique they needed. A paper published in 1956 determined the optimum time in mice when embryos should be transferred to guarantee that the uterus was at its receptive stage.

A letter, written by Donald and Anne, was published in the April 10, 1954, issue of *Nature* questioning whether anything was gained by using inbred lines in experimental studies. They studied the variability of three types of mouse to the narcotic pentobarbital sodium: an inbred strain (C57BL), and an F1 hybrid between two inbred strains (C57BLfemale × C3Hmale) and an outbred (randomly bred) strain. They found the inbreds were the most variable, the hybrids the least variable, and the outbreds in between. The work was stimulated by results obtained by Professor Hans Grüneberg, a colleague at University College London, who found a similar phenomenon in studies on morphological variation, and who made the suggestion that this phenomenon be taken into account in the design of experiments. Donald and Anne were clearly interested in the biological mechanisms underlying this result, for the next year they published a little-known speculative review in a Penguin Series called New Biology, entitled 'The importance of Being Cross-bred'. In it they arrived at the following conclusion:

> When for a given environment the means of both parental strains fall short of the optimum value for the character concerned (whether monotelic or polytelic), the inter-strain hybrids raised in that environment will exceed both strains in the direction of the optimum.

This review is well worth reading for it clearly carries the mark of Donald's clear and incisive way of analysing problems.

I began a long association with Donald and Anne as the result of two unanticipated events. In a totally independent study Peter Claringbold and I, at the University of Sydney, Australia, had found out that inbred mice were more variable in their response to oestrogens than outbred mice, and that the most uniform responses were obtained with F1 hybrids between inbred strains. We sent a paper to *Nature* entitled 'Why Use Inbred Lines?' challenging the current dogma that the best animals to use in experimental work were genetically uniform inbred lines. The paper was published on September 25, 1954, five months after Donald and Anne's paper. Little did we know that the following year Donald, Anne, and I would find ourselves in adjacent laboratories at the Royal Veterinary College, London, where we found facilities to investigate experimentally the generalization proposed by Donald and Anne in their New Biology article. Our common interest in the control of variation in experimental animals resulted in two papers on the effect of environmental temperature on the growth of mice. It was during this collaborative work that I came to appreciate the incisive way in which Donald could formulate and analyse any problem of a quantitative nature. We finally wrote an article for *Nature* entitled 'Variance Control in the Animal House'.

Recently I was reflecting with Donald about this early work we did together, and he was lamenting that many younger researchers no longer know about it, although F1 hybrid mice are widely used today experimentally.

It was during this time that Anne McLaren and I successfully cultured mouse pre-implantation embryos in vitro, after which we transferred them to surrogate mothers to obtain grossly normal newborn mice. To do this we made use of the technique for transplanting mouse embryos that Donald helped optimize. It was this work that helped open up the possibility of experimentally analysing early mammalian development and in vitro fertilization and embryo transfer so widely used in the treatment of human infertility. Donald actively participated in the discussions that led Anne and I to do this work, but when time came for its publication he declined having his name on the paper since he had not done any of the experimental manipulations.

Donald was an inspiration to work with and I count myself lucky that I was able to actively work with him early in my career. I always found it a stimulating experience when we met in subsequent years and discussed new problems in research.

* * *

Donald's Contributions to Artificial Intelligence

Claude Sammut

School of Computer Science and Engineering, University of New South Wales

I still remember the title of the first talk that I heard Donald Michie give. It was called 'Artificial Intelligence: The First 2,400 Years'. Only partly tongue-in-cheek, Donald provoked his audience into considering the long tradition behind AI, starting with Aristotle, through to mathematicians and philosophers like Leibniz and Frege, and on to the twentieth century. Looking back on Donald's career in AI, we can see the extraordinary contribution that he made in the continuation of this tradition. His immediate predecessor was Alan Turing, with whom he had many conversations about AI while working as a code-breaker. The years spent at Bletchley shaped much of Donald's thinking and echoes of his conversations with Turing can be found in much of his later work. Donald was especially taken by the ideas that Turing presented at the end of his 1950 paper on computing machinery and intelligence. The 'child-machine' was to be an educable machine, capable of learning and accumulating knowledge over time. It is, therefore, not surprising that learning became one of the dominant themes in Donald's research.

Today, journals and conferences on machine learning are filled with papers on what we now call 'reinforcement learning', that is, a computer program that improves its performance on some task by conducting trial-and-error experiments. The program is rewarded for success and punished for failure and continually modifies its behaviour until it achieves the desired level of performance. Turing had suggested this form of learning, but, in the early 1960s, Donald was the first to make a learning machine of this kind. His accomplishment was all the more extraordinary because he did this without a computer. His MENACE machine for playing noughts and crosses was a collection of hundreds of match boxes, each representing a state of the game. Beads in the boxes represented a move in the given state. With MENACE, Donald foreshadowed the main elements of future reinforcement learning systems, including random selection of actions, gradually being more and more biased towards those that will give a higher expected reward. Eventually, the BOXES algorithm was implemented on an electronic computer and became the benchmark for future work on reinforcement learning.

The work on reinforcement learning took Donald to Stanford University, and a visit with Bernard Widrow, who was working on learning a control task by imitating another agent. Later, while working with Roger Chambers, Donald returned to this theme, which would occupy him for many years. Using the graphics computers that were just emerging in the 1960s, Chambers and Michie developed a learning system that was a symbiosis of human and machine. A human could seed the BOXES algorithm with starting knowledge by demonstrating a skill, like balancing a pole. Donald would come back to this work in the 1990s, coining the term 'behavioural cloning' to mean that the machine learns to reproduce a human skill by observing performances of the skill. Behavioural Cloning began at the Turing Institute, with Mike Bain and Jean Hayes-Michie, and continued in our lab at UNSW, which Donald and Jean visited frequently, and also in Ivan Bratko's group in Ljubljana. Many other laboratories have also adopted some form of learning by imitation. So again, Donald's work became the foundation for very fruitful lines of enquiry, years later.

The Edinburgh days of the Experimental Programming Unit and the Department of Machine Intelligence and Perception were amazingly productive. The 'Graph Traverser', with Jim Doran, was yet another piece of fundamental research that has had far-reaching impact. The project developed over several years and the capabilities of the Graph Traverser evolved in different ways; but most importantly it laid the foundations for much of our understanding of heuristic search methods. The Graph Traverser was later taken up by Austin Tate, who made major contributions to modern planning systems.

Game-playing is a natural test bed for search methods. MENACE solved problems in noughts and crosses, the Graph Traverser was demonstrated on tile puzzles, but the real challenge for search and problem-solving was chess. It was clear that with the enormous search space of a chess game, an uninformed search would not do well. Ivan Bratko, Danny Kopec, and Donald developed an 'Advice Taker' language that could be used to represent chess knowledge to guide the game tree search. As well as trying to improve search techniques, much work was done to try to understand the thinking of chess masters. In this, Donald took to heart Turing's notion of trying to educate a machine in the same way that a human is educated. He enlisted the help of psychologists in this endeavour, among them Jean Hayes, who would become Donald's wife and partner in research.

Although domain knowledge could be used to aid a problem-solver's search, the acquisition and coding of this knowledge can be tedious. This led to a consideration of machine learning as a means of automatically building knowledge bases. This brings us back to the title of Donald's talk: 'Artificial Intelligence: The First 2,400 Years'. The occasion was the G. A. Miller lecture that Donald was invited to give at the University of Illinois at Urbana-Champaign in 1983. I had recently joined the Department of Computer Science at the invitation of Ryszard Michalski. The connection between the three of us was machine learning. Ryszard had been one of the champions of the emerging field and following my PhD on machine learning, I had gone to Illinois to work with him. Donald's interest in Ryszard's work was to find a means of acquiring expert knowledge by example and so, we crossed paths for the first time. Donald had been living in part-exile from Britain following the loss of funding in the post-Lighthill years. He spent one semester each year in the USA teaching graduate courses at Illinois and also at Stanford. It was there, in 1978, that another Australian, Ross Quinlan, happened to be in Donald's class. Donald challenged his students to learn whether a chess end-game would result in a loss for one side. Rather than use one of Michalski's algorithms, Ross wrote his own, a decision tree learner. The subsequent work that Ross did profoundly altered the direction of machine learning research. Sadly, Ryszard Michalski, who had been ill for some time, died just two months after Donald's tragic accident.

Most machine learning researchers aim to make their systems as autonomous as possible, but Donald took the view that knowledge discovery was a cooperative venture between human and machine. So he preferred learning systems that allowed the human to guide the mechanical development of a theory to explain the data. He supervised Alen Shapiro's PhD on 'structured induction', in which the trainer provides the high-level structure of a decision tree and then allows the computer to expand the nodes below, given the data. This was successfully used for learning chess concepts and also became a cornerstone of later industrial applications of machine learning techniques.

Donald's contributions to AI are certainly not limited to his technical work. He was instrumental in bringing to the attention of the British government the importance of computing research and especially non-numerical computing, and he new the value of building a strong team. After setting up his own small group in the Experimental Programming Unit, he attracted other researchers of the highest calibre, who went on to make their own ground-breaking contributions in theorem proving, logic programming, planning, programming languages, theoretical computing, and much more. The most controversial team that Donald directed was the group that built the FREDDY robots. In the mid-1960s, Donald and Richard Gregory had begun discussing the possibility of a robot that, like Turing's child machine, would be able to perceive and act on its environment and be educable to some extent. Such a machine was eventually realized by a team including Pat Ambler, Harry Barry, Christopher Brown, Rod Burstall, and Robin Popplestone. More than 35 years later, FREDDY is still an impressive achievement, combining machine vision, tactile sensing, and planning, all assembled in a programming system that was, itself, highly influential. In doing my research for this foreword, I reviewed the recording of the 1973 BBC broadcast of the debate between Sir James Lighthill, Donald Michie, Richard Gregory, and John McCarthy. Lighthill made many claims about the worth, or lack of worth, of robotics research and what was and was not possible. With the passage of 35 years, we can see how Lighthill's objections have all fallen away.

At the end of one visit to our laboratory, Donald left me a gift of Dava Sobel's book, *Longitude*, the story of John Harrison's quest to build an accurate clock for determining longitude. I think the story appealed to Donald for two reasons. One was that he probably identified strongly with Harrison's lifelong struggle against bureaucracy. The other reason was his respect for tool makers, which he considered to be the unsung heroes of science. Many of the most important discoveries ever made would not have been possible unless someone had invented the right tool. So Donald was full of admiration for the POP-2 programming language that Burstall and Popplestone had developed for the FREDDY project and also for the libraries that made possible software development for a complex system. Robotics researchers today still struggle with this problem.

One of Donald's contributions to POP-2 was the idea of 'memoization', that is, caching the results of function calls so that they do not have to be recalculated for the same arguments. This can be thought of as a form of 'speed-up' learning and foreshadowed explanation-based learning and partial evaluation in logic programming.

The years following the release of the Lighthill report were difficult for Donald since funding was scarce, so he resolved not to rely on public funding and instead seek support from industry. This was a necessity but it also made Donald one of the first AI entrepreneurs and the first to record a major win for machine learning. A consultation for Westinghouse, in Pittsburgh, led to them using machine learning to improve the yields of a Uranium sinter plant. A letter to Donald, stating that this was saving the company millions of dollars per year, became machine learning's first big success story. This also led to Westinghouse providing research funds for the Turing Institute, which Donald founded in 1984 in Glasgow with Tim Niblett and Peter Mowforth.

In naming the institute Donald was again acknowledging the debt he owed Turing for stimulating the intellectual pursuits that would occupy most of his life. The institute itself became a stimulus for new and exciting research, including Stephen Muggleton's work on Inductive Logic Programming. And it was a place to which one could send one's ex-students, confident that they would flourish, as did Ashwin Srinivasan.

By the early 1990s, Donald had spent much of his time as a director and fundraiser and wanted to pull back from these duties and return to more research. With Mike Bain and Jean Hayes-Michie, Donald had returned to his early work on learning by imitation, and in a visit to Australia in 1992, worked with us on learning a pilot's flight skills by recording his behaviour and applying machine learning to build a 'behavioural clone'. This was a continuation of a theme that Donald returned to regularly, which was to use machine learning to help articulate expert knowledge. He pursued this with us and with Ivan Bratko and his colleagues in Ljubljana.

In 1998, at the age of 75, Donald was still ready to start a new research programme. As the 50th anniversary of Turing's *Mind* paper was approaching, he wanted to do something to commemorate it. So how about building a conversational agent to pass the Turing test? This became the focus of his intellectual pursuits for the next nine years, until 2002, much of it spent at UNSW. In July 2007, he was working with Richard Wheeler, in Edinburgh, on a system that was almost ready for demonstration. Unfortunately that demonstration never took place.

This Foreword has turned out longer than intended, but that is because Donald's career was so long and eventful. I have mentioned many names of people who have been influenced by Donald, and left out many, many more for lack of space and a lack in my own knowledge. But everyone who knew Donald knew him as a force of nature. He was relentless in his pursuit of knowledge in many areas and he never let obstacles impede that pursuit. He has left a great legacy in the research he did, but I think an even greater legacy is the inspiration he has given to those of us who had the privilege of knowing him and working with him.

* * *

Donald Michie—The Person

Stephen Muggleton

Department of Computing, Imperial College

I had the great privilege to be supervised in my PhD by Donald Michie in Edinburgh during the early 1980s. From that time up until his death I knew and admired him as a close colleague and friend.

Donald was indeed a great scientist as all the tributes to him attest. However, he was also a great and honest man, and a true friend to many people around the world. He was an unusually gifted human being with many admirable human qualities. I remember his late wife Jean saying that he viewed himself as a hero out of an epic poem, much like Odysseus or Jason leading his argonauts to find the Golden Fleece. And I must admit that those in his lab often felt ourselves to be like the Argonauts, battling through adverse conditions to find the Fleece, with Donald at the helm.

Donald was larger than life and always exciting to be with. He was always on the lookout for adventure. As a teenager he was keen to be dropped behind enemy lines in China. Shortly afterwards he was to be found battling with the new Colossus at Bletchley Park, finding ways to rapidly and automatically decode German High Command messages, with a consequent massive reduction in Allied casualties. Following the war Donald found the most exciting new scientific area he could to work in by pursuing the new science of genetics. His pioneering work here with Anne McLaren led to the test-tube baby technology used in clinics today. As soon as computers were available Donald founded the first Artificial Intelligence lab in the world, heading a team in Edinburgh which built the world's first intelligent assembly robot. He then continued to design and develop creative and intelligent computer programs right up until the end of his life.

In everything he did Donald showed an amazing and overwhelming sense of determination. In particular, he never let politicians get in the way of what he perceived as being important goals.

He was always immensely supportive of all those students and colleagues whom he committed himself to. For this reason he had many friends and colleagues all over the world, to whom he provided influence and encouragement in their work. I remember an impromptu after dinner speech which he was asked to give at an international conference in former Yugoslavia. The conference was on artificial intelligence, but Donald chose to speak on the human capacity for 'wisdom'. He described wisdom as a mixture of intelligence and kindness. Donald was certainly highly intelligent, but also extremely kind.

All those who knew Donald will judge that he helped make the world a greater and more exciting place to live in. We will all miss him greatly.

Acknowledgements

This book has been made possible because of the goodwill of many individuals and institutions. A debt of gratitude is owed to Barbara Harriss-White, whose encouragement and good counsel helped the book take its first steps. It is an honour when an eminent scientist writes the Foreword for one's book. To have four contribute in this way is rare indeed, and I am immensely grateful to Jack Good, John Biggers, Claude Sammut, and Stephen Muggleton. A special thank you also to Leslie Pendleton of Virginia Tech, who worked with Jack Good, after he had been hospitalized, to get his contribution to me. Throughout the enterprise, the Michie family, especially Chris and Susan Michie, were extremely supportive of my efforts. Joining them in generously giving time and resources were Katrina Dean of the British Library, Latha Menon and Emma Marchant of the OUP, Betty Higginbotham of Virginia Tech, Arlene Newlands and Edith Atkinson of Edinburgh University, Anita Kumari and Laurent Mignet of the IBM India Research Lab, and my friends and colleagues in the UK: Ross King, Steve Moyle, Simukai Utete, Andre Stern, Sumeet Agrawal, and David Gavaghan. Naresh Kumar helped convert many of the articles in this volume into an editable form. I have been supported throughout by the IBM India Research Laboratory, and by my academic homes in the Computing Laboratory at Oxford, and the Department of CSE and the Centre for Health Informatics at the University of New South Wales.

And to Ruhi Saith, who has been through thick and thin with me, I can only offer this *ruba'i* (not Khayyam's or even Fitzgerald's):

> *See how the rose effuses until the last*
> *Whilst the thorn, uncaring, presses fast*

Such is the world we have inherited
That his is the essence of a paradise past.

Truly, خوش نصیب ہیں ہم

A. S

The Editor wishes to thank the copyright holders for permission to reprint the articles that appear in this book, free of charge in all instances. They are listed below in the order in which they occur in the book. For articles 31, 32 and 33, every effort has been made to trace and contact the copyright holders, and the publisher and author apologize for any errors or omissions. If notified we will rectify these at the earliest opportunity.

1. Special Minute of the Senate, Edinburgh University. Reproduced with permission from the University.
2. 'At Bletchley' from 'Colossus and the Breaking of the War-time 'Fish' Codes' (2002). *Cryptologia*, 24(1), pp. 17–58.
3. Turing's Vision (1985). *The Creative Computer*, by Donald Michie and Rory Johnston, Pelican, pp. 133–6.
4. 'Fifty Years After' from 'Fifty Years After Breaking the Codes: Interviews with Two of the Bletchley Park Scientists' (1995). *IEEE Annals of the History of Computing*, 17(1), pp. 32–43.
5. Machines That Can Play Games (1963). *The Scotsman*, 11 July.
6. Where Britain Lags Behind (1963). *The Scotsman*, 12 July.
7. Edinburgh Will Set the Pace (1966). *The Scotsman*, 17 February.
8. Clever or Intelligent? (1969). *Cybernetics*, XII, 4.
9. Recollections of Early AI in Britain. Reproduced with permission from the Artificial Intelligence Applications Institute, University of Edinburgh, and M. Bain.
10. 'Tokyo–Edinburgh Dialogue' from 'Tokyo–Edinburgh Dialogue on Robots in Artificial Intelligence Research' (1971). With H. G. Barrow, R. J. Popplestone, and S. H. Salter, *Computer Journal*, 14(1), pp. 91–5.
11. Machine Intelligence in the Cycle Shed. (1973). *New Scientist*, 22 February.
12. 'Of Bears and Balls' from 'Explaining it to Governments' (1985). *The Creative Computer*, ibid., pp. 203–5.

13. 'Comments on the Lighthill Report' from 'Comments on the Lighthill Report and the Sutherland Reply' (1973). *Artificial Intelligence*, Science Research Council, London.

14. 'The Turing Institute' from 'The Turing Institute: An Experiment in Cooperation' (1989). *Interdisciplinary Science Reviews*, 14(2), pp. 117–19.

15. Slaughter on Seventh Avenue (1997). *New Scientist*, 7 June.

16. Human Window on the World (1985). *The Creative Computer*, ibid., pp. 64–72.

17. 'Rules from Brains' from 'Building Symbolic Representations of Intuitive Real-Time Skills from Performance Data' (1994), with R. C. Camacho, *Machine Intelligence*, 13, pp. 385–417.

18. Turing's Test and Conscious Thought (1993). *Artificial Intelligence*, 60(10), pp. 1–22.

19. 'Strong AI': An Adolescent Disorder (1995). *Informatica*, 19, pp. 461–8.

20. Return of the Imitation Game (2001). *Electronic Transactions on Artificial Intelligence*, 5(B), pp. 203–21.

21. 'Keeping Mice' from 'Keeping Mice' (1961). *Daily Worker*, 12 April; 'Mrs. Mouse and Baby' (1961). *Daily Worker*, 13 April; and 'Plain or Coloured' (1961). *Daily Worker*, 19 April.

22. Maternal Inheritance in Mice (1955). *Fur & Feather*, 15 December.

23. 'Super-pregnancy' from 'Superpregnancy in the Mouse, I (1959). Implantation and Foetal Mortality after Induced Superovulation in Females of Various Ages.' *J. exp. Biol.*, 36, 281–300 (with Anne McLaren). Published by permission of the Company of Biologists.

24. 'The Transfer of Fertilized Mouse Eggs' from 'Studies on the Transfer of Fertilized Mouse Eggs to Uterine Foster Mothers. I. Factors Affecting the Implantation and Survival of Transferred Eggs' (1956). *J. exp. Biol.*, 33, 394–416 (with Anne McLaren). Published by permission of the Company of Biologists.

25. The Importance of Being Cross-bred (1955). *New Biology*, 19, 8–69. Harmondsworth: Penguin (with Anne McLaren).

26. 'Immunological Tolerance and Chimaeras' from 'An Investigation of Immunological Tolerance Based on Chimaera Analysis' (1961). *Immunology*, 4, 413–24 (with M. F. A. Woodruff and I. M. Zeiss).

27. Scientific Advice to Governments (1981). *New Scientist*, 23 April.

28. Song and Dance Story (1979). *New Scientist*, 24 May.

29. 'The Black Death of Our Times' from 'The Black Death of Our Times—And Some Antidotes' (1981). *Computer Weekly*, 5 February; and 'The Black Death of Our Times (2)—Re-skilling the Works' (1981). *Computer Weekly*, 19 February.

30. Keeping One Jump Ahead (2006). The *Spectator*, 25 February.

31. What They Read and Why (1960). *Discovery*, March.

32. Sciencemanship (1959). *Discovery*, 20, pp. 259–60.

33. 'The Tramp's Charter', from 'Camping Through the Curtain (1957). *Autocar*, 15 November.

34. Descent into Unreason (2003). *Stop The War Coalition*, London.

All proceeds from this book will go to The Donald Michie Memorial Fund. Details of the fund are available by writing to: Professor J. Michie, Rewley House, 1 Wellington Square, Oxford OX1 2JA, UK.

A Lifetime in a Minute

Every life is interesting in a myriad different ways, and all biographical sketches necessarily incomplete. How then does one fit the story of a life-time into one page or even three, especially when it was as varied and eventful as Donald Michie's? Fortunately, I found about sixty years of it had already been fitted into a minute. On 23rd January, 1985 a Special Minute was seen (as these things are) by members of the Senate of Edinburgh University, on the occasion of Donald Michie leaving the University. Here it is in full:

SPECIAL MINUTE

Professor Donald Michie MA, DPhil, DSc, FBCS, FRSE

Donald Michie leaves Edinburgh after 26 years and a career of extraordinary diversity. He was born in Falkirk in 1923 into a family with strong banking connections. During his education at Rugby he demonstrated marked talents for golf, squash, and chess. From Rugby he won, in 1942, an open scholarship to Balliol College, Oxford, to read classics, but this had to be delayed because of the unfortunate state of international affairs. After setting a record for the shortest time as an infantry private, he was posted to Station X, the cypher school at Bletchley Park, where good use could be made of chess-playing open scholars. Events at Bletchley were a closely guarded secret until the thirty-year rule allowed the release of a part of the story in 1975.

The details have an extraordinary fascination. All German military signals were encoded by a machine named Enigma. The output of a keyboard was transposed by a set of wheels carrying a pattern scrambling wires, which connected keys to different letters. The wheels were rotated with each character typed, which meant that a fresh transposition code was in use for every letter. With the right wheels and initial settings, decoding was instantaneous but without them the task appeared impossible. The Germans were confident that their signals were absolutely secure. However, a set of wheels was stolen by members of the Polish underground movement and smuggled to Britain. The cypher school at Bletchley was given the task of breaking Enigma and had priority to employ the finest minds in the country. Michie was an obvious recruit. He worked with Alan Turing on machines, which tested random Enigma settings to see if intercepted messages could be turned into recognisable German text. The machine that they produced would today be called a computer. As a result of their work the supreme allied commanders were able, for most of the war, to read any German signal nearly as quickly as the intended recipient. It is difficult to imagine how the war could have been won without the results from Bletchley, and all too easy to see how it could have been lost.

Despite the dazzling success in war, when peace returned it was officially decided that there would be few industrial, commercial, or scientific uses for the new technology. One of the reasons was that it was expected that a computing engine might need as many as a thousand bits of memory and that it would never be possible to achieve adequate reliability! The team was dispersed to civilian life. Michie took up his delayed scholarship at Oxford, but switched from classics to medicine.

Following the visit to St. Giles' Fair he acquired some pet mice, which he bred in the kitchen of his digs. The observation that the patterns of the fur of successive generations of Michie mice did not correspond with received views on genetics prompted discussions with eminent professors of the subject, a DPhil, and later a DSc.

After a period of work as a research associate at University College and the Royal Veterinary College in London, he was offered a non-teaching Senior Lectureship in Immunology at Edinburgh in 1961. He developed statistical tests for tissue matches in kidney transplants that are the standard technique today. In 1962 he was awarded a Readership in Surgical Science. His computing interests remained at the hobby level but involved a spectacular bet. Michie was challenged to build a machine which would learn to play noughts and crosses. His apparatus consisted of an array of match boxes containing beads to represent each possible position and the options open. Successful moves were reinforced by the addition of beads so that the probability of winning (or at least not losing) steadily increased. In the early sixties the idea was revolutionary in its implications. The bet was won.

Michie's interest in machines which could learn won him an invitation as visiting Professor in Electrical Engineering to Stanford. During this visit to America his involvement with computing was rekindled while visiting a USAF project for the machine analysis of language. On his return he persuaded the Chairman of Elliot Automation to give Edinburgh a generous discount for a computer and set up the second multi-access time-sharing system in the country. (This was shortly after the time at which official estimates put the number of computers needed in Britain at five.) Edinburgh's pre-eminence in artificial intelligence can be traced to Michie's Experimental Programming Unit, which was set up after his transfer from Surgical Science in 1965. He gathered a dedicated group of junior researchers and instilled in them the highest levels of enthusiasm for the new subject. He was closely associated with Bernard Meltzer's Meta-Mathematics unit, which did pioneering work in the computer proof of mathematical theorems. From 1966 they organized a series of Machine Intelligence Workshops, which have produced a regular stream of books. Michie was awarded a Personal Chair in Machine Intelligence in 1967.

In 1968 the group set about the construction of robots with vision, touch, and mobility. By 1972 the system was envied by leading laboratories in America and Japan. Indeed even today leading car producers are astonished at the date of the Edinburgh achievement. Unfortunately it was officially decided that there would be few industrial or commercial uses for the new techniques, the project was closed, and the team was dispersed.

Michie moved on to the development of expert systems, and in 1979, in company with John McCarthy, lost by a narrow margin a bet about computer chess. The bets had been laid in 1969 in response to comments from David Levy, the current Scottish chess champion, that computers would never be able to approach the best human players. Opinion amongst the artificial intelligentsia was fairly evenly divided. But very few people except Michie ever imagined that a machine that would fit in your pocket and cost less than a tankful of petrol could play respectable chess. David Levy won his bet in 1979. It would be interesting to know if he would accept a second.

A career, which covers classics, code-breaking, genetics, kidney transplants, electrical engineering, computers, and robots requires many mid-stream jumps. Donald Michie manages to make original contributions to a new field of interest in an astonishingly short time. His predictions about the progress of personal computing and robots have proved correct. Shortly to be fulfilled is one about the success of computers at medical diagnosis. His next achievement will be unpredictable as the output of an Enigma machine. The only features that can safely be excluded from its description are dullness and tranquillity.

There are some mistakes and some omissions, but why quibble. I can, however, add twenty seconds worth of additional information. Donald Michie left Edinburgh when he was 60 ('premature retirement' was how he described it). The Machine Intelligence Research Unit at Edinburgh transformed itself into the Machine Intelligence Research Affiliates at the University of Strathclyde. His goal was to conduct long-term research in Machine Intelligence with funds derived primarily from industry. This idea, unusual even now, was remarkably successful for about 10 years, taking shape in the form of the Turing

Institute—of which Donald was the Chief Scientist—and its associated software development and consultancy company, Intelligent Terminals Limited.

In 1988, long-overdue recognition of his path-breaking work in mouse embryology with Anne McLaren followed in the form of a Pioneer Award from the International Embryo Transfer Society. In a dazzling sequence of experiments over 10 years in the 1950s, McLaren and Michie established much of the basis of modern in-vitro fertilization techniques. With the 1990s also came, finally, recognition of his contributions to machine intelligence in the form of several awards. In 1995, he co-founded the Human Computer Learning Foundation, with the aim of exploring ways in which computers could be used to assist and improve human skills. Now over seventy, he continued active experimental research with Jean Hayes-Michie and others in the area of extracting models of human skills. In the 2000s, more honours followed: the IJCAI Award for Research Excellence and a Lifetime Achievement Award from the British Computer Society. By now, his attention had turned to developing conversational software agents, a task that continued to occupy his research to the end. On 7th July 2007, he and Anne McLaren died together in a car accident, on the road from Cambridge to London. And so ended not just one, but two, remarkable scientific lives.

Machine Intelligence

The Beginning

Although chronologically, Donald Michie's involvement in machine intelligence may appear to have occurred after his work in biology in the 1950s, we now know that much of this interest stemmed from wartime work as a cryptographer at Bletchley Park. His friendship with Alan Turing and their discussions on intelligent machines are well documented. But it is the time he spent in M. H. A. Newman's group (the 'Newmanry'), in the company of I. J. Good and others, that possibly played the greatest influence on him. In letters written to Max Newman in 1978 (these are available at the beautifully catalogued Newman Archive, which is accessible on the Web), he says: 'My years in the Newmanry were the most thrilling experience of my life, and also most formative...' Revealingly, along with a paper on automatic chess-playing, he writes:

> I promised to send you a reprint on our chess stuff, and here is one, from the Proceedings of the conference on Artificial Intelligence, which has just ended in Hamburg. But as I said, robots and computer chess and all that, and especially any contributions of mine, have always seemed quite piddling compared to the excitement of our war-time project.

This is interesting, since it suggests that some of the best academic research done in the late 1970s was still lagging substantially behind what had been done at Bletchley nearly 40 years earlier. It seemed only natural therefore to start this section with excerpts from an essay on that time. 'At Bletchley' (the title is mine), from 'Colossus and the Breaking of the Fish Codes', was written much later (in 2002), but it still captures some of the excitement of a young scholar involved in exciting research. Much later, many who spent time at the Turing Institute started by Donald Michie, felt similarly. Perhaps the Institute was modelled, at least in spirit, on the Newmanry.

I have also included a short segment entitled 'Turing's Vision', from Michie and Johnston's *The Creative Computer*. Turing's name is associated with three main topics: a solution to a problem in the foundations of mathematics using an abstract machine now called a Universal Turing Machine; a physical realization of these abstract machines in the form of general-purpose electronic computers; and the use of these computers to simulate human cognition. The parts of Turing's 1947 lecture to the London Mathematical Society, reprinted here, describe the latter two and laid the foundations for much of Donald's machine intelligence programme, and he returns often to this lecture at various stages of his research. Under the last of these three headings is the famous 'Turing Test'—more on this later.

In this section and in the following, interspersed amongst the essays are some interviews. Interviews are, admittedly, a strange kind of conversation. Mark Twain disliked them intensely, claiming there was something wrong in principle with the whole business, and as a result 'in interviews as a rule men seem to talk like anybody but themselves.' Despite this Twainian warning, I think readers will find 'Fifty Years After'—ostensibly, an interview with I. J. Good and Donald Michie— quickly becomes a conversation between two old friends.

At Bletchley
(2002)

PERSONAL PREHISTORY

In late 1941, following my 18th birthday, a normal next phase would have been two further terms at boarding school, with an option for scholarship holders to proceed to a shortened university degree course before joining up. But over that Christmas my teenage imagination was fired by a tale from my father concerning a mysterious establishment at Bedford. He had it on the authority of the then War Minister, Sir James Grigg, that as preparation for doing something unspecified but romantic behind enemy lines there were opportunities to sign up for a Japanese course starting in a couple of months' time. I duly journeyed to Bedford and presented myself at the address given.

Sorry, wrong info

My request to enroll elicited from the Intelligence Corps officer who saw me a somewhat puzzled reply: 'Who told you that we have a Japanese course now? That particular exercise is planned for the Autumn.' Noting my confusion he added: 'But we have courses on code-breaking. There's a new intake just starting. Would that interest you instead? I'll have someone find you a billet nearby. Make sure to be back here at 9 a.m. Monday.'

In the Second World War one did not mess about. Returning to the London suburbs just long enough to pack a suitcase, I was back and signed in to the School of Codes and Ciphers, Official Secrets Act and all, on the Monday morning. With the rest of the new class I was soon held in thrall by our instructor, a certain Captain Cheadle, and by the black arts of codes and ciphers.

With nothing to occupy my evenings, I arranged to have my own key to the building and classroom. My habit became to return after hours to the texts and exercises. The resulting accelerated learning curve made my selection inevitable when a Colonel Pritchard arrived from Bletchley. He was on a mission to recruit for the new section that was being formed by Ralph Tester to follow up John Tiltman's and William Tutte's successive coups. The hope was that breaking and reading Fish traffic could be placed on a regular basis. The Pritchard interview lasted no more than a few minutes. I was to present myself within 48 hours at the entrance to Bletchley Park with a sealed letter.

After admission and a visit to the billeting office, I was parked in the Mansion House. My first task was to memorize teleprinter code until I could fluently sight-read punched paper tape. Pending completion of the Hut assigned to Major Tester's new section I sat as an ugly duckling in a large room filled to capacity by members of the Women's Auxiliary Air Force. What were they doing? Who knows? New arrivals were imprinted with a draconian DON'T ASK DON'T TELL principle in regard to anyone's immediate business but their own. I did, however, discover that those whose boyfriends were on active service felt only contempt for an apparently fit young male in civilian attire. Some of them had lost boyfriends in the RAF, and many had boyfriends still alive but in daily peril.

CHARM OF A SECOND LIEUTENANT

The experience did nothing to ease my sense of disorientation in the new surroundings. Relief appeared in the person of a uniformed and exquisitely charming Intelligence Corps officer, Second Lieutenant Roy Jenkins. My task was to bring him up to my own recently acquired sight-reading skills. Roy's post-war career was to include Cabinet Minister and Chancellor of Oxford University. In my isolation, his company was rescue and balm. We departed to swell the ranks of Tester's new section, in my case via a most curious diversion.

FORTY MEN AND A TEENAGER

On reporting to Ralph Tester I was immediately dispatched to take charge of a room like a small aircraft hangar. It was located at some distance from his new Hut. Within it there sat at tables several dozen uniformed men who remain in my memory as being all of the rank of Lance Corporal. What I can attest beyond error is that I quickly became convinced of the infeasibility of the operation which it was now my job to supervise…

TO THE TESTERY

The dogged endeavours of my well-drilled force of crib-draggers, in due course, generated sufficient documentation for me to report that the 'human wave' assault was unlikely to contribute effectively and best disbanded. After this interlude, depressing for all concerned, I gained the long-sought shore of the Testery proper. I was turned over to a young graduate, now the internationally distinguished mathematician P. J. Hilton, for instruction in the earlier mentioned method known as 'Turingery'.

Peter knew all the Testery hand-procedures backward and forward, and played a massive part in perfecting them. My first and vivid memory was that, although only a year or two older than me, he smoked a pipe. My second was of his didactic strictures on my fetish of tidiness and aesthetics in paper-and-pencil work. I should say 'my then fetish'. With efficiency and speed at an unimaginable premium, not to mention justified awe of my new mentor, I was cured of this kind of perfectionism for life!

Other vivid images of my first encounter with the Testery are first and foremost of Major (later Colonel) Ralph Tester himself. I recall his mesmeric impact on female spectators in the lunch break as he leapt, daemonic and glowing, about the tennis court with an animality that I had only ever envisaged as radiating from the great god Pan. Yet a year later when I was already in the Newmanry, engaged in a machine-based attack on the same Fish ciphers, the same man was ashen under his tan. He had had to summon me (presumably at Newman's request) to reprove my conduct. Why had I been canvassing the cryptographic staff of both Newmanry and Testery for signatures to a petition for the administrative merging of the two sections? With the naivety of a nineteen-year-old I was oblivious of such facts as that, even if a Foreign Office section and a War Office section could have been merged, one or other of Tester and Newman would have had to be dumped, and that it would not have been Newman. An ingenious administrative compromise resulted. A fictional 'Mr. X' appeared on Newman's books whose fake identity four selected Testery staff assumed for periods in rotation, acting as a species of internal consultant. This gave good technical liaison, previously absent.

Tester had the sense of purpose and personal humility of an outstanding leader. At the time of Rommel's retreat to Tunisia, we suddenly found that some mysterious change in the system had locked us out of the Berlin–Tunis channel. A group of us offered to go flat out round the clock. Ralph's cryptographic skills were really too unpractised to be of material help, as he and we knew. But he sat among us, bolt upright as was normal for him, unflagging as the hours raced by. In the end the hours were not racing, and we young Turks were drooping and nodding. Ralph, focused and refulgent as ever, saw this: 'You know,' he said tactfully, 'it's easy for me. Most things go downhill with age. Stamina for some reason goes the other way. So you're no good at this sort of thing until you're at least forty. Another coffee, anyone?'

During the glory days of the American space programme, when the mean age of space vehicle commanders seemed to be getting more and more venerable, I recalled Tester's words.

STRANGE INCIDENT, BEST FORGOTTEN

The Testery's machine operators were ATS girls ('Auxiliary Territorial Service' I think). One of them, Helen Pollard (now Currie*) in her reminiscence of the Testery speaks not only of the thrill of it all but briefly hints at a romantic

---

* See Helen Currie, 'An ATS Girl's Memories of Bletchley Park at War and After' (undated). BP Trust, the Mansion, Bletchley Park, Bletchley, MK3 6EF, UK.

attachment. That attachment outlasted the war. If there is to be a dedication of this memoir then let it be to her.

For all the attractions of the new life, or perhaps because of them, I could not drop from my mind the initial 'white feather' impact of that roomful of WAAF girls. While on leave visiting my home in Weybridge, I learned from my father of questions from his peers at the St. Georges Hill golf club about what his son was doing for the war effort. Apart from knowing that I was not after all learning Japanese, his mind was unavoidably blank on what I was now up to. It was out of the question to give information of any kind to any person outside the wire beyond 'sort of clerical work' or the like. He asked me whether I had ever considered active service.

Back in BP I asked for an interview with Colonel Pritchard, and requested a transfer to the North African desert. Pritchard let me finish. Then he said: 'Who's been getting at you?' Taken off guard, I waffled. 'No one?' he enquired politely, and let his question hang in the air.

Eventually I blurted out that my father had mentioned such a possibility, but had applied no pressure. Anyway, I maintained, it had nothing to do with my decision. There was another uncomfortable pause. Then: 'I have to instruct you to return to duty. You see, Mr Michie, we have a war on our hands. Inconvenient, but unfortunately true. Unless you have further questions, you are free to return at once to your Section.' Pause. 'And by the way, I do not expect you to raise such matters again.' Pause. 'Either with me or with anyone else.' Longer pause. 'As for your father, I do not anticipate that he will raise them either.'

I returned to the Testery and I confess I felt relieved. I don't believe I gave it a further thought. But many years later my mother told me that my father had received a visit at his place of work in the City of London from an army colonel, who presented himself as my superior officer. Did I know anything about it? I shook my head. For a decade or two after the war, to reveal anything whatsoever about Bletchley Park and its activities continued to be embargoed under the Official Secrets Act. Inevitably its subjective restraints weakened over long time. None the less, 25 years passed before any mention of British use in 1943–5 of electronic computers for a cryptanalytic purpose appeared in the open literature.

CHESS, TURING, AND 'THINKING MACHINES'

It was through needing to consult the originator of Turingery on some point that I first met Turing. We soon discovered a common interest in chess, and also the fact that we were both sufficiently poor players to be able to give each other a level game. At BP a person was either a chess master, having been recruited for that reason (similarly with winners of national crossword competitions) or he did not count chess among his interests. We formed the habit of meeting once a week for a game of chess in a pub in Wolverton. On the pervasive need-to-know principle we never discussed his work in the Naval section. When I was demobilized I still knew nothing about Enigma, except possibly its name. Our shared topics of interest were (a) the possible mechanization of chess-playing and (b) learning machines. These interests were inspired in me by him, and were shared with Jack Good, now internationally renowned in mathematical statistics. In the post-war years, 'thinking machines' continued to occupy the three of us in occasional correspondence and meetings until Turing's death…

TURING STYLE AND BP STYLE: BOTH UNUSUAL

The Naval section had originally been founded to support Turing's great Enigma breakthrough. Hence it was natural that he be asked to head it. Unfortunately his uncanny intellectual gifts were tightly interwoven with an at least equally uncanny lack of what are ordinarily called 'social skills'. The predictable result was administrative chaos. Rapid *ad hoc* extemporizations came to the rescue from one of his brightest lieutenants, the one-time British Chess Champion Hugh Alexander. He had made his pre-wax living (there was in those days no money in chess) as an experienced and fast-thinking manager of the John Lewis London department store. So a little job like quietly and tactfully reorganizing Turing's bewildered section was to him an interesting challenge. In short order Alexander flowed into the *de facto* headship. Turing continued happily as *de jure* Head, no longer distracted by these matters.

One day Turing arrived at the gate of the Park late for work. On such occasions one signed oneself into a book with ruled columns and headings that included 'Name of Head of Section'. Turing unexpectedly wrote 'Mr. Alexander', and proceeded in to work. Nothing was said. But somewhere wheels turned silently. Records were updated. Alexander continued his miracles of inspired and often unorthodox deployment of human and material resources, but now as the official Head of Naval section.

I had this from a third party, and never asked Turing about it. I think he would have found my question uninteresting...

GOOD COMPANIONS

A common enterprise of comrades: many people of both sexes and of every rank and degree have spoken or written of their WW-II experiences, and of the exhilaration of 'Each for all and all for each'. At BP, friendship and mutual enjoyment continued in the more than half of each twenty-four hour cycle that was passed outside the wire, at dances with Wrens or ATS, sing-songs in the transport coaches, group expeditions to cinemas and pubs, daytime discussion walks in the countryside on coming off a night shift.

Far from being shouldered aside by the urgency of work-time preoccupations, in wartime Britain every kind of cultural interest, educational activity and entertainment blossomed. Twenty-first-century leisure notions of dumbed down amusements, of mindless hanging out, ganging up, or freaking out, would have seemed like bad news from another planet. Work-place politics, turf wars, and petty spites lay in the future. Later, often much later, people of my generation came upon them for the first time and made belated adjustment. I am not alone in the impression that our new world seems sometimes locked in joyless pursuit of the transient, or of the unattainable. We and our juniors elbow each other under ever more unpredictable competitive conditions. Yet memory tells us that today's gathering ills do not necessarily spring predestinate from unalterable flaws. There are other modes of living and working together. We know. We were there.

Turing's Vision
(1985)

There is much scepticism about the assertion that computers can actually create something new. People do not readily credit machines with creativity, partly because creativity has always been a thing of mystery, of essentially human quality, and they are offended to see it apparently brought down to the level of nuts and bolts. The cry is still heard that 'You only get out what you put in.' Many serious academics as well are bothered by the central role played by induction in computer creativity. The distinguished philosopher of science Sir Karl Popper denies that induction can be the source of new knowledge. Now, the evidence of concrete results is turning against the doubters. But we can also cite the vision of the man who in effect devised the whole theory of modern computing, years before electronic computers were technically feasible: the English mathematician Alan Turing, who died in 1954.

Turing's great achievement was to show, by a thought experiment in 1937, that a general-purpose computing machine was logically possible and would be capable of solving an unlimited variety of problems. He did this by conceiving a hypothetical device, since dubbed the 'Universal Turing Machine', that would wander up and down a tape on which was inscribed the data and a program, peering here, overwriting there, until an answer had been output onto the tape. As befits a person of such originality, Turing had an extraordinary turn of mind, and a carefree disregard of how the rest of the world behaved or thought. He used to cycle to work wearing a gas-mask as a protection against pollen. While working at the top-secret code-breaking centre at Bletchley Park during the Second World War, he buried some silver in the woods nearby as a precaution against the liquidation of bank accounts in the event of a successful German invasion, and later forgot where the hiding place was. He recruited a youthful Donald Michie after the war to help find it, with the aid of a gimcrack metal detector he put together himself, but to no avail.

Turing's own attempts at building machinery were inept, but his foresight about how others might do so was unsurpassed. He described before any real computers were operational a great deal about how these machines would be used, including many concepts which are now commonplace in data processing: loops, subroutines, boot-strapping, remote access. In a lecture to the London Mathematical Society in February 1947 he uttered some prophecies that strike a modern-day computer technologist (or user) as uncanny:

> Roughly speaking those who work in connection with the Automatic Computing Engine will be divided into its masters and its servants. Its masters will plan out instruction tables for it, thinking up deeper and deeper ways of using it. Its servants will feed it with cards as it calls for them. They will put right any parts that go wrong. They will assemble data that it requires. In fact the servants will take the place of limbs. As time goes on the calculator itself will take over the functions both of masters and of servants. The servants will be replaced by mechanical and electrical limbs and sense organs. One might for instance provide curve followers to enable data to be taken direct from curves instead of having girls read off values and punch them on cards. The masters are liable to get replaced because as soon as any technique becomes at all stereotyped it becomes possible to devise a system of instruction tables which will enable the electronic computer to do it for itself. It may happen however that the masters will refuse to do this. They may be unwilling to let their jobs be stolen from them in this way. In that case they would surround the whole of their work with mystery and make excuses, couched in well chosen gibberish, whenever any dangerous suggestions were made. I think that a reaction of this kind is a very real danger. This topic naturally leads to the question as to how far it is possible in principle for a computing machine to simulate human activities.

EVOLVING THE TABLES

Turing describes in detail how the machine holds in its memory both data and 'instruction tables' (the program). These tables would be worked out in detail in advance by mathematicians, but this mode of working would leave much to be desired. 'What we want,' Turing asserts, 'is a machine that can learn from experience.' He explains: It has been said that computing machines can only carry out the processes that they are instructed to do. This is certainly true in the sense that if they do something other than what they were instructed then they have just made some mistake. It is also true that the intention in constructing these machines in the first instance is to treat them as slaves, giving them only jobs which have been thought out in detail, jobs such that the user of the machine fully understands in principle what is going on all the time. Up till the present, machines have only been used in this way. But is it necessary that they should always be used in such a manner? Let us suppose we have set up a machine with certain initial instruction tables, so constructed that these tables might on occasion, if good reason arose, modify those tables. One can imagine that after the machine had been operating for some time, the instructions would have been altered out of all recognition, but nevertheless still be such that one would have to admit that the machine was still doing very worthwhile calculations. Possibly it might still be getting results of the type desired when the machine was first set up, but in a much more efficient manner. In such a case one would have to admit that the progress of the machine had not been foreseen when its original instructions were put in. It would be like a pupil who had learnt much from his master, but had added much more by his own work. When this happens I feel that one is obliged to regard the machine as showing intelligence.

The technique of having a program change part of itself is already used to a certain extent with low-level languages. It is, however, frowned upon as untidy. Only one or two experimental AI languages have facilities for operating on code as data, or executing data as code. Turing himself though knew where he stood, and characteristically it was not on the side of convention or tidiness. The closing passage of the 1947 lecture brings this home with eloquence and force, and with a clear affirmation of the principle that machines should learn by inductive modification of their instructions in response to the behaviour of humans:

> It might be argued that there is a fundamental contradiction in the idea of a machine with intelligence. It is certainly true that 'acting like a machine' has become synonymous with lack of adaptability. But the reason for this is obvious. Machines in the past have had very little storage, and there has been no question of the machine having any discretion. The argument might however be put into a more aggressive form. It has for instance been shown that with certain logical systems there can be no machine which will distinguish provable formulae of the system from unprovable, i.e., that there is no test that the machine can apply which will divide propositions with certainty into these two classes. Thus if a machine is made for this purpose it must in some cases fail to give an answer. On the other hand if a mathematician is confronted with such a problem he would search around [and] find new methods of proof, so that he ought eventually to be able to reach a decision about any given formula. This would be the argument. Against it I would say that fair play must be given to the machine. Instead of it sometimes giving no answer we could arrange that it gives occasional wrong answers. But the human mathematician would likewise make blunders when trying out new techniques. It is easy for us to regard these blunders as not counting and give him another chance, but the machine would probably be allowed no mercy. In other words then, if a machine is expected to be infallible, it cannot also be intelligent. There are several mathematical theorems which say almost exactly that. But these theorems say nothing about how much intelligence may be displayed if a machine makes no pretence at infallibility.

To continue my plea for 'fair play for the machines' when testing their IQ: a human mathematician has always undergone an extensive training. This training may be regarded as not unlike putting instruction tables into a machine. One must therefore not expect a machine to do a very great deal of building up of instruction tables on its own. No man adds very much to the body of knowledge; why should we expect more of a machine? Putting the same point differently, the machine must be allowed to have contact with human beings in order that it may adapt itself to their standards. The game of chess may perhaps be rather suitable for this purpose, as the moves of the machine's opponent will automatically provide this contact.

Now, three decades later, it is clear that the amount machines will eventually be able to add to the body of human knowledge may outreach even Turing's imagination.

Fifty Years After*
(1991)

LEE: What part did Turing play in the design of the Colossus?

MICHIE: Jack wrote to me recently and said 'surely not'. The only positive evidence that I have is that on occasion I did see Tommy Flowers, Max Newman, and Turing having conversations—and was told that this was what they were talking about. That's all—hearsay.

LEE: The implication that Hilton made is that Turing applied his knowledge of logic to the design.

MICHIE: I wrote to Jack recently about the input that Turing made. I believe it was rather peripheral.

GOOD: Well, Peter certainly got it incorrect. There can be no doubt that Newman was the main strength. I thought that Newman had been perhaps unconsciously influenced by his background in Boolean logic and by his

---

* From the introductory section of the original article:

'These interviews were conducted over a three-month period in early 1991 [by John A.N. Lee and Golde Holtzman] in preparation for making a series of videotaped interviews that were to be conducted by David Kahn, Karen Frenkel, and Perci Diaconis. It was not the intention to prepare a script for the videotaped interviews but instead to explore subjects and themes that could be woven effectively into the short periods available for taping. Because of security restrictions, we did not break any new ground in understanding the methods of codebreaking, but we did learn more about Good's and Michie's associations with Alan Turing and the development of some very early concepts of computer design. What follows then is a set of extracts from these interviews, not all of which were covered in the televised interviews.'

knowledge of 'Turing Machines'; he denied it.* Of course ... people are not aware of what goes on in their subconscious mind.

MICHIE: I am afraid that just doesn't sound like a plausible account from Max, because it would be impossible for Max to design that machine, of that character, without a background in logic.

GOOD: Oh, he had a background in logic—yes—Newman. He gave the course on logic which led to Turing's great paper. GCCS [the Government Code and Cipher School] chose Tommy Flowers and the Telephone Research Establishment (TRE) to build the Colossus, because Turing had had contact with them earlier about the possibility of building Bombes.

LEE: [Quoting Hilton] 'Much has been written in recent years about the scientists' success in "Britain's secret weapon." Others of us shared the excitement of successful achievements; some, like mathematician Max Newman, deserved great credit for providing the organizational framework essential to the full exploitation of that success. But Turing stood alone in the full comprehension of the name of the solution, and devising the solution—essentially by inventing the computer.'

MICHIE: It is true, Jack, that Turing used a kind of combinatorial brute-force approach which was embodied in the Bombe, and you can see it in the Colossus. But when Peter Hilton talks about Turing inventing the computer, he must be talking about inventing the 'Universal Turing Machine' in his pre-war paper.

GOOD: Right. Well, Turing was a bit secretive about his sources, I think. I mean I only discovered that the Poles had made a contribution by asking a question about something I didn't need to know. I think it was Arthur Chamberlain was sitting next to him [Turing], and myself were in the office, they had their backs to the window (I could draw a picture of their positions) and I said, 'How on earth did we discover the wiring of the [Enigma] wheels?' And Turing, giving this other person, I thought, a kind of meaningful look, said, 'I suppose the

---

* **Good:** He told me that he had worked in the 'Testery' [Major Tester's section] where Fish was attacked 'by hand' and that he was poor at that work and thought it should be mechanized.

Poles.' And I said, 'and perhaps a pinch?'* which of course was certainly possible. And then we stopped the conversation. But I had never heard of the 'Poles' before.

MICHIE: What was it then that Max Newman denied?

GOOD: Well, he stated that he suggested the machine—the Colossus machine. He thought that it was the sort of thing that ought to be mechanized, because he hated doing it by hand.

MICHIE: That being true, he said something to me, very, very similar, when I was in his home in the 1970s; he said, 'Well, I arrived and I was expected to do some cryptography and be very good at it. and I found out that I wasn't. I tried hard and I couldn't. So I got interested in why don't we mechanize the bloody thing.'

GOOD: Did he say 'bloody thing'?

MICHIE: Something to that effect, that was the spirit of it. You know, he spoke very combatively.

GOOD: Oh yes, but I don't think he would have said 'bloody thing.'

MICHIE: Well, those are my words, but … I was trying to get him to put the record straight.

GOOD: I know that he didn't like having to mess about when he thought that lecturers were bad. When he and I went to NPL to take some lessons from Turing. Turing had designed the control circuit of the ACE …

LEE: This is post-1945? While you were at Manchester?

GOOD: This is after the war—1946, I think. And we were there for nearly a week and Turing's method of explaining this was bad. He wasn't really all that very

---

* British slang for 'steal'.

good at lecturing. Instead of from the top down (a good expository is top down) it was bottom up. He began by talking about little pieces of the circuitry, and how to do an addition, and things like that. And gradually the picture emerged. But Newman would have none of that—in a sense he was Turing's social superior; he was just not going to stand this nonsense from Turing. The result was that I learned much faster, because Turing was my social superior and I was prepared to put up with it. So eventually I was able to get my first program right. Turing gave me a theorem that said 'No one gets their first program right.' So of course that put me on my mettle and I was extremely careful, checked very carefully. It wasn't a very long program, just 30-odd instructions. Newman said that programming the ACE was 'like trying to catch a mouse just as it was going into a hole.' He also foresaw that the cost of programming would far outstrip the cost of hardware, and that program development would be a 'massive industry'.

Regarding Colossus:

MICHIE: The [history of Bletchley Park] has one gap. They talk about the sudden change of urgency in getting the Colossus manufactured, and [having] 10 operational by D-day, as though that arose solely from the preparation for D-day. Actually there was a technical breakthrough which has never appeared, never been referred to, in any public account. The fact is that it was Jack and I, and only us two, that did that. And it had a quite radical [effect].

GOOD: I mentioned it—the main credit was yours for using the machine to help to determine the wheel patterns. Tom Flowers has already referred to the fact that there was a real breakthrough in breaking the wheel patterns … and I think that might have been in my discussion of his paper. It's in print …

MICHIE: I am not only concerned about myself, because if you recall, having got the idea, you and I immediately set to work and on the spot, and we worked very hard doing experiments with one of us behind the machine and the other looking at the other side.

GOOD: And you were behind the machine.

MICHIE: Pulling and pushing these wires. And I remember my doing something very dumb…

GOOD: Well, you made a mistake in sign, you forgot which way the wheel was going…

MICHIE: Anyway, the fact is, Jack, we may very well have got it right, because it did actually trigger a cascade process, and this is not generally known.

GOOD: Oh yes, it was very important: it was a very central idea, but it was simple.

MICHIE: I just want to know if it is going to come up at all.

GOOD: You know I mentioned it the other day—an important idea can be so simple as to seem totally trivial. The idea of a half-deciban,* which I introduced, which probably saved 50 percent of the time of Banburismus.** Such a simple idea that a schoolboy could have thought of it. (Of course, I had to estimate how much information would be lost.)

LEE: *Afterwards.*

GOOD: Yes, but here were these high-class people who had been working hard for some time without thinking of it. It is something to do with changing what's ongoing. There is a tendency for people to get into a rut. I can imagine a maintenance engineer on an automobile saying, 'of course force is proportional to acceleration.'

MICHIE: There's this hiatus in the Colossus story when people don't and can't say 'we've always known it' because almost nobody does know it.

---

* See I.J. Good, *Good Thinking: The Foundations of Probability and its Applications* (Minneapolis: University of Minnesota Press, 1983), p. 159: 'Turing used the term *deciban* by analogy with the acoustic term decibel for a unit of a weight of evidence, and we called the weight of evidence "decibannage", a clumsy term.'

** Named after the town Banbury, where the punched sheets used for decoding were manufactured.

LEE: In your case, what did you know about machines, and what did you know about the things you were doing—on which you built the ideas? Wasn't it Newton who talked about 'standing on the shoulders of giants'?

MICHIE: Well, the giant on whose shoulders everybody was standing, including Alan Turing, was Bill Tutte—he got the original break.

GOOD: The mistake that the Germans made was, I think, [to send] two messages at the same setting of the wheels. And that meant that it was then possible for a linguistic type like Wittgenstein or Turing to read the same language of both messages. Then that could be stripped off, and you have pure key. Which was then handed over to a mathematician to ...

MICHIE: You had two hypotheses about which would solve the problem. You had a key and one of them was right.

LEE: Well, you had the ultimate 'crib'?

MICHIE: Yes, but you didn't know which plain language went with which. Having got that right, you were 'in clover'.

GOOD: We worked on it for two or three months.

MICHIE: Later it was just done before breakfast.

GOOD: Yes, yes, three times before breakfast! [Laughter]

MICHIE: The task that Jack has just described is a pure task, in which all the cyphers have just gone away, because the two transmissions have the same key but different texts. If you add them together, by Boolean addition, the key cancels out and you are left with some gobbledegook, which you know however is the superimposition under Boolean addition of two texts. What would take Briga-dier Tiltman months, which was an incredible pioneering intellectual achievement, if and when the same thing popped up again, people would do it just in no time. But that was characteristic of acquiring the skill. Once you know it can be done, then you do it again.

GOOD: Peter Hilton was very good at adding two teleprinter letters together in his head, he could see them getting added together, he had good visualization—which may be one reason why he is a good topologist. He had a very quick mind. We were once standing outside a cinema, do you remember? And they were talking about the seats—they said, 'two [seats] at one [shilling] and six [pence]' and he would *immediately* say 'nine'. [Laughter] And each time when the man at the door announced how many seats there were at a certain price, instantly Peter would shout out the answer. I don't think anybody except the few of us around knew what joke he was making.

LEE: I was reading the script for the play *Breaking the Code*, and there is a conversation between Turing and Knox, when he first arrived at Bletchley—in the play—he is taken over by somebody else who explains about the Enigma, and he is talking about the wheels and the rotors, and so forth, and in the play, at least, Turing is doing the multiplication, apparently in his head, as to how many combinations that is. This one is so many thousands, and then [Pat] says, 'they added two more wheels, and now we get three out of five,' and Turing replies that there are 'so many'.

GOOD: Oh yes, I'm not sure that's a true story. There were originally only three wheels, then five in the 'library', and then it was raised to eight wheels on the Naval Enigma, so the number of possible wheel orders rose from 6 to 60 to 336 (equaling $8 \times 7 \times 6$). He wasn't that good at mental arithmetic. He was a very slow thinker!

MICHIE: Yes, and his mental skills were, in that environment, fairly normal, whatever that might be [at Bletchley Park].

Regarding a question on the authenticity of the story that BP cracked the message which targeted Coventry for a blitz starting on November 14, 1941, and that Winston Churchill had the difficult decision to protect the source of the break by allowing Coventry to be ravaged:

GOOD: That was denied, especially by Ronald Lewin; there simply wasn't time to do anything in the way of an evacuation.

LEE: There was also the feelings that if Churchill did know, (a) he could not break the silence and (b) there was no way you take 250,000 people and move them into the countryside.

GOOD: But apparently the official story is that there wasn't time. It was known but only a few hours ahead, whereas Winterbotham was given the impression that it was *only* that he [Churchill] couldn't reveal the secret so he had this horrible decision to make, to save thousands of lives perhaps, or reveal the secret—the Ultra secret.

MICHIE: It isn't even known that there is anything in this story at all—that there ever was a decrypt which gave notice of the attack on Coventry.

LEE: Of course the alternative clue was the possible existence of the directional [radio] beams [for the aircraft to follow] which could be detected.

GOOD: Yes, but only within an hour or so of the attack.

MICHIE: Cryptographers like Jack and me are the last ones in the world to be able to throw any light on this, because (a) we never acquainted ourselves, or were acquainted, with any of the content [of the messages], we were too busy breaking, which was our job; and secondly (b) even if we had, or even if we were the recipient of a rumour or report from somebody in the intelligence hut, it was our training to expunge it from consciousness! We really could do that.

GOOD: We certainly had no information on that. Anything I received concerning Coventry was learned from a book or from a meeting with Ronald Lewin, who interviewed me in Blacksburg.

MICHIE: Whether he was the source of any of these rumors, I cannot say. He is the source of the Coventry story, isn't he?

GOOD: Not the original Coventry story; no, that was Winterbotham's mistake apparently. Ronald Lewin was much more careful. He didn't just rush into print. He had contacts in high places and was a conscientious professional historian.

Discussion of Turing's homosexuality:

[In 1947 Good and Turing essentially exchanged locations, Good returning to work with the Foreign Office in London and Turing leaving NPL to join the computer-building group at Manchester.]

GOOD: ... we walked down King's Parade [Cambridge] with Turing, [to M.] do you remember?

MICHIE: After we read that passage that we weren't supposed to read?

GOOD: That's right! Turing was very angry with us.

MICHIE: He wasn't around in his room.

GOOD: He wasn't around and Donald began reading this manuscript. I don't know whether you read very much of it—I think you just said, 'Oh, this looks interesting,' perhaps something like that, and then Turing came in and said, 'What the heck are you doing?'

MICHIE: I think I requited him in due course because I think I published that paper later. It was about neurons and neural nets and doing computations with such constructions.

I published the typescript in *Machine Intelligence* in the 1960s.

GOOD: That was posthumous, of course.

MICHIE: Yes, I got permission from the estate. it was a matter of achieving subgoals.

GOOD: I probably looked at it for a couple of minutes, and you perhaps looked at it for five, and then Turing came back. I remember he was very angry. He didn't shout, but he was obviously pretty angry...when we walked down King's Parade that was the first time I discovered that he was homosexual. That was when he said that he was going to Paris to 'see a boy'. It was obvious that he was admitting or proclaiming his homosexuality.

MICHIE: He certainly wasn't [open about it] during the war, for some of us, including both of us, were quite unaware … I took quite seriously his engagement to …

GOOD: Joan Clarke?

MICHIE: At the same time, I was thoroughly aware that the whole problem of converse with women was a great burden, and problem, for him. And I recall him explaining to me once, I didn't think he was homosexual as a result of this conversation, because I [saw him through] the eyes of a rather priggish young person (me) who had just left school and was just experimenting with female company—I had grown up to look on women as undereducated relative to men, which perhaps to some extent was the case in those days. But he put it in a very grotesque way to me and said, 'You know, the problem is that you have to talk to them…If you take a girl out, you have to talk to her. And then so often when a woman says something, to me it is as though a frog has suddenly jumped out of her mouth.' It was an extremely unpleasant metaphor.

LEE: Hilton quotes you, Jack, as saying, 'It was fortunate that the authorities did not know during the war that Turing was a homosexual, otherwise the Allies might have lost the war.'

GOOD: Yes …

MICHIE: Oh, but that's absolute nonsense because Bletchley had some flamboyant homosexuals—Peter's ideas that security people were down on homosexuality itself is absolute nonsense. I can't think how he could write that. The most flamboyant case was Angus Wilson—he later became a very successful novelist, and he had a boyfriend called Beverly. Angus was about that high [indicating small] with flowing yellow hair (I remember it went white later) and Beverly (I forget his second name) was very 'weed-like', very tall. They could be seen shambling along the horizon, a daily sight, as they took their walk around lawns after lunch.

GOOD: I never knew that. I know that Angus Wilson ran around the pond in the nude when he had a nervous breakdown.

MICHIE: He was also said to have poured ink on his head on another occasion; it was the first sign he was going nuts again. I had not heard about the nude bit.

GOOD: I assumed they [the BP authorities] were down on homosexuality.

MICHIE: I think that's a retrospective color, actually. Because Henry Reed*—you remember Henry Reed—you knew he was a homosexual, didn't you'?

GOOD: No!

MICHIE: I must have known him better than you. He was always complaining to me about how his current affair was, or was not, prospering.

GOOD: Well, I was in digs** with him, and with David Rees.

MICHIE: Perhaps he regarded you as . . .

GOOD: Well, he never said anything about his affairs. He complained about the food. He said we ought to get together and complain to Mrs Buck, who was the landlady, about the food.

MICHIE: I had some links to a more literary set. There was a literary set in Bletchley, and I was fresh from a wholly arts education. There were these two cultures—the mathematicians' culture was another—I worked all my time in the mathematicians culture but I retained, certainly for a year or two, quite a lot of social links to various classics dons and literary people like Henry Reed. And in that group, things like whether Henry Reed was a homosexual—everybody knew. And the same with Angus Wilson.

GOOD: I had no idea.

Discussion about the people and organization at Bletchley Park:

MICHIE: I am not sure to what extent they made an imprint, a lasting imprint, on you, Jack, but my whole professional life really was fundamentally affected

---

* Reed was a poet who had composed a poem entitled 'Naming of Parts'.
** British slang for 'a rooming house'.

by those three years, and I am sure by the people. The formal organization, in the case of the Newmanry, was quite extraordinary. I don't think any of us realized until we got into ordinary peacetime organizations (sometimes called bureaucracies) what a dynamic, democratic, but efficiency-oriented community could be like. Just how incredibly effective was the hut compared to almost anything that is possible to organize in peacetime conditions. There are various sociological reasons how people change their effective priorities when the emergency goes. Now it so happens that I had the opportunity or it was placed in my lap, in 1963 to recreate an organization of that kind. There was a sense of urgency but from a different source. This was originally an unofficial group which finally won recognition—the experimental programming unit—and it was run by what we called 'The Round Table', which I set up and modelled exactly on Newman's tea party. The tea party was the authority and also the tea party could work fast and could decide something—that was it, and if Max Newman was out of town at the time—too bad—he would just have to read in the book and find out what the tea party had been up to. My Round Table was based exactly on that and the psychological conditions in that period of trying to start AI in Britain when there wasn't any. So all the prejudices and mechanisms were against it, and all my people were extremely untried, so they had to establish themselves. They were all juniors and dropouts—people who are well known now—like Rod Burstall, for example—people who were very talented, as they subsequently proved. But under those conditions, events reproduced that atmosphere and fire, and at the same time showed me and made me understand why in general you can't do it under normal conditions.

GOOD: To some extent Newman carried forward that method to Manchester. We had round-table discussions about the syllabus; he was a little more dictatorial there...less democratic, but everyone could have their say.

MICHIE: But that's a pretty normal academic practice—but the effectiveness bit tends to get lost. People do not feel obliged either to do it or to report back that they haven't done anything. They don't feel obliged to say when their action items are completed.

GOOD: In a way there was more freedom…

MICHIE: There is a particular mix which creates a group psychology certainly in which extraordinary freedom and extraordinary discipline are combined—and then you can go like a bomb.

GOOD: Of course, we were preparing decision trees for the WRNS ['Wrens']—things like that—who were not present at these meetings, so it was not democracy all the way down. We told them what they should do and that they were to carry out exactly what you wanted them to do.

LEE: Then those were your original programs, Jack?

GOOD: Yes, but these were executed by people.

LEE: Did you take the same idea into Colossus?

GOOD: Yes. What at first was research was reduced in many cases to trees which the WRNS were to carry out. We had a duty officer who would receive the print out…Usually the decision tree worked, but when it didn't, the duty officer would suggest what to try next.

Discussion of the uneasiness that Good and Michie felt, since no one knew the importance of what they were doing and their 'public' friends inferred that they were shirking their duty:

HOLTZMAN: You hear about the wartime groups who missed the good old times in the war because of the excitement, presumably; afterwards, you missed that urgency.

MICHIE: The same can be said of a great number of 'boffin' groups: They had a tremendous amount of special science that sprang from experience of scientists—radar, operations research, many other things—and many, many of these groups report the same kind of thing … of course, it can't help but be exciting.

LEE: Except you were cut off from your ultimate goal, achievement—the direct impact on the war. You were doing the decryption but did not necessarily see the messages, or did not know what the results were.

GOOD: But that was the thing to do. In the same way that the girls who operated the Bombes, if they got a machine 'stop', that was for them a success. That was their job and it was rare enough that it was very encouraging to them.

LEE: It was self-satisfying in the task itself, as opposed to knowing that you had influenced (say) the Normandy Invasion in some way ...

GOOD: Exactly.

MICHIE: We knew the very high priority on what we were doing—that was good enough. We were satisfied with that.

GOOD: I was disappointed when we were told that 'Jellyfish' was what we should go for, which is what Harry Hinsley said in his history. But 'Jellyfish' was one of the easier cyphers to break—'Tunny' was harder to break—it was more of a challenge to break 'Tunny' than 'Jellyfish'.

LEE: In some respects you were isolated from the real war. As opposed to the aircraft mechanic who was putting a plane into the air, knowing that the aircraft is going to go off and do something ...

MICHIE: Somewhat like an artillery man—who doesn't know what his shell is going to hit.

LEE: But he does get some satisfaction when he sees the bumph on the horizon.

MICHIE: Of course, but we got our satisfaction when we cracked the next day's coder.

GOOD: And of course at Los Alamos when they exploded the first atomic bomb they realized that they had at last achieved what they had been working on for years.

LEE: With a lot of people not knowing what their piece was!

GOOD: Yes, they achieved their engineering goals. You can say it was a matter of achieving subgoals.

MICHIE: It was not the same as people who were out dying in the desert.

GOOD: No, but we might have died nevertheless. I was once in an 'Anderson Shelter'* in London when a time bomb exploded about nine yards away.

MICHIE: One or two of the ATS** girls whose boyfriends were on active service felt that we were in a kind of 'funk hole.' Fairly soon after I arrived I was made to feel that by one or two of them. Before I mucked in with the Testery, I had a few weeks, first of all learning things like reading punched paper tape, and secondly teaching young Roy Jenkins—whom you probably remember...

GOOD: The Roy Jenkins?***

MICHIE: Yes, he wasn't very studious, I am afraid. In any case, it began to prey on my mind after a while. I didn't do anything about it to start with, but after I guess a month or so, particularly since my father dropped a remark which made me feel worse, I brooded over it. Finally I went to Colonel Pritchard, who was the one who recruited me from the cypher school in Bedford, and said to him that I wanted to apply for a reposting. He said, 'Yes, really? Tell me more.' So I said, 'Well, I want to be reposted'—I was on the books of the Army—'for active service, preferably in North Africa.' There was a very long silence and then he said, 'Who's been getting at you?' [Laughter] And I said, 'Well, my dad, as a matter of fact.' And he said, 'I will pay very careful attention to what you have told me, Mr. Michie. Thank you. Good-bye.' So I pottered off, and never heard or thought much more about it, but after a while I discovered, from my father, that very shortly after that Pritchard had suddenly appeared at my father's office in London. He had a talk with him; I certainly heard no more about it from my father...

---

* 'Anderson Shelters' were corrugated steel, inverted U-shaped enclosures which families buried in their own gardens for protection.
** Auxilliary Territorial Service.
*** Jenkins was later Chancellor of the Exchequer, and President of the European Commission.

Early Promise

Of the early days of computing and machine intelligence research, I have chosen three essays from the early 1960s that appeared in the *Scotsman*, and one from the late 1960s. The first three are popular articles, but they do capture something of what was going on in the early days of the Experimental Programming Unit at Edinburgh. They also describe a growing frustration at the lack of government support—resulting in Donald's report surveying the needs of computer scientists in Britain—and the excitement that followed the promise of sustained funding following that report. The reader will have to look to Donald's technical articles for his own contributions during this period. The 'graph traverser', developed in 1966 with J. E. Doran, was the first example of using a heuristic search function and a precursor to the famous A* algorithm of Hart, Nilsson, and Raphael. MENACE, made out of matchboxes in 1963 and possibly the first trial-and-error learning machine, learned to play noughts and crosses. It led to the subsequent development of BOXES in 1968, that learned to master motor tasks based on the principles of rewards, punishment, and trial-and-error, laying the basis for the field of reinforcement learning. Glimpses of these can be found in 'Clever or Intelligent?'.

'Recollections of Early AI in Britain' is, in fact, a transcript of a video recording that can be obtained on the Web (details are in the Publications section). Finally, there is the 'Tokyo–Edinburgh Dialogue'. In 1971, Japan was taking its first steps in robotics. Members of Tokyo's Electro-technical Laboratory visited Edinburgh and presented Donald with a list of 35 questions. The answers start where 'Recollections' ends, and give perhaps the most complete picture of the FREDDY project. There may be too much of the nuts-and-bolts for some, but this only helps remind us that robotics poses as many questions to the engineer and programmer as it does to the philosopher. It is, of course, this robotics work at Edinburgh that was to come under the glare of Sir James Lighthill's damning assessment of artificial intelligence.

Machines That Can Play Games (1963)

The last ten years have seen a silent revolution—the computer revolution. I believe that is likely to affect mankind as much as the invention of language, the discovery of the wheel, or the control of fire.

Every area of our lives has already been affected. The enormous burdens of accounting and clerical work of all kinds, under which every business or administrative enterprise tends to become buried, is beginning to be lifted by the automation of white-collar work. Road and air traffic systems are coming within the reach of computerized control. At the advancing wave front of new development are such feats as machine translation of foreign languages, machine reading of the printed word, and machine recognition of human speech.

Increasingly complicated tasks, requiring great experience and judgment, are yielding to mechanization. A good example of this is the task of the weather forecaster. Most readers would agree about the need to improve upon merely human powers in this respect! Computer programs for weather forecasting have already reached, and are just beginning to surpass, the level of accuracy attained by human forecasters.

Of special interest are results obtained by a group at Stanford Electronics Laboratories, led by Bernard Widrow, the inventor of a device called the Adaline, which 'learns' to classify patterns. One of his students, M. J. C. Hu, has turned his attention to the complicated patterns of atmospheric pressure, etc., with which the weather forecaster has to work. Preliminary results reported this month to the American Association for the Advancement of Science are extremely encouraging, showing 83 per cent accuracy for next day forecasts, compared with 67 per cent for the US Weather Bureau forecasters.

BEHAVIOUR

I believe that only be the first wave of the computer revolution has yet broken upon us, and that the impact of the second wave will be even more dramatic than the first. What I have in mind are current attempts to program computers so that they show qualities of 'learning', 'originality', and 'intelligence'—in other words, forms of behaviour which we would call 'intelligent' if we observed them in a human being.

For example, Mr John Martin, of Ferranti Ltd, has written program to my design which causes a Pegasus computer to play noughts and crosses against itself at the rate of roughly a game per second. The interest of the behaviour of the computer while under the control of this programme is *not* that it plays noughts and crosses but that it *learns* to play, and improves its game with practice.

The reader may feel that this is all very amusing but of no conceivable practical importance. He may be right, just as were those who laughed at the early balloonists. The idea of using hot air to lift a manned basket into the skies has not had any significant impact on civilized life. But he may be wrong, just as were those who scoffed at the Wright brothers' first attempts at the heavier-than-air flight.

There are today in our increasingly complex industries all manner of problems requiring elementary trial-and-error learning. In a chemical factory the objective may be to confine a reaction within certain limits by turning knobs on a control panel. The knobs may control such things as temperature, rate of flow, concentration of chemicals, etc.

HUNCHES

Such systems are often so complicated that it is not possible fully to analyse them, so that we cannot lay down precise rules in advance for turning the knobs. In such cases we normally employ a human being, who over a long period of trial-and-error acquires a semi-instinctive skill at manipulating the system.

Today, however, computer scientists are beginning to design programs which show the requisite 'learning' behaviour, and thus set the human operator free to employ his time in more interesting ways.

A common reaction to somebody researching in machine intelligence is to say that he is trying to do the impossible. 'After all the computer can only do what you tell it to do.' We are prepared to believe, at a pinch, that trial-and-terror learning can be mechanized, but how on earth can machines show originality? In other words could a machine have a 'hunch'?

Work in this is field has already disposed in general of the point about originality. Computers have produced new proofs for old theorems in school geometry, which have much surprised the human designers. A computer program written by L. A. Hiller and L. M. Isaacson at the University of Illinois has composed music in various styles ranging from church music to modernistic. The machine's compositions when played by an orchestra were as normal to the ears of the inventors as to members of the audience, who had no special knowledge of the computer program.

What about 'hunches'? Most readers will have seen the children's puzzle consisting of a square frame containing numbered tiles, one space being empty so that the tiles can be slid about. The object is to slide them around in order to achieve some pattern of numbers.

Let us assume that the pattern is the one shown in the photograph.* It is interesting to watch the behaviour of a human being when first confronted with this puzzle. His earlier efforts at the solutions are usually painfully fumbling with many retracings and wasted moves. As he gains experience, he tends to arrive at solutions by way of shorter and shorter paths. But usually there is a more or less sudden transition at which his performance takes a sharp turn for the better. The transition marks the point at which he has hit upon some 'hunch' on how to

---

* The photograph could not be reproduced here for technical reasons. The pattern shown in it is this (here, each number represents a tile and '-' represents the blank space):

```
1  2  3
8  -  4
7  6  5
```

tackle the problem, e.g., some way of classifying a given configuration as 'nearer to' or 'further from' the desired configuration.

Two questions immediately arise: (1) Is it possible to program a computer so that it will perform well at this puzzle? (2) Is it possible to program it so that it will have good hunches on how to solve it?

Question (1) presents no particular difficulty, and the answer is 'Yes'. I have myself investigated the behaviour of a machine based on a very simple puzzle-solving strategy. In rough terms the strategy consists in working out a score for the 'distance' from the current configuration of the puzzle to the target configuration. The score has two components. One component measures the number of squares separating each tile from the place where it should be, and the other measures the degree to which the tiles are in the right sequence in clockwise order round the central square.

All that the machine has to do at each stage is to make the move, out of those available, which gives the smallest distance score. The machine's performance is quite good; that is to say, better than my own but worse than my secretary's!

But, one may ask, where did the rules come from calculating the distance score on which the machine's decisions are based? The answer is of course that they came from a human brain, which means, in the last analysis, from a hunch. What are the prospects of also mechanizing this elusive process of 'hunching' or concept formation?

This is the point at which research into mechanized thought-processes, or 'artificial intelligence', is currently stuck. One can only marvel at what has been already achieved by computer programs, none of which has been endowed with concept-forming capabilities. For instance, last summer a former draughts champion of Connecticut was beaten by a computer program written by A. L. Samuel of IBM Research Laboratories, Yorktown Heights. Yet Samuel told me soon after the event that be was still fumbling without success for a way to enrich his computerized draughts player with the capacity to form new concepts—as opposed to merely manipulating and attaching weights to concepts fed in from outside.

PROBLEM

It may be that the problem is so difficult that attempts to tackle it using models of intelligent behaviour as complicated as draughts-playing are over-ambitious. In collaboration with Dr Bernard Meltzer, of Edinburgh University, I am currently trying a more modest approach using the simple 3 × 3 puzzle referred to previously. It is too early for us to be able to say very much as yet, except that some definite progress has been made.

How to computerize concept-formation has also been under study for a number of years by the US Air Force's multi-million-dollar research establishment, the Rand Corporation. One team in particular has been attempting to design a 'General Problem Solver', which should be capable of tackling a mental task regardless of its particular nature; that is to say, if equipped with the rules of chess, it should begin to work out how to improve its chess; if given the axioms of Euclid it should be able to look for proofs of theorems.

Up to date the General Problem Solver has been richer in promise than in performance, but this is a characteristic of much of the effort in this very young subject. Future developments of the Rand program should be well worth watching.

Not only the Rand Corporation, but dozens of American military and other government agencies are pouring money into new ways of using computers. In the US large-scale studies of advanced methods are also being made by forward-looking private enterprises such as the huge Bell Systems, inventors of Telstar.

In Britain the picture is one of the early post-war promise, slowly starved to death by Government apathy and sheer lack of funds. In tomorrow's article [which follows below] I shall discuss some aspects of this sad story, and take a look into the future.

Where Britain Lags Behind
(1963)

It is often thought that the main impact of the new 'electronic brains' is upon commerce and industry. Commercial applications are indeed of very great importance, but equally spectacular are the possible effects of high-speed computing methods upon the range and tempo of scientific advance.

It is therefore easy to understand the excitement aroused in scientific circles by the recent initiation in Scotland of a pioneering experiment. Edinburgh University has been wired up, by 200 miles of telephone cable, to one of the largest and most powerful computers in the world.

In attempting a popular account of the new computer sciences one is handi-capped by many misconceptions about the subject. Most people are under the impression that without a thorough knowledge of advanced mathematics it is not possible to use a computer (i.e. 'program' it, in the technical jargon). This is not true. The only quality which is important for a programmer to possess is the ability to think clearly and logically.

The misconception has grown up because the main use to which computers have been put in the past is the handling of mathematical problems. Naturally anyone who wants to tackle such a problem with a computer must have a grasp of the mathematics involved in that particular problem. Today, however, some of the most exciting developments in computer usage are concerned with such essentially non-numerical problems as the decipherment of ancient languages, automatic translation, decision-making in business, the solution of problems in logic, the simulation of learning processes, the playing of games such as draughts, and so on.

Further than this, as indicated in yesterday's article, the first steps have been taken towards the mechanization of thought itself.

AWARENESS

We may look to a future in which man can turn to the computer not only for aid in making routine evaluations and decisions but even for new formulations and approaches. There is a most conspicuous difference between America and Britain as regards awareness of what is happening today in this field. In the past five years hundreds of active research projects have been springing up all over the United States devoted to attempts to mechanize, in one way or another, some of the processes of human thought. Britain, however, where much of the pioneer work was done a decade ago, is showing a mysterious slowness in catching on.

It was possible for an authoritative article published in the *Observer* last year to state that not a single British university supports research work in 'artificial intelligence'. By contrast, in the Massachusetts Institute of Technology no fewer than 150 research workers are engaged in this field alone.

This is a state of affairs which seems all the more tragic to those who know that the mathematical foundations of computing were laid by a Briton, A. N. Turing, whose untimely death ten years ago robbed the world of one of the geniuses of our century.

Not only was Turing remarkable for the depth and originality of this mathematics. Equally astounding was his ability, years before even the most primitive digital computer existed, to foresee in considerable detail the whole future development, including the visionary possibilities of 'artificial intelligence'.

Turing contributed actively to the enterprising post-war efforts, at the National Physical Laboratory in London and at Manchester University, in designing and building prototype machines. Just at what point the rot set in is difficult to pinpoint. But by the mid 1950s momentum had already been sadly lost.

It was during this period that at London University two men—both of whom today occupy leading positions in the computer world—toiled for years unassisted on a shoestring budget to bring into existence what could have been at that time the world's most advanced computer. By 1956, this daring project was within a few thousand pounds of completion. The money to push on was not forthcoming. The project was dismantled and today their unfinished handiwork survives as a museum specimen.

A scandal like this is not likely to be repeated, if only because a ship cannot he sunk unless it has been floated in the first place. In the realm of machine building, the scale and pace of development today require monetary investment far beyond what our lethargic British policies could ever authorize. Even commercial research and development may at this moment be singing its swan song. The next generation of computers, performing calculations in ten-millionths rather than millionths of a second, will be arriving in our midst in perhaps two years or three. But they will be arriving from across the Atlantic.

The electrical and physical side of computing, the development of new ultra-fast switching components, the design of ways of assembling and organizing complicated circuitry—all this is known in the computer world as 'hardware'. As implied above, work on hardware can be expensive. It is still cheap at the price, when assessed against the tens of millions which can be absorbed by a single research project in nuclear physics.

By 'software' is meant the development of new ways, not of building computers, but of using computers. It is when we turn from 'hardware' to 'software' that the arithmetic of official cheese-paring becomes entirely laughable. The simple fact about 'software' research is that its speed of advancement is dependent on little else than the energy and brains of those engaged in it. Little more is required in the way of cash than salaries and the rental of time on a computer.

This is why it is one of the fast-expanding fields of scientific research in which a small and hard-up nation like our own stands a chance to challenge the two giants, America and Russia. But the men who could be helping to build the research teams to make this challenge, are being forced to look overseas for surroundings more congenial to research initiative.

Among the more serious effects is the weakening of Britain in world markets. The industries hit are precisely those in which a small country, rich in know-how rather than material resources, might hope to make its mark. The whole tempo of automation, crucially dependent on the computer sciences, has lagged painfully. Lacking a fresh impetus from home-grown sources of new ideas, Britain may decline to the point where her only export is frustrated scientists and engineers.

The root of the trouble, as I see it, is a particular frame of mind on the part of the older generations of our scientists and administrators. This state can best be described as a special blend of ignorance and bliss. The full force of the trance-like condition strikes one with renewed impact on returning form touring in America. There, the entire scientific and commercial community seems fully alive to the opening of a new era by an invention more revolutionary than the development of the steam engine nearly 200 years ago.

Where is this attitude most entrenched and what is to be done? Are the universities to blame? I don't think they are. In general universities and technical colleges are most willing to give shelter and encouragement to any lively research programme that can attract money from outside.

Are the research councils to blame? Yes and no. Yes for being so slow to catch on. No, in that, having once caught on, such bodies as the Department of Scientific and Industrial Research are at last making serious studies of what is to be done.

Is the Government to blame? Yes and again yes. The first 'yes' is for the Treasury, which has the power to blight any scheme, whatever its timeliness and promise, by mere refusal to make available the necessary cash. The second 'yes' is for the new Ministry of Science. By founding this body, the government gave itself a great opportunity to wake up.

The only immediate hope which I see arises from the impending general election. Whichever party is successful, a new man is likely to take over this potentially vital ministry. These are some of the steps that I would like to see him take.

FIVE POINTS

1 Endow at least a dozen research fellowships in computer science for young men who have recently finished their university or technical training. I see no reason why the only such research fellowships at present available in this country should be those offered by an American corporation, International Business Machines.

2 Enable by appropriate subsidies British computer companies to second members of their own staff for two or three year periods to join academic research projects. This has been tried in America with much benefit to both universities and companies.

3 Demand Treasury support for the research councils on a scale permitting a four- or five-fold increase in spending on pioneering work, especially in 'software' research.

4 Get the Treasury, through the Universities Grants Committee, to facilitate the founding of university departments in the computer sciences throughout the country. It may soon seem as archaic that a university should have only one department in the subject as the idea of having only one department in a medical school (Edinburgh has about 30).

5 Finally, he prepared to spend at least a million pounds (the Festival of Britain cost more than two million) in capitalizing, in a university setting, a permanent centre of advanced studies.

It is no use merely fiddling with the problem. If the next Minister of Science wants to secure the future of computer science in Britain and to start the urgent business of counter-attracting from America some of our lost talent, then he must be prepared to launch a programme on something like this scale.

Edinburgh Will Set the Pace (1966)

Two and a half years ago, when I wrote on 'The Computer Revolution', my theme was that hopes for Britain as a leading technological nation were being blighted by official ignorance and apathy. Lack of money, lack of men, and lack of adequate machines was bringing research initiative to a standstill in a key sector of science.

Summarizing some of the extraordinary advances of computer science in America, I called for prompt and far-reaching official action, before the potentialities of British brains and initiative in this new field became fatally stunted.

FRUSTRATION

The following year I toured over 20 British universities on behalf of the Science Research Council (then the DSIR) to investigate the truth of my own allegations. I had to report an almost universal sense of frustration, despair or, in some cases resentment provoked by the Governments past computer policy. The keener and more dynamic the research worker, the more intense tended to be his sense of being let down by 'his own side' in the international arena, and I concluded that 'expenditure during the next five years on computer-provision for the Universities will have to be at many times the level of the past five years.'

The Council for Scientific Policy and the University Grants Committee subsequently launched a further investigation, to assess the computer requirements of British Universities and research establishments. The investigating Committee, led by Professor Flowers of Manchester University, submitted its report last summer.

Suspense about its contents has now been broken by a historic announcement in the House of Commons by the Minister of Education and Science, Mr Anthony Crosland. He has outlined a six-year policy, to cost £30 million. The major feature is the setting up of three regional computer centres at the Universities of London, Manchester, and Edinburgh, with very large computers to which research workers from other university and research institutions would have access.

The magnitude of the new departure can be judged by comparing this average rate of planned spending—£5 million a year—with the expenditure over the past three years—half a million pounds per year!

This decision is, I believe, one of the most important steps ever taken in this country's scientific development. Let us look at some of the questions which it raises.

Why should we have a few very large computers rather than many small ones? What is 'computer science' and why should it he developed? Can computers do anything else except arithmetic? How will the new technology affect the world in which our children will grow up?

The argument for large machines is economic. A large and more expensive computer works faster, and the gain in speed more than counter-balances the increased cost. So it's cheaper to have large numbers of users 'plugging in' to one big central installation than equip them all with little machines of their own.

The phrase 'plug in' is not as fanciful as it sounds against the background of recent advances in computer technology. Users will soon be able to converse with a machine many miles distant over the ordinary telephone network, the computer appearing to give each user its undivided attention. The 'console' or control panel for this purpose need not consist of anything more elaborate than a special electric typewriter.

It is also becoming possible to connect many small computers by telephone link to a few larger ones. The concept of a 'national computational grid' begins to emerge, in which the citizen of the future will command the services of mighty computing machines merely by dialling his nearest center. He will then call upon problem-solving power and information resources in much the same way as he now avails himself of water, gas, and electricity piped to him through our nation-wide utility networks.

NEWBORN BABY

Many people imagine that a computer is somehow inherently capable of everything when it first arrives from the manufacturer. Actually in its newborn state the computer is capable of almost nothing. Like a newborn baby, its possibilities depend upon the education which is fed into it.

In computer terms this takes the form of complicated 'programs'. Only under the guidance of programs can computers even do arithmetic, let alone make logical deductions, communicate with each other or with human users, or show the first few sparks of 'intelligence' which can today be achieved by a few very sophisticated programs.

Having understood that the role of programming is crucial, the next difficulty for the laymen is to form an idea of the mountains of human labour which go into it. Writing a big computer program is the modern equivalent of building the pyramids, and can consume hundreds of man-years.

Depending on the skill with which a program has been written, and the imagination and experience which has gone into it, the result can be worth a fortune, or absolutely nothing at all. A program to design the routes of a cargo fleet, or to help a bank to choose its investments, or to control machine tools in a factory, can save millions of pounds or it can simply pour money down the drain. Everything then turns on the art and craft of programming, and this is, indeed, what computer science today is mainly about.

The chief work of computers for years to come will be essentially doing schoolroom sums on a gigantic scale and at an inconceivable rate, for physicists, doctors, engineers, architects, statisticians, demographers, chemists, geologists, astronomers, and so forth.

But a new way of using computers will gradually take over the central place during the coming ten years. I refer to the simulation by computer of human thought-processes, in particular the ability to generalize and learn by experience. What are the new domains which will be opened up when we can make a computer think and converse 'like a human'?

Long-term applications in such fields as information retrieval and machine translation are obvious. I shall instead mention a few of the more humdrum and immediate benefits which I foresee.

SOUNDS SIMPLE

Think for a moment about the kind of problem which sounds like a mathematical one, but which mathematicians do not know how to solve. For instance a manufacturer has to send lorries on a round trip so that they visit each of, say, 20 towns. He wants to find a route on the map which will make the total mileage covered as small as possible. It sounds simple, but no mathematical technique is known which will give the answer.

Perhaps he could look at all possible routes, adding up the distance for each one. There are too many possibilities—even for the world's fastest computer—to tackle by this 'brute force' method. In practice the manufacturer hires a human intelligence, a flesh-and-blood designer, to sit down with a map and a slide-rule and drawing materials and do the best he can. The designer relies upon guesswork, common-sense, and accumulated 'know-how'. An unsatisfactory and expensive method!

Again, consider the problem of drawing a network on the map to give a pattern of electricity transmission lines for a power grid. Transmission lines cost the taxpayer over £100 million per annum, so that the fewer and shorter the lines the better. In my own research group, Mr Burstall has written an 'intelligent' computer program which will design electricity networks about as well as a human designer employed by the Central Electricity Generating Board.

Suppose that Burstall's program were better than human skill by a margin of only one or two percent. This could represent a national saving of a million pounds or more per annum, about equal to the whole of last year's expenditure on providing scientific computers for the entire nation!

Are there other intellectual problems measurable in pounds, shillings, and pence? Constructing efficient time-tables, whether for schools, or universities, or railway or bus services, is something which we do the way we do because we don't know any better! Here again computer programs of the new sort—i.e. using a flexible kind of 'reasoning' rather than mere brute-force calculation— are coming to the rescue.

Finally, consider problems of control. We are beginning to be able to program a computer not only to give answers to questions but also to give decisions. I refer particularly to the second by second decisions needed to control complicated factory procsses.

Particularly important is the possibility of adaptive control, whereby the computer system improves its performance by using its own past experience. If really effective means of 'learning' can be built into automatic systems then the way will be clear for a runaway process. Learning systems will be used to design better learning systems!

A striking feature of computer science is the way that far-fetched or even frivolous-sounding projects may give clues to vital practical problems. The American scientist Minsky is currently trying to program a computer to play ping-pong, having connected to the machine a photo-electric 'eye' and an electrically, operated 'hand'. In my own laboratory, in collaboration with the Atlas Computer Laboratory at Chilton, we are programming a computer to learn by trial-and-error to do pole-balancing tricks.

Mastering the formidable technical difficulties of a toy problem is often the first step to the solution of a real and important problem—in the present case the use of computers to augment human manual skills in industry.

RECREATIONAL PUZZLES

The same is true of more intellectual sports. My colleague J. E. Doran and I have been using recreational puzzles as an aid in developing a general problem-solving program. Now, however, the same program has been found useful by a colleague, R. J. Popplestone, in his study of theorem-proving by machine.

The recent Government announcement throws the way open to a great advance of computer science. There is no reason why Britain should not lead the world in computer science, as she has done in radio astronomy, molecular biology, and plasma physics. The only danger is that the Government having done one good deed may now heave a sigh of relief and say 'Thank goodness! This new baby previously neglected, is taken care of! It can be left to grow up on its own.'

This would be like putting aeroplanes into the air, but forgetting to train and commission pilots for them. In the past ten years much money has been lost through failure to install computers. Very much more money has been lost by installing computers without the programmes and programming staff needed to put them to work.

Whatever is done elsewhere, I am confident that Edinburgh University, chosen as the base for one of Britain's three planned regional centers, is going to set the pace.

Clever or Intelligent?
(1969)

It is fashionable to talk of the computer revolution as the second industrial revolution. The first revolution mechanized muscle power, and today motor cars, ships and aeroplanes, power stations and factories sustain a population which has multiplied fivefold since the lifetime of James Watt. But now we see the beginning of the mechanization of brain power. It is even possible that just as machines have outstripped muscles, so computers may some day outstrip brains.

The fact that we are still in the first onrush of the second revolution tends to blind us to the pace and acceleration of change: even now a third revolution is gathering momentum—the harnessing of mechanized brain power to mechanized muscle power—i.e. intelligent robots. I am not going to speculate about the uses to which these new and rather awesome creatures will be put. The early guesses in the case of horse-less carriages or heavier-than-air machines seem half-baked when we look back. I am going instead to talk about the work of a few laboratories scattered around the world, including our own in Edinburgh, where scientists are trying to develop a design philosophy for automated intelligent behaviour. Just as at earlier stages in technological history one would find groups developing the hovercraft philosophy, the jet philosophy, the flying-machine philosophy, or the philosophy of the horseless carriage, so now a number of American laboratories, and three in Britain—at Edinburgh, Aberdeen, and Sussex Universities—are trying to develop machine intelligence.

In fields like space exploration, which require billions of dollars of expensive equipment, American supremacy is perhaps inevitable. But machine intelligence is open for rapid development with a research budget of relatively modest size.

It may therefore be of interest to talk about what research workers in this field are actually trying to do and what are the problems of programming a robot to act intelligently.

It was an Englishman, Alan Turing, who first suggested in 1953 that board games like chess or draughts could provide models through which the design principles for intelligent robots could be investigated. The basic idea is shown in Figure 1. Here the interaction between the machine and its environment is depicted as a game against Nature. One player's strategy (Nature's) is fixed. We can't do anything to change it. What about the other player's strategy? Inventing strategies for the machine side of the game is precisely the research worker's craft, just as inventing stories is the novelist's craft, or inventing music is the composer's. Figure 2 shows the general structure of a game. In such a tree diagram the blobs represent states of the board and the lines represent legal moves. To put this in terms of the game against Nature, Figure 3 shows a fragment of a decision tree describing an imaginary problem from real life. Each node on the diagram represents a possible state of affairs and the lines represent legal moves. The lines radiating from each node indicate possible reactions of

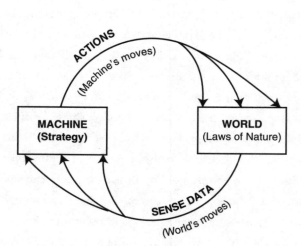

Figure 1. The interaction between machine and its environment depicted as a game against Nature. Equipping the machine with strategies for this game is the subject matter of machine intelligence.

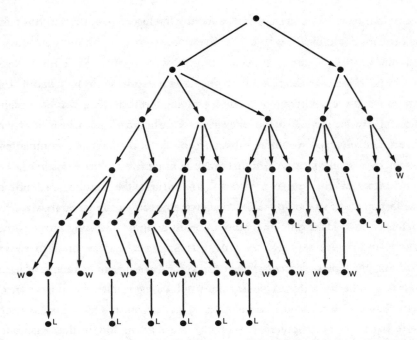

Figure 2. A game tree. Here the blobs represent states of the board and the lines represent legal moves. The terminal nodes have been labelled with W for a won game (for the first player) and L for a lost game.

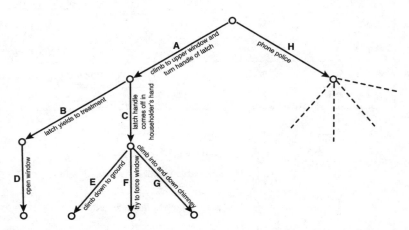

Figure 3. Part of a planning tree for a householder locked out of his house. Each node represents a state of affairs and the lines represent possible courses of action or reaction on the part of the house-holder or the environment, according to whose turn it is to play.

the world, or possible lines of action for the intelligent planner, according to whose turn it is to play.

As indicated in Figure 4, strategies come in two sizes: (1) clever but mindless and (2) intelligent. An example of category A in the realms of games would be a noughts-and-crosses strategy in the form of a look-up table: that is, a table showing a recommended move for every possible board position. In an adaptive version, table entries would be subject to change in the light of accumulating results of past plays. A working example is a machine which I made out of matchboxes (Michie, 1963) many years ago to illustrate the principle. Each box is in effect an item in a look-up table, corresponding to a particular board state. In each box are beads of different colours, corresponding to different moves. By a reward-and-punishment regime involving adding or subtracting beads for those used in a given play, elementary trial-and-error learning can be demonstrated. It turns out that even this elementary kind of learning results, on a purely automatic basis, in surprisingly complex forms of behaviour. Figure 5 shows the performance of a computer program constructed roughly on the matchbox principle (see Michie, 1968) learning to master a quite difficult motor task, which

Type of strategy	Type of behaviour
A only	reflex
A + B	adaptive
A + B + C	simple cognitive
A + B + C + D	complex cognitive

Key

"Clever but mindless" { A : fixed stimulus–response tables
                         B : modifiable stimulus–response tables

"Intelligent" { C : cognitive maps using lookahead
                 D : inductive reasoning and planning

Figure 4. Diagram showing two types of strategy, 'clever but mindless' and 'intelligent', together with the types of behaviour they give rise to.

it had never seen before, namely balancing a pole on a motor-driven cart. This task was originally formulated, in a different context, by Donaldson in 1960. Here the pole-and-cart system is simulated in a second computer connected to the learning computer by a high-speed data link. Every fifteenth of a second the pole-and-cart system sends a signal across the link, and the learning program must immediately reply either 0 or 1. The reply imparts either a leftward or rightward drive to the cart's motor. No interpretation of the state signals is given to the learning program, nor any information as to the significance of the 0 (left) versus 1 (right) choice. But as can be seen, it manages to piece together an adequate control strategy.

In the robot realm an early triumph in this category was Grey Walter's electronic tortoises which were capable of quite involved goal-seeking behaviour. Latter-day descendants include a wide variety of automatic control and guidance systems used in space navigation, ballistic weaponry, and the like. Why do we call these clever machines mindless? What is the equivalent of a 'mind' when furnishing a robot? The key feature is the ability to construct and store internal models of the world from the fragmentary incoming stream of sense data, and to use these as the basis of planning. We

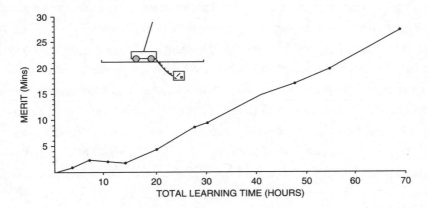

Figure 5. A 'clever but mindless' strategy which shows adaptive behaviour using a simulated pole-and-cart system harnessed to a learning computer. The curve shows average time-until-crash plotted against learning time. Thus after 70 hours of pure trial-and-error learning, the pole is balanced for approximately 30 minutes.

owe this formulation to Craik (1943) the gifted experimental psychologist whose early death in 1945 robbed Britain of one of her brightest scientific hopes.

An example of an intenal model is the 'cognitive map' which we construct when we learn to find our way through a maze, or even our own house. A table of situation–action pairs will get us just so far until something goes wrong— like finding ourselves locked out. It is then crucially important to us that *in our model*, as in outside reality, the chimney connects the roof to the inside of the house. This is what makes it possible for us to include for example the move 'climb into and down the chimney' in the planning tree of possibilities shown in Figure 3.

Growing planning trees inside the computer is something we now under-stand moderately well how to do. Teaching the machine to construct useful cognitive maps from fragmentary sense data is less easy, but a beginning is being made in the various laboratories. At Stanford University the Artificial Intelli-gence laboratory is developing a computer program to coordinate one sensor (TV camera) and one effector (mechanical hand) to perform a fairly stereotyped task of the sort that a 2-year-old child can manage (piling bricks). None the less, the program must perform elaborate feats of model construction and verifica-tion as the basis for planing each move. This is even more true when we come to integrated behaviour, as planned by Stanford Research Institute, whose robot is shown in the accompanying photograph (Figure 6).* Figure 7* shows a local essay on a related theme in the form of Freddy, the newly constructed 'real world interface' for our research computer. Designed and built in Edinburgh by Steve Salter, it has now been successfully connected to the computer by Harry Barrow. We talk to it through a teleprinter terminal in the programming language POP-2, developed by Rod Burstall and Robin Popplestone. The kind of task which we are attempting to teach it is to find and identify simple objects in its world, to move them so as to satisfy stated conditions, and to make and print out maps of its world from time to time.

---

* These photographs could not be reproduced here for technical reasons.

In Figure 4, I distinguished lower and higher forms of intelligent behaviour. The kind of planning described so far is still at the lower level, a level extensively explored in research on computer programs for games such as chess. Here a plan takes the form of a chain of moves or at most a branching sequence. But there is a higher level of problem-solving in which this kind of planning is simply not good enough. At this higher level, planning actually takes the form of generating new programs, later to be executed when the moment for action arrives. The idea of a computer program clever enough to write and execute its own programs has flitted across the machine intelligence scene since early days. We are now, I think, beginning to see how to handle what was always an exciting concept but is at last becoming a practical one. Imagine a robot equipped with wheels, steering wheel, etc., in other words a cognitive automobile. Suppose it is now hundreds of miles from San Diego. John McCarthy has suggested the following problem, which might be put to our robot:

1) At each filling station a map is obtainable on request;
2) Each map has an arrow pointing towards San Diego;
3) Each quadrant of each map contains at least one filling station;
4) Kindly produce and execute a plan for planning and getting to San Diego.

Figure 8 shows the winning answer. Of course this plan is just an outline scheme and in practice some of the constituent boxes themselves pose problems for which miniature plans of the same form would have to be generated, e.g. for selecting the nearest filling station in a quadrant of the map, let alone for handling the actual driving.

We do not as yet fully understand how to program a computer so that it will generate high-level plans of this type. But thanks to some rather abstract work on methods of proving things mathematically about computer programs, lines of approach are beginning to come into view. In the United Kingdom active schools both of machine intelligence research and of abstract programming theory have been rapidly gaining momentum, and through the annual series of Machine Intelligence Workshops which we hold in Edinburgh and through many other media, these schools are keeping in lively touch with each other.

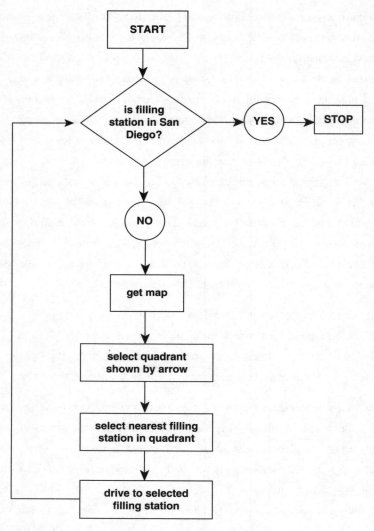

Figure 8. Answer to the San Diego problem, shown as a flow diagram.

With a little luck we may see the new insights being applied during the next few years to endow experimental 'real-world' devices with powers of learning and planning which may seem surprising even to their inventors.

Although we cannot say now in 1969 precisely how advances in machine intelligence will transform our society and the lives of our children, we know that the transformation will be far reaching, whether through the automatic control of factories, or intelligent machines for operation in remote environments like space or the ocean bed, or the arrival of the conversational computing terminal in the home as an intelligent extension of the domestic television set. There is a chance for Europe to move into the lead in this exciting area of new technology, the foundations of which were in fact laid in Europe some thirty years ago.

REFERENCES

13440. SRI project 5953. Menlo Park, California, Stanford Research Institute.

Barrow, H. G. and Salter, S. (1969). Design of low-cost equipment for cognitive robot research. *Machine Intelligence* 5 (eds. B. Meltzer and D. Michie). Edinburgh: Edinburgh University Press.

Craik, K. (1943). *The Nature of Explanation*. Cambridge: Cambridge University Press.

Donaldson, P. E. K. (1960). Error decorrelation: a technique for matching a class of functions. *Proc. III International Conf. on Medical Electronics*, pp. 173–8. J. McCarthy, Personal communication.

Michie, D. (1961). Trial and error. *Science Survey*. Part 2. pp. 129–45. London: Penguin.

Michie, D. (1963). Experiments on the mechanisation of game learning. Part 1. Characterisation of the model and its parameters. *Computer Journal* 6, pp. 232–6.

Michie, D. (1968). 'Memo functions' and machine learning. *Nature*, 218, pp. 19–22.

Nilsson, N. J., Rosen, C. A., Raphael, B., Forsen, G., Chaltin, L., and Wahlstrom, S. (1968). Application of intelligent automata to reconnaisance: Final report. Prepared for Rome Air Development Center, Griffith Airforce Base, New York.

Turing, A. M. (1953). Digital computers applied to games. *Faster than Thought* (ed. B. V. Bowden). London: Pitman.

Recollections of Early AI in Britain: 1942–65

BAIN: What was your earliest contact with the idea of intelligent machinery?

MICHIE: Arriving at Bletchley Park in 1942 I formed a friendship with Alan Turing, and in April 1943 with Jack Good. The three of us formed a sort of discussion club focused around Turing's astonishing 'child machine' concept. His proposal was to use our knowledge of how the brain acquires its intelligence as a model for designing a teachable intelligent machine.

BAIN: What was his basic idea?

MICHIE: Turing's belief about intelligence was that the propensity is innate, but the actuality has to be built. For him the crux was the brain's ability to make sense of its inputs, that is to understand them. And how would we tell whether we had succeeded? To assess degrees of machine understanding he was later to propose what is celebrated today as the Turing Test.

BAIN: So how did he see AI's task?

MICHIE: AI's first task was to build a propensity, which means a general learning program. The second task would be to train and educate this 'child machine'.

BAIN: How did Turing's conception affect you?

MICHIE: It gripped me. I resolved to make machine intelligence my life as soon as such an enterprise became feasible. During the 15-year wait for hardware facilities, I became a geneticist. In summer 1948 I was spending my days at

R. A. Fisher's lab in Cambridge, and my evenings on the Machiavelli challenger for Turing and Champernowne's blue-print for playing chess. Turing called it a 'paper machine'. With my wartime colleague Shaun Wylie—he was now back in Cambridge as a don at Trinity—we developed our own rival paper machine. Turing was intrigued, and decided to play the two off by programming the 'Manchester Baby'—precursor of the Ferranti Mark 1. He was thwarted (rightly) by its designer and the guardian of its scarce resources, Tom Kilburn.

BAIN: What happened next?

MICHIE: In 1950 I visited the National Physical Laboratory (NPL) where the pilot Ace was engaging all comers with its faultless play of the game of tic-tac-toe. The experience encouraged me to hope that technical feasibility of experimental work might be in the offing. In 1959 the NPL symposium on the Mechanization of Thought Processes came out. Around the same time an Edinburgh colleague, asserting that learning machines were an impossibility, challenged me to prove him wrong. In response I built a contraption of matchboxes and glass beads, the Matchbox Educable Noughts-And-Crosses Engine. It won me my bet and an invitation from the US Office of Naval Research to visit Stanford.

BAIN: What did you do at Stanford?

MICHIE: I programmed in FORTRAN a general trial-and-error learner based on MENACE for the IBM 7090, using an IBM 1620 for hands-on interactive program development. Bernard Widrow, who developed the Adaline Perceptron-like machines, had a student using them to study machine learning by imitation. The task was to balance a pole on a motor-driven cart; I wondered whether machine learning of such a task by unaided trial-and-error might be possible.

BAIN: And did such reinforcement learning prove to be possible?

MICHIE: Eventually. But full success did not come until after my return to the UK. Still short of funds and facilities, I ported my program to the Ferranti Pegasus with the help of one of their staff programmers, John Martin. The algorithm, BOXES, was published in the British *Computer Journal*—the first-ever working demonstration of reinforcement learning by machine. But I was more than ever frustrated and upset by the lack of University provision of electronic computing. The then Minister of Science and Education thought that 'computing' meant desk calculators. The wartime Bletchley Colossus machines were still an official secret. This early UK development of high-speed electronic computing was quite unknown.

BAIN: How long did the Colossus machines remain secret?

MICHIE: Until 1972, when the fruits of a brilliant piece of sleuthing by Brian Randell surfaced in his paper in the seventh volume of *Machine Intelligence*.

BAIN: So what came after Stanford?

MICHIE: On my return I had secured a few hundred pounds from the Royal Society for initial experiments. Concerning the national computer-blindness I lobbied everyone in sight. Finally in Whitehall I waylaid Christopher Jolliffe, a senior official of the Department of Scientific and Industrial Research (DSIR). An immediate by-product was an invitation to apply for funds for my own experiments.

BAIN: And did you apply for the money?

MICHIE: The Department of Surgical Science in which I was employed as an immunogeneticist lacked floor-space for such work. With the connivance of the Dean of Medicine, John Brotherstone, later Chief Medical Officer of Health for Scotland, I moved into an abandoned University cottage in Hope Park Square, paying my handful of students and other helpers from the fast-shrinking Royal Society funds. The Head of my Department, Prof. Michael Woodruff, was eventually calmed, and his Department was later compensated with a new Readership in place of the one I had hijacked. But the survival of the Experimental Programming Unit, as we styled our band of irregulars, hung in the balance.

BAIN: So what happened to the infant Experimental Programming Unit?

MICHIE: The worst. Christopher Strachey had long been campaigning for 'nonnumerical analysis' as the wave of the future for computing. But numerical analysts still dominated all matters involving calculation. The hoped-for DSIR grant was declined. The Hope Park Square irregulars now faced imminent extinction. I threw myself on the mercy of my Vice-chancellor, Edward Appleton, a distinguished physicist known for the 'Appleton Layer' of the upper atmosphere. He cleared his morning appointments and diligently grilled me on 'machine learning' and 'heuristic programming', notions then unheard of. Finally he turned back to my troubles. 'Tell me,' he enquired gently, 'does anybody know of this DSIR problem?' On hearing that the news had not gone further than myself and my secretary he continued: 'Ah well! I do not think you should consider it necessary to *burden* your colleagues with this knowledge. Meanwhile you seem to be going about things in the right way. There is nothing much that I can do. But I'll make a few enquiries.' He also mentioned a fact which was quite new to me, namely that his previous job had been as Head of the DSIR.

BAIN: Did he say to whom he planned to make enquiries?

MICHIE: No. But things suddenly started to happen, first with a visit from a Fellow of the Royal Society, Ian Sneddon, head of the Glasgow mathematics department. He looked keenly through what we were doing. Jim Doran was visiting from Oxford on funds from Norman Bailey's MRC Statistics Unit and he and I were looking at ways of mechanizing best-first searches of problem graphs. Our Graph Traverser algorithm I believe still plays a humble role at the heart of Austin Tate's impressive suite now in world-wide use for automated planning. On the cognitive side two psychology students, Jean Hayes (who later became my wife) and Kay Pole, were collecting comparative data on human tactics over the very same set of problems. An early stalwart of our little group was Andrew Ortony. After an unsatisfying brush with the science faculty's undergraduate chemistry course, he had concluded that there must be more to life! Ten years of fruitful work in Edinburgh were followed by a cognitive science career of international distinction. All these were inspected by our visitor, Professor Sneddon. I explained to him Turing's notion of mechanizing human generic methods as preliminary to educating and training the machine.

BAIN: And did Sneddon buy this interpretation of Turing's 'child machine'?

MICHIE: I don't know. But the miraculous news followed that DSIR had received new advice. The money was after all to be granted, and our expanding payroll was secure. This freed me for what followed—namely a 4-month release from the university to conduct a nation-wide survey and to report to DSIR on the state of university-based computing research in the United Kingdom.

BAIN: What did your survey for the DSIR conclude?

MICHIE: The survey revealed stunning talent and intense eagerness among Britain's scientific under-40s to get into two areas of computing research in particular:
1. Man–machine communication; 2. Machine intelligence.
The report also uncovered an equally stunning wastage. These young brains were draining across the Atlantic in search of enablement. DSIR meanwhile had been re-formed, budding off the Science Research Council for handling the academic end of the research spectrum. It was this new body's Computing Science Committee under Lord Halisbury's chairmanship that received my report. With a generous budget they settled down to implement its recommendations. For the two above-listed and (as Turing foresaw) intimately connected research areas, and for the Experimental Programming Unit, it was a godsend.

BAIN: How was that?

MICHIE: From my country-wide travels my remit to identify frustrated research talent was now reinforced with the means to recruit. Rod Burstall from Birmingham, Robin Popplestone from Machester, and John Collins from London all joined the ranks. The story of Rod's enlistment seems worth recalling. Armed with the new funds, I put to Christopher Strachey, himself one of programming's most gifted practitioners, the following question: 'Who is the best programmer in the country?' Without hesitation he replied 'A Birmingham student called Rod Burstall'. I went to the phone and after a while located the young man himself. 'I have urgent job information for you' I said, 'Where shall we meet?' A puzzled voice proposed a local Chinese restaurant and gave me directions. I sped up the motorway, and in two hours was there. The restaurant meeting that followed took a little longer: Rod Burstall's approach has has always been conspicuous for its care and deliberation. At the conclusion he threw in his lot.

BAIN: What was the new team's first move?

MICHIE: With the newly delivered Elliott 4120 machine, the new-formed team lost no time in embarking on what was later to become Britain's second time-sharing system, operational only a few weeks after Maurice Wilkes at Cambridge. We had been pushed, however, into radical innovation by dire necessity.

BAIN: So necessity became the mother of invention?

MICHIE: Indeed yes! Our own efforts soon out-ran conventional bounds set by a RAM of some 72 Kilobytes and a backing store of punched paper tape files—Elliott Automation's disc development had crashed! In a response to the emergency, Burstall, Popplestone, and Collins designed the innovative POP-2 language. They sought to unify the best of Algol and Lisp with stack-oriented and super-economical interactive execution of functions. A starkly unitary design made the POP-2 language the basis at all levels—operating system, programmer's interface, and user interface. A teleprinter in every room connected to the machine room, of which a bird's-eye view was conveyed by a TV camera feeding a small monitor on every desk. I recall that when one typed a POP-2 command to the operating system, one could see on the monitor the 'system response', in the form of the operator Margaret Crosby instantly mounting or dismounting this or that paper-tape file or magnetic film. But the Multi-POP system worked. After upgrading to an Elliott 4130, with disk-handlers to take over from Margaret Crosby, it came to support over thirty remote users throughout the United Kingdom.

BAIN: Back in 1965, what were the other significant developments?

MICHIE: The incoming University Vice-chancellor, the biologist Michael Swann, had been sweeping with a new broom. As a former friend and colleague from my genetics days, he was enthusiastic for the new studies. 1965 saw offical university recognition of the Hope Park Square irregulars, and the Unit's establishment as a full-fledged department of the university offering a post-graduate Diploma in Machine Intelligence. Our newly recognized department was able to colonize sufficient of the cottages around the square to be able to throw a line to a new unit which Bernard Meltzer was set on founding. As the Reader in Electrical Engineering, he had found no echo in his own department. But his new Metamathematics Unit in Hope Park Square carried seeds of outstanding intellectual creation. One has only to mention the mechanized theorem-proving work of Boyer and Moore, the conception and demonstration of the principles of logic programming by Robert Kowalski, and the later work of Alan Bundy and his school—all of which flowed over into new academic developments of AI. These flower today in Edinburgh's multi-disciplinary Informatics School, presided over by the same Alan Bundy. Although I have set 1965 as my chronicle's horizon, two other conspicuous processes had been initiated, with marked future consequences.

BAIN: What were these processes of the mid-1960s?

MICHIE: First was our bond with Ted Elcock and Michael Foster's group in Aberdeen. They early prefigured, and implemented in software, some of the core ideas latent in Kowalski's later logic programming. Much can be traced and deduced from the first few volumes of the *Machine Intelligence* series of which the first was launched in that same year. The key Aberdeen insight was to move the craft of programming from the idea of imperative commands towards a declarative style. The programmer should specify to the machine a set of goals and sub-goals, leaving it to the system to fill in the details of how best to achieve them. The second consequential event was a chance encounter with the noted engineer-psychologist Richard Gregory then at Cambridge. From this the basic concepts emerged for the subsequent Edinburgh robot project. In some respects of teachability and world modelling, by 1973 it had surpassed even the most versatile offerings of the robotic world of today. We called that robot FREDERICK.

BAIN: Another acronym?

MICHIE: Yes. It stood for 'Friendly Robot for Education, Discussion and Entertainment, the Retrieval of Information, and the Collation of Knowledge'! Alan Turing would have understood exactly what we meant!

Tokyo–Edinburgh Dialogue (1971)

At the Conference of the International Federation of Information Processing Societies, which was held in Edinburgh in 1968, E. A. Feigenbaum of Stanford University, USA, delivered a paper entitled 'Artificial Intelligence: Themes in the Second Decade'.[1] In it he said:

> History will record that in 1968, in three major laboratories for AI research, an integrated robot consisted of the following:
>
> (a) a complex receptor (typically a television camera of some sort) sending afferent signals to...
> (b) a computer of considerable power; a large core memory; a variety of programs for analysing the different video signals and making decisions relating to the effectual movement of...
> (c) a mechanical arm-and-hand manipulator or a motor-driven cart.

The intensive effort being invested in the development of computer controlled hand-eye and eye-cart devices is for me the most unexpected occurrence in AI research in the 1963–68 period.

Since then research on computer-controlled robots, as a major aid to artificial intelligence research, has proceeded apace, for example in the three laboratories mentioned by Feigenbaum, directed respectively by M. Minsky at MIT, McCarthy at Stanford University, and C. Rosen at Stanford Research Institute.

Recently, Japanese groups have been entering the field in strength, notably the Electro-technical Laboratory in Tokyo. This laboratory was represented by S. Tsuji on a survey team of robot engineering recently sent on a world tour by the Japan Electronic Industry Association under the leadership of Prof. Y. Ukita. The team paid a visit, among other ports of call, to the Department of Machine Intelligence and Perception, University of Edinburgh, and submitted a list of thirty-five questions concerning the project in progress here. We found it an extremely useful and clarifying exercise to answer these questions, which seem to us wide-ranging and shrewd.

Since the aims and content of artificial intelligence research, and of experimentation with robot devices in particular, are not yet widely known outside a very few specialist groups, there may also be benefit in making the dialogue available to a wider scientific readership. We reproduce the text of the exchange below:

GENERAL

(1) **Q** *What is the purpose of your research on intelligent robots* ? **A** To investigate theoretical principles concerning the design of cognitive systems and to relate these to the theory of programming. To devise adequate methods for the formal description of planning, reasoning, learning, and recognition, and for integrating these processes into a functioning whole. in terms of application (long-range) we can envisage a possible use of an intelligent robot as a teaching machine for young children. But our project is a research project, not an application project. Robots for us play the role of test gear for the adequacy of the formal descriptions referred to above.

(2) **Q** *Which do you think most important in your research scene analysis: problem-solving, dexterous manipulation, voice recognition or something else?* **A** Problem-solving.

(3) **Q** *Do you have a plan for developing any new hardware for manipulators, locomotion machines, or special processors for vision?* **A** We plan to use equipment already developed by ourselves and others, and we prefer to simulate locomotion by movement of the robot's world as first suggested to us by Mr Derek Healy. The present 'world' is a 3-feet-diameter sandwich of hardboard and polystyrene which is light and rigid. It rests on three steel

balls and is moved by wheels, driven by small stepping motors, mounted on the anchored robot. A pair of bumpers, one in front, one behind, operate two microswitches to determine contact with obstacles. Our next piece of equipment is a platform 5 feet square which may be moved anywhere in an area 10 feet square by flexible drive wires from two servo-motors. The platform can carry weights of 200 lbs and will move at up to 10 inches per second with accelerations of 1/10 g. Various types of hand–eye systems may be hung from a bridge above the platform.

(4) **Q** *We assume that the speed of available digital computers is still too slow for real-time processing of complex artificial intelligence problems. Is this true? If so, do you have any ideas for solving the difficulty?* **A** We agree that the speed of available computers is still too slow, especially for sophisticated peripheral processing such as vision. Dedication of satellite processors to sub-tasks (e.g. pre-processing the video signal) is one approach. Special-purpose hardware could of course increase the speed of processing, but it seems doubtful whether it can exhibit behaviour of great logical complexity which a digital computer is capable of doing. An improved instruction set, or more parallel computation (multi-processor) may yield significant improvements. But the immediate obstacles lie in fundamental problems of software design, rather than in hardware limitations.

(5) **Q** *Which language do you use in robot research, Fortran, Algol, PL./1, Assembler, LISP, or other list processing language? What would be the features of robot-oriented languages?* **A** We use POP-2.[2,3] The nearer a programming language is to a fully general mathematical notion, the more open ended its structure, and the more flexibly adapted to conversational use, then the better the language for robot research. We feel that an ideal robot-oriented language would be one that dealt in relations as well as functions, and would have deductive and inductive capabilities.

(6) **Q** *Can you describe the software hierarchy structure in your robot system?* **A** The mechanism of hierarchy is simply that of function call and a typical hierarchy might be (example taken from the vision hierarchy) *top—* program for guiding object recognition. *middle—*region-finding program

and program for matching relational structures. *bottom*—eye control program.

(7) **Q** *What performance capability do you predict for intelligent robots in 1975?* **A** We expect demonstrations of feasibility before 1975 in the child teaching machine application; that is a system able to recognize and manipulate materials used in teaching children the elements of arithmetic, sets, properties and relations, conservation laws, etc.

(8) **Q** *Will there be any chance of applying the newly developed techniques in research on intelligent robots to some industry (for example assembly lines) in the near future?* **A** We see possible industrial applications in the late 1970s including assembly lines. Other conceivable applications are luggage handling at airports, parcel handling and packing, machine tool control and repair, and various exploratory vehicles, e.g. for pipe-laying in deserts, forest clearing in remote areas, ocean-bed work, and planetary exploration. Applications for cognitive vehicles will probably remain restricted to work in environments which are essentially intractable.

(9) **Q** *What do you think of the control of many industrial robots by a mini-computer? What level of 'intelligence' would such a computer-robot system have?* **A** We would certainly expect to see the control of many 'fixed program' robots by a mini-computer. Such a system would not show much intelligence.

(10) **Q** *May we know the budget and manpower available for your project?* **A** We have £500 per annum from the Science Research Council for 'construction of models for on-line control experiments', supplemented by small sums earned as revenue through consultancy and rental of computer time. In addition the GPO Telecommunications Headquarters have awarded a contract for £10,000 over two years specifically for the robot research. The mechanical engineering for our Mark 1 robot, costing about £1,000 to construct, was largely the work of Mr Steve Salter of the Bionics Research Laboratory of this Department, at that time directed by Professor R. L. Gregory and supported by the Nuffield Foundation. The electronics, interfacing, and software have been mainly done in the Experimental Programming Unit by one grant-supported research

scientist working part-time on the robot work (Dr Harry Barrow) and one University Lecturer (Mr Robin Popplestone). But the work is being carried out in the general context of a large-scale study of machine simulation of learning, cognition, and perception, financed on a generous scale by the Science Research Council (£260,000 over five years) and by the University of Edinburgh. The POP-2 software and conversational computing system has received support also from the Medical Research Council to the amount of about £70,000 over five years. About a dozen research scientists are employed in the general project. Seven of these constitute a 'Robot Working Party' which meets fortnightly under the chairmanship of Professor Donald Michie, and plans the robot work, but this is a side-line activity for them with the exception of the workers mentioned above.

EYE

(1) **Q** *What are the aims and targets of your research in the context of vision?* **A** Picture-processing performance should be sufficient for forming plausible recognition hypotheses concerning members of a limited repertoire of simple objects (e.g. ball, pencil, cylinder, wedge, doughnut, cup, spectacles, hammer) as a basis for experimental verification or modification of such hypotheses by the robot through action (changing angle of view or interfering with objects manually).

(2) **Q** *Which input device do you use: vidicons, image dissector tubes, or other special devices?* **A** We use vidicons but are investigating image dissectors.

(3) **Q** *What is the performance of the input devices in areas such as resolution, dynamic range, sampling rate of A to D converters? In such areas are there any possibilities of improving the input devices?* **A** Present resolution of TV sampling system is 64×64 points and 16 brightness levels. Speed of conversion of A to D converter is approximately 100 KHz. This system is to be improved to 256×256 points and 64, or more, levels. A to D conversion should be about the same rate. Sampling time for a picture point is largely

determined by the time taken for the TV scan to reach the point (up to 20 ms maximum). We are considering image dissectors, which have negligible settling time.

(4) **Q** *Do the eyes of your robot move (electronic or mechanical movement)? What are the merits of eye movement?* **A** The eye does not move relative to the main frame. We are considering relative movement of two eyes for depth perception. Also, we are considering using one camera for wide angle views and a second camera with a long-focus lens for investigation of details. Merits, obvious; demerits, complication.

(5) **Q** *Is there any processor for visual input? Is it special hardware? What is the role of the preprocessor?* **A** We have installed a small processor for pre-processing visual input and thus reducing the load on the multi-access system. Later on we may build special hardware, for instance for doing ranging by stereoscopic or focusing methods. In the case of the stereoscopic method we would probably use hardware correlators. We might also build hardware contour followers for the region analysis approach, if it could be shown that a very significant saving in processing time would result.

(6) **Q** *Do you use linguistic methods to recognize the picture input? Is there any trouble when the line drawing of the solids suffers noise? How do you solve the shadow and hidden line problems? What is the most complex solid which your robot can recognize?* **A** We are experimenting with a method which involves describing pictures in terms of properties of regions and the relationship between regions.[4,5] We believe that the system will be moderately immune to noise. The shadow problem will be solved initially by allowing the combination of regions of different intensity level to form a new region and trying recognition again. Later we might attempt to decide whether something was a shadow or not by measuring differences in texture or distance on each side of boundaries between areas of different light intensity. At present the robot is capable of recognizing the simple objects described under heading (1) of this section, under controlled lighting conditions and viewing them from a roughly standard position.

(7) **Q** *Does your robot have colour sensing? What are the merits of this?* **A** No. Colour sensing would, however, undoubtedly aid region analysis and also facilitate communication with the human user concerning a given visual scene. It would be easy to have a single colour-sensitive spot in a moving eye system.

(8) **Q** *How do you solve the difficulties of texture?* **A** At present we have no method of coping with texture. In the future we will think of dealing with it by ideas like spatial frequency and spatial correlation, e.g. for distinguishing between textures like wood grain and textures like sand.

(9) **Q** *Which do you think best for range measurements: stereoscopic cameras, range finders as with SRIs robot, or sound echo method?* **A** Possible methods of range measurement that we are considering are: stereoscopic cameras, focusing adjustment with a monocular camera, and a touch-sensitive probe. Focusing has the advantage over stereoscopy in that it cannot be deceived by vertical stripes. However it is probably less accurate. We did a little investigation of sound echo ranging techniques but rejected them. The wave-lengths of practical generators are too long for good resolution on our scale of equipment.

(10) **Q** *How does your robot measure a parameter such as size or position of the objects? Are the accuracy and speed of measurement satisfactory for real-time manipulation?* **A** At present it does not make such measurements. We are prepared to be satisfied with errors of approximately 5 percent. Speed limitations are likely to be more severe for vision than for manipulation.

ARM AND HAND

(1) **Q** *Describe the hardware specifications of the manipulators such as degrees of freedom or sensors.* **A** A manipulator has been designed and is under construction. Two opposed vertical 'palms' can move independently towards and away from each other over a range of about 18 inches and can move together vertically through about 12 inches. Objects may thus be gripped between the palms, lifted, and moved a small distance laterally, in a linear Cartesian frame of reference. Absolute accuracy of positioning will be about

0–2 per cent of full range of movement, but backlash, rigidity, and repeatability should all be only a few thousandths of an inch. Later, it is intended to add rotation of the manipulator about a vertical axis, and rotation of the palms to turn objects over. Strain gauges at suitable points will give indications of the forces exerted by the arms and the strength of grip.

(2) **Q** *How dexterous will manipulation be and will it be successful?* **A** Too early to say.

(3) **Q** *How do you design the control loop of the manipulators?* **A** The controlling computer will output positional information as 10-bit digital words. These will be converted to an analogue voltage to control a DC servo motor. Potentiometers will be used to measure position and tachogenerators to measure velocity.

(4) **Q** *Do you have any suggestions for a system with two hands which would cooperate in a job with human beings?* **A** Not at this stage in terms of implementation. As an application area we have already mentioned teaching aids for children.

(5) **Q** *Do the manipulators have any reflex actions? Is there any need of a small computer for the exclusive use of the manipulators?* **A** A peripheral loop will stop movement if an unexpected force is sensed by the strain gauges. Exclusive use of a satellite computer is not necessary. We shall, however, be using such a machine to pre-process visual information and we will make use of it in controlling reflex movements.

LOCOMOTION

(1) **Q** *Is there any great need to use legs instead of wheels?* **A** No.

(2) **Q** *How does the robot direct its position in the real world?* **A** Combination of dead-reckoning with landmark recognition is possible, and has been examined by simulations.

(3) **Q** *Does your robot have balance-detecting and controlling equipment?* **A** No.

(4) **Q** *What are the application fields of robot-like machines with locomotive ability in the near future?* **A** Mowing lawns! If by 'near future' is meant the next two or three years we do not see commercial applications above a rather trivial level.

COMMUNICATION

(1) **Q** How *does your robot communicate with the digital computer?* **A** The robot communicates with the computer as a peripheral of the Multi-Pop time-sharing system, running on an ICL 4130 computer. Communication is via transfers of single 8-bit bytes. The output byte is decoded as a command to sample the picture or drive the motors. The input byte contains the state of the bump detectors and brightness of the picture point. When the satellite is installed, communication will be via a high-speed link with the ICL 4130. The robot will be interfaced to the satellite, essentially as it is now to the ICL 4130.

BRAIN

(1) **Q** *What performance and abilities does the brain of your robot have? Does it have self-learning ability?* **A** We have engaged in the past in experiments involving developing various abilities in isolation and have not yet finished building an integrated system using these abilities. For instance there is the Graph Traverser program for problem solving (Doran and Michie[6]; see Michie and Ross for an adaptive version[7]). Boxes and memo functions for rote-learning,[8-10] programs for deduction and question answering,[11] and the Induction Engine.[12] Full learning ability requires what is learnt to be expressed in a language more powerful than simply a sequence of weights, as in Perceptrons or Samuel's checkers learning program.

(2) **Q** *What can the question-answering system in your robot do?* **A** We have implemented a number of approaches to question-answering. We have theorem-proving programs, which, as Cordell Green has shown, can be modified for question-answering. We also have a program called QUAC based on relational combinators.[13]

(3) **Q** What *would be the best interface between robots and human beings?* **A** The best interface from the human's point of view would be spoken and written natural language, together with the ability to point at things with

the robot watching through its television camera. In the immediate future, for research purposes, typewriter and visual display using a flexible command language: e.g. 'imperative mode' POP-2.

(4) **Q** What *is the most difficult problem in future artificial intelligence research?* **A** Possibly the internal representation of the robot's world, which will certainly involve automatic methods for inductive reasoning from a very large mass of (mostly irrelevant) data. It seems to us that, to be usable by the robot for serious planning, internal models must involve both direct representations in the form of appropriate data structures, as when a map is used to model a terrain, and indirect representations in the form of axiom systems and sentences in a formal language such as predicate calculus. Facts are retrieved from the former by look-up and from the latter by reasoning procedures. What is lacking at present is any general theory concerning the relative economics of these two forms of representation, or any principles for automatic transfers of knowledge from one to the other. We are inclined to think that present work on automation of induction will help in the required direction.

On the deductive side, we would mention the problem of discovering the relationship between solving a problem by logical inference and solving it by an algorithm (i.e. no redundant inferences made), so that opportunities for reducing an inference process to an algorithm may be automatically detected and exploited.

A certain confluence is now apparent between work on robot cognition and the field known as theory of programming. This is because formal equivalences can be set up between proving that a plan will be adequate to bring about a given result in the real world and reasoning as to whether a program will compute a given function.We attach importance in this connection to recent advances in the theory of formal proofs about programs.[14–17]

In terms of implementing systems capable of operating within reasonable time constraints, methods for handling highly parallel processes will be crucial, and these are still in their infancy.

ACKNOWLEDGEMENTS

The Edinburgh work has on the hardware side mainly been conducted in the Bionics Research Laboratory (of the Department of Machine Intelligence and Perception) founded by Professor R. L. Gregory. The basic software and interfacing work has been done in the Experimental Programming Unit of the same Department. The authors have been greatly assisted by their colleagues on the Robot Working Party: Dr R. M. Burstall, Reader in Machine Intelligence, Dr J. A. M. Howe, Director of the Bionics Research Laboratory, and Dr H. R. A. Townsend, Senior Consultant Neurologist in the Western General Hospital and part-time Senior Lecturer in the above department.

A special debt is acknowledged to an overall philosophy contributed by Professor R. L. Gregory. His dictum, 'The cheapest store of information about the real world is the real world itself', was a major part of the original motivation, and the emphasis laid upon the role of internal models in Gregory's analysis of perception continues to be central to our work.[18]

REFERENCES

1. E. A. Feigenbaum (1968). Artificial intelligence: themes in the second decade. *Proc. IFIP Congress* 1968, 10–24. Amsterdam: North Holland Publishing Co.

2. R. M. Burstall & J. S. Collins (1971). A primer of POP-2 programming. *Programming in POP-2* (ed. R. M. Burstall). Edinburgh: Edinburgh University Press.

3. R. M. Burstall & R. J. Popplestone (1971). POP-2 Reference manual. *Programming in POP-2* (ed. R. M. Burstall). Edinburgh: Edinburgh University Press. Also in *POP-2 Papers*. Edinburgh: Edinburgh University Press (1968).

4. C. L. Fennema & C. R. Brice (1969). A region oriented data structure. *Technical Note* no. 7, SRI project 7494. Stanford: Stanford Research Institute.

5. C. L. Fennema & C. R. Brice (1969). Scene analysis of pictures using regions. *Technical Note* no. 17, SRI project 7494. Stanford: Stanford Research Institute.

6. J. E. Doran & D. Michie (1966). Experiments with the Graph Traverser program. *Proc. Roy. Soc.* A, 294, 235–59.

7. D. Michie & R. Ross (1970). Experiments with the adaptive Graph Traverser. *Machine Intelligence* 5 (eds B. Meltzer & D. Michie), 301–18. Edinburgh: Edinburgh University Press.

8. D. Michie & R. A. Chambers (1968). Boxes: an experiment in adaptive control. *Machine Intelligence* 2 (eds E. Dale & D. Michie), 137–52. Edinburgh: Oliver & Boyd.

9. D. Michie (1968). 'Memo' functions and machine learning. *Nature*, 218, 19–22.

10. D. L. Marsh (1970). Memo functions, the Graph Traverser and a simple control situation. *Machine Intelligence* 5 (eds B. Meltzer & D. Michie), 281–300. Edinburgh: Edinburgh University Press.

11. A. P. Ambler & R. M. Burstall (1969). Question-answering and syntax analysis. *Experimental Programming Report* no. 18. University of Edinburgh: Department of Machine Intelligence and Perception.

12. R. J. Popplestone (1970). An experiment in automatic induction. *Machine Intelligence* 5 (eds B. Meltzer & D. Michie), 203–15. Edinburgh: Edinburgh University Press.

13. C. C. Green (1969). Theorem proving by resolution as a basis for question-answering systems. *Machine Intelligence* 4 (eds B. Meltzer & D. Michie), 183–205. Edinburgh: Edinburgh University Press.

14. C. C. Green (1969). Applications of theorem-proving to problem-solving. *Proc. Intern. Joint Conf on Artificial Intelligence* (eds D. Walker & L. M. Morton), 219–39. Washington DC.

15. R. W. Floyd (1967). Assigning meanings to programs. *Mathematical Aspects of Computer Science*, 19–32. Providence, Rhode Island: Amer. Math. Soc.

16. Z. Manna & J. McCarthy (1970). Properties of programs and partial function logic. *Machine Intelligence* 5 (eds B. Meltzer & D. Michie), 27–37. Edinburgh: Edinburgh University Press.

17. R. M. Burstall (1970). Formal description of program structure and semantics in first order logic. *Machine Intelligence* 5 (eds B. Meltzer & D. Michie), 79–98. Edinburgh: Edinburgh University Press.

18. R. L. Gregory (1966). *Eye and Brain*. London: Weidenfeld and Nicolson.

Disaster and Recovery

In title, if not in tone, the 'Lighthill Report' was intended to be a general survey of AI research in Britain. But it was clear from the outset that Donald Michie and his team, then leading this research, would be substantially affected by its conclusions. The first essay in this segment appeared on the day that the Science Research Council's Board visited Edinburgh to decide on the future of the robotics work being done there (presumably, by then with a copy of Sir James's report). At this time, machine intelligence in Edinburgh was indeed being done in a cycle shed. A reporter in the Scottish *Daily Mail* in March 1964—remember that by now, slick Bond films had affirmed the possibility of rows of computer consoles and smoothly spinning tape-drives—was somewhat startled by the reality: 'To find Dr. Michie, you first have to find (no easy job) 4 Hope Park Square, Edinburgh. It is a trickle of old buildings, with a double wooden gate which hasn't been opened in the last decade if the rusted baling-wire which holds it loosely closed is anything to go by ... it looked, laboratory-wise, the equivalent of a thatched slit-trench.'

I will let readers look elsewhere for the events leading up to the presentation of the Lighthill report, which resulted in the robot program at Edinburgh being discontinued, and Donald Michie's research group being dissolved. Donald himself remained reticent on this topic: he talks a little bit about it in his last lecture ('Mechanization of Thought: Early AI Adventures', which is available on the Web). He did however respond in writing to the criticisms in the report. 'Of Bears and Balls' (the title is mine) from *The Creative Computer*, has been included here as a short background to the contents of Lighthill's assessment.

The reader can get to the original document easily enough, which is now available on the Web: but here is a summary of what Donald made of it's contents. 'Comments on the Lighthill Report' is the actual rebuttal that appeared in the Science Research Council's report.

Just as interesting as the written record is a 'debate' (it is not clear if this really was one in the true sense of the word), held at the Royal Institution, between Sir James Lighthill on the one hand, and Donald Michie, John McCarthy, and Richard Gregory on the other. An edited version of this debate, released by the BBC, can now be obtained from the Web. In one of its lighter moments, Donald Michie confesses to a bet with the chess grandmaster David Levy—that a machine would be able to defeat him by the end of the decade—and invites Sir James to be part of the wager (it is not known if this invitation was taken up). He lost the bet, as he later acknowledges in 'Slaughter on Seventh Avenue'. But that he saw computer chess as the *Drosophila melanogaster* (fruit fly) of machine intelligence is made abundantly clear in much of his writing during the period. He was equally confident though that machine intelligence would not be achieved simply as a result of a chess program defeating a grandmaster, a point that he emphasizes in his report of Deep Blue's victory over Gary Kasparov. His argument for machines capable of communicating usefully with humans was a long-standing one: 'Human Window on the World', from of a chapter with the same title in *The Creative Computer*, is consistent with the principal points made in 'Clever or Intelligent?' nearly 20 years earlier.*

---

* It would appear that the reasons why chess was proposed as a *Drosophila*-equivalent may have been lost in the race for building cleverer, but not necessarily more intelligent, chess programs. John McCarthy, in his review of the Kasparov v. Deep Blue match in *Science* (7 June, 1997) summarizes this thought: 'In 1965 the Russian mathematician Alexander Kronrod said, "Chess is the Drosophila of artificial intelligence." However, computer chess has developed much as genetics might have if the geneticists had concentrated their efforts starting in 1910 on breeding racing *Drosophila*. We would have some science, but mainly we would have very fast fruit flies.' Donald Michie also appears to have foreseen some of this. In an article written in 1979 in *Practical Computing* ('Preserving the Vital Link of Comprehensibility', later re-published as 'Artificial Intelligence in the Micro Age') he writes that there are two ways in which problems like chess-playing could be addressed: by methods modelled on the human style of cognition, or by brute-force technology comprised of very fast processors and large memories. He writes that he expected the latter approach would be preferred by 'an institution with clout'.

In some senses, recovering completely from the setback of the Lighthill episode took Donald nearly a decade. He would later write: 'Work of excellence by talented young people was stigmatized as bad science and the experiment killed in mid-trajectory. This destruction of a cooperative human mechanism and of the careful craft of many hands is elsewhere described as a mishap. But to speak plainly, it was an outrage. In some later time, when the values and methods of science have further expanded, and those of adversary politics have contracted, it will be seen as such. The persons will be long forgotten.'*

But in fact, all of this happened sooner rather than later. Although not directly about machines or machine intelligence, I have elected to include 'The Turing Institute'– the 'TI' to many – here: it is the phoenix arisen from the ashes of the old Experimental Programming Unit. Unfortunately, there isn't room enough here to describe the Machine Intelligence Research Unit that, between 1973 and 1983 in Edinburgh, acted as the nest for the TI. It was during this period that Donald's great interest in the area of 'structured induction' was kindled: more on this in a later essay. 'Rules from Brains' are fragments from a longer article on 'behavioural cloning'—a term he gave to the use of machines to extract understandable descriptions of inarticulate skills ('I just do it: don't ask me how.'). It is in this area that he did much hard experimental work with Jean Hayes-Michie—most of it remained to be written up—and contributed vigorously to research in Australia and Europe.

* Donald Michie, *Machine Intelligence and Related Topics* (New York: Gordon and Breach, 1982), 220.

Machine Intelligence in the Cycle Shed (1973)

During the 1970s, computing in its various forms is expected to be the world's third largest industry, with the software business predominating. Thereafter, the development of self-programming systems exhibiting some degree of 'intelligence' promises ultimately to transform our whole economic and cultural life. But these opportunities will not come unbidden.

Britain is both well qualified and ill qualified to play a leading part here: well qualified because of its rich concentration of talent in advanced computer science; ill qualified because most of the sites of concentration are in the enchanted playgrounds of the universities, where criteria of unstructured excellence are paramount and cost–benefit considerations not always felt to be in the best of taste.

It is no solution to seek to re-locate these brain-banks in industry where the payback horizon is of the order of three years. In advanced computing, 'strategic research'—with a horizon of 10 to 15 years—plays dominant role. And in any case, some aspects of the 'playground' ambience of the university constitute a real aid to creativeness. The problem of providing appropriate and stable conditions for this kind of work is receiving attention from the Research Councils as part of the post-Rothschild debate. One can trust with fair confidence that the right administrative framework will be engineered eventually. But I want here to consider some of the more intangible difficulties.

Improvement of contemporary programming systems in the direction of 'learning' and 'problem-solving' represents a deliberate encroachment on the functions of the human intellect. To some, this conveys an aura of the exotic, the audacious, even blasphemy. The research seems hard to relate to any existing field. Difficulties of placing novel fields, and indeed individual discoveries, are by no means new or uncommon; they are probably related to the notion of prematurity. In his perusals of the scientific literature and consultations with the grape-vine, every scientist comes across the phenomenon of premature discovery—meaning the acquisition of new knowledge which is destined for ultimate recognition, but which is so far ahead of its time as to be overlooked or dismissed. Most scientists regard such mishaps as regrettable but not significant. After all, if X didn't discover it or obtain recognition for it. then Y and/or Z would have anyway.

This phenomenon was re-analysed in last December's issue of *Scientific American*, by Gunther Stent, professor of molecular biology at Berkeley. Stent related scientific innovation to innovation in art and literature. He contended that new work, whether in science or in art, can gain acceptance only if it can be connected to contemporary 'canonical' knowledge. Unless, and until, such connections can be constructed, a scientist's discovery (such as Mendel's 1867 paper, rediscovered in the early 1900s) or an artist's creation (such as Picasso's first cubist painting *Les Demoiselles d'Avignon*, done in 1907) will remain unappreciated. This is not because the professional world is wicked or foolish, but because the innovator's product—though it may be sound or even brilliant—is in a rather literal sense useless.

Stent also considers the possibility that an entire field of enquiry may lack connection not with its own canonical body of knowledge (this would be a contradiction) but with the body of knowledge possessed by the scientific community at large. This is precisely the situation of machine intelligence research today, where techniques of computing are used to investigate questions not of natural science but of philosophy. The fact that the search for formal (and hence mechanizable) definitions of phenomena of thought and knowledge may yield technological rewards is irrelevant to the present argument: the established specialism to which machine intelligence most logically belongs is too remote from practical science to facilitate general acceptance.

Has this done any particular harm so far? The following circumstances seem relevant.

1) Advances in nuclear physics (with the possible exception of plasma physics) are not expected to be of industrial, military, or social significance.

2) The Science Research Council's budget for nuclear physics runs at about £20 million per annum.

3) The SRC's expenditure on research in computer science is less than £1 million per year (of which perhaps a tenth is devoted to machine intelligence).

4) Computing is the example *par excellence* of a brains-intensive industry; whatever hopes Britain has of economic revival must lie in such areas.

By contrast, when a technology has a well-established canon into which novel concepts can be absorbed, eagerness to invest may outweigh considerations of a project's expensiveness and likely unprofitability. (An unkind observer of Concorde's present plight might propose it as a case in point.)

	Inexpensive	Expensive
Economically profitable	A	B
Economically unprofitable	C	D

Contemplate the diagram above. A reasonable man might expect national priorities to be in the order A, B, C, D. But there is a peculiarly British mannerism of government, whereby a virile ability to spend £500 million is matched by maidenly prudishness about pennies. Northcote Parkinson has decribed a related phenomenon—the time taken to reach a decision being in inverse proportion to the sum involved. He illustrates this with an imaginary committee meeting:

Allowing a few seconds for rustling papers and unrolling diagrams, the time spent on Item Nine will have been just two minutes and a half. The meeting is going well. But some members feel uneasy about Item Nine. They wonder inwardly whether they have really been pulling their weight. It is too late to query that reactor scheme, but they would like to demonstrate, before the meeting ends, that they are alive to all that is going on.

Chairman: 'Item Ten. Bicycle shed for the use of the clerical staff. An estimate has been received from Messrs Bodger & Woodworm, who undertake to complete the work for the sum of £350. Plans and specification are before you, gentlemen.'

Mr Softleigh: 'Surely, Mr Chairman, this sum is excessive. I note that the roof is to be of aluminium. Would not asbestos be cheaper?'

Mr Holdfast: 'I agree with Mr Softleigh about the cost, but the roof should, in my opinion be of galvanized iron. I incline to think that the shed could be built for £300.'

Mr Daring: 'I would go further, Mr Chairman. I question whether this shed is really necessary. We do too much for our staff as it is. They are never satisfied, that is the trouble. They will be wanting garages next ... '

And so on. I am not suggesting that machine intelligence research is, like the bicycle shed, of trivial importance; quite the contrary. What it shares with the shed is that it is of trivial cost when measured on an appropriate scale—relative to, say, nuclear physics. If the world of government science were like the world which Parkinson delights to caricature, we could imagine discussion of Item Ten spinning out interminably—decision is postponed from meeting to meeting; a special panel of bicyclists studies the shed building proposal for a year, and then reports positively; an eminent Cambridge physicist is called in and pronounces the whole concept to be unsound; eventually the feeling takes root that 'shed' has become a four-letter word and that the wise man should steer clear.

Happily we are not imprisoned in Parkinson's world. Returning to the 'A, B, C, D' table we should confidently (1) assign advanced computing science, including machine intelligence an 'A' for top priority, (2) terminate discussion of Britain's bicycle shed, and (3) get on with it.

Of Bears and Balls
(1985)

Scientists are often faced with this dilemma: should they try to explain their real technical concerns, knowing that their reward may be fidgets, yawns, and puzzled frowns, or should they use the knee-jerk tactic and hit where they know they can get a response? References to scientific goals, and attempts to explain them, are often wasted breath. Hitting the technology button, on the other hand, seems to buy us something. The knee-jerk tactic is known in the AI business as 'yellow perilling'. Everyone, after all, can understand that intelligent robots could be useful in the industrial struggle against Japan. But to understand why the scientists themselves consider the work important—that is not easy to convey to busy people. But it is often just not appropriate for scientists to justify their work in terms of immediately visible benefits.

The Dutch government's advisory group on the social impact of microtechnology has been afflicted with a similar worry. The group noted that 'the speed of innovation makes it increasingly difficult for governments to follow developments'. Except that the statement covers only a small part of what could be said, scientists may well feel: 'At last someone has said it.'

To those concerned to see that the potential of the synthesis of new knowledge by computer is fully exploited, this situation presents a major obstacle. Substantial investment of money and political commitment is going to be needed to make the creative computer happen. Yet in Britain there is not even one national laboratory for long-range computing research. The field of artificial intelligence specifically has had particular difficulty in gaining acceptance in the UK political and scientific establishments. Its existence over the last twenty-five years has been punctuated by influential cries that the whole exercise is an infantile disorder. In 1972–3 the Science Research council received two reports on long-range policy for computing science and machine intelligence. One, the careful work of experienced computer professionals, said 'Build it up!' The other, which said 'Wind it up!', came from an outsider, Sir James Lighthill: distinguished as a fluid dynamicist, a controversial government expert, and the departing occupant of Cambridge University's Lucasian Chair of Applied Mathematics.

Advice to government has traditionally emanated from past holders of this chair, some of it of uneven quality. Professor Sir George Biddell Airy once advised Queen Victoria that if the Royal Salute were fired outside the Crystal Palace, the building would collapse. More pertinently to us, Airy's advice secured the withdrawal of government support for Charles Babbage's Difference Engine.

In the case of AI, Lighthill's recommendations emboldened the SRC to dismantle the coherent structure of UK work in the field, with effects which were felt even across the Atlantic. The long-term cultural and economic damage wreaked by this decision has been very serious.

BEARS AND BALLS

We must believe that Lighthill's advice did not spring from shallow roots. Some of it was, however, a little strange. In considering the question 'Why build robots'?' he remarked:

> We have to remember the long-standing captivation of the human imagination by the very concept, as shown by its continual prominence in literature, from medieval fantasies of the Homunculus through Mary Shelley's 'Frankenstein' to modern science fiction. To what extent may scientists consider themselves in duty bound to minister to the public's general *penchant* for robots by building the best they can?
>
> Incidentally, it has sometimes been argued that part of the stimulus to laborious male activity in 'creative' fields of work, including pure science, is the urge to compensate for the lack of the female capability of giving birth to children. If this were true, then Building Robots might indeed be seen as the ideal compensation! There is one piece of evidence supporting that highly uncertain hypothesis: most robots are designed from the outset to operate in a world as like as possible to the conventional child's

> world as seen by a man; they play games, they do puzzles, they build
> towers of bricks, they recognize pictures in drawing-books ('bear on rug
> with ball') . . .

The 'bear on rug' reference was to a paper on computer vision published in 1972
by Harry Barrow, Pat Ambler, and Rod Burstall. One of the simple pictures used to
test their program had 'Bear on rug with ball' as its caption. Lighthill continued:

> Nevertheless, the view to which this author has tentatively but perhaps
> quite wrongly come is that a relationship which may be called pseudo-
> maternal rather than Pygmalion-like comes into play between a Robot
> and its Builder.

Lighthill divided the field of AI into: A—Advanced Automation; C—Computer-
based Research into the workings of the central nervous system; and B—Bridge
activities intended to link A and C, or alternatively, Building Robots. He asserted
that while progress in A and C had been disappointingly slow, they were nevertheless legitimate areas for research. B on the other hand, he argued, was getting
nowhere and ought to cease. It had 'grandiose aims' which it had failed to reach,
he said, adding, 'This raises doubts about whether the whole concept of AI as an
integrated field of research is a valid one.'

The nature of Lighthill's misunderstanding is at root the same as that encountered by Robert McGhee. As was pointed out at the time, B should really stand
for 'Basic', the fundamental research that constitutes the heart of the subject. It
was as if Thomas Hunt Morgan and his colleagues who pioneered modern
genetics had been told: 'You have the mathematical theory of Mendel to play
with. You have breeding work to do for the community's good in improving
crops and farm animals. You are also free, and we will even fund this modestly,
to investigate the broader matrix of biological processes in which the genetical
phenomena are embedded. But frankly, we see no need to be breeding fruit flies.
Better switch to cows!' Being able men, Morgan and his colleagues would doubtless have made more than adequate cattle breeders, and could indeed have found
one or two shrewd applications for already formulated principles of academic
genetics. But the chromosome theory of heredity would have had to wait, and
everyone, including farmers, would have been the losers.

Comments on the Lighthill Report (1973)

Two contrary attitudes are common. In the first place there is a widespread, although mostly unconscious, desire to believe that a machine can be something more than a machine, and it is to this unconscious urge that the newspaper articles and headlines about mechanical brains appeal.

> On the other hand, many people passionately deny that machines can ever think. They often hold this view so strongly that they are led to attack designers of high-speed automatic computing machines, quite unjustly, for making claims, which they do not in fact make, that their machines have human attributes.
>
> (M. V. Wilkes, 'Can a Machine Think?' in *Discovery*, May 1953)

Sir James Lighthill's report speaks of *the ABC of the subject*, categorizing it as follows:

- A - *Advanced Automation*
- B - *Building Robots*
- C - *Computer-based CNS Research*

The report regards A and C as worthy activities which, however, have made disappointing progress. B is regarded as unworthy, and as having made very disappointing progress indeed. B, it should be noted, is really used in the report to denote any experimental programming which lacks obvious application to either A or C. Thus computer chess is included in *B* whereas robot parcel-packing is put into A.

Most people in AI who have read the report have had the feeling that the above classification in misleading. Sir James has arrived at his position by interpreting AI as consisting merely of outgrowths from a number of established areas, viz.:

- A as an outgrowth from control theory,
- B as an outgrowth from science fiction,
- C as an outgrowth from neurobiology.

These interpretations are remote from those current in the field itself.

A number of questions accordingly pose themselves, including the following:

1. Was this report based on as thorough a survey as it should have been? In particular, was opportunity taken to invite the views of the international leaders of the field?

2. How successful has the author been in overcoming the difficulties inherent in his inexperience of the field, and in putting aside his own professional biases?

3. Has accepted practice been followed in documenting subjective opinions wherever possible and in providing factual sources and references which others can check?

4. What is the validity of the ABC classification? Would the computing science community accept it?

5. Are the report's assessments of work in the B category—Building Robots—intended to apply to experimental robotics conducted in the United Kingdom? If so, should not the author
   i. have said so plainly,
   ii. have asked to see the experimental robotics work during his visit to Edinburgh?

INTERNATIONAL OPINION NOT CONSULTED

The first of these questions is so critical as to merit a brief note to the effect that the leading American workers, such as McCarthy, Minsky, Nilsson, Raphael, and

Robinson, were not in fact consulted. The appearance of their names in the list of fifty given in the report's third paragraph derives from the fact that the author has read scientific writings of theirs, not that he invited their opinions. Since the field in question was pioneered in the United States of America, which supports to this day an effort on at least twenty times the scale of that in the United Kingdom, it is well to bear in mind this fact when assessing Sir James's evaluations.

INTELLIGENCE THEORY

Space does not allow a review of the remaining questions of the above list; a detailed critique is available elsewhere. (D. Michie (1972) 'On first looking into Lighthill's Artificial Intelligence Report' (unpublished).) Instead I will briefly indicate two themes which arise from Lighthill's implicit question: *If you throw A and C away, what is left, if anything?* Lighthill's answer is *Building Robots*. An alternative answer, which many will prefer, is *Intelligence Theory*. By this we mean attempts to systematize the design principles of intelligent systems wherever they may be found, whether in the A or C application areas.

Having fixed on *Building robots,* Lighthill paints a picture of this pursuit which must strike those actually engaged in experimental robotics as somewhat unfamiliar. In studies of actual robot work the role of the equipment is plainly seen as test gear for putting certain types of theoretical ideas to experimental test.

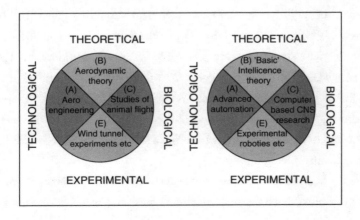

A pertinent parallel is the building of wind-tunnels as an aid to aero-engineering—as illustrated in the figure at the bottom of the previous page.

This figure brings into relief the reason why Building Robots is an unhelpful choice for the role of Bridge between A and C. It is surely more fruitful, if one seeks inter-disciplinary connections, to choose a common body of theory rather than to seize on a piece of laboratory equipment. One feels that Sir James would be among the first to agree that to speak of building wind-tunnels as the Bridge between aero-engineering and the study of bird flight, would direct attention away from the true bridge, namely the science of aerodynamics. The equivalent science in the case of AI is at a primitive stage. It is the hope of every AI professional to contribute in some way to bringing the required theory into being. This, as I see it, is the burden of Sutherland's re-definition, in his contribution to this symposium, of B as standing for *Basic*.

ENCOURAGEMENT OF RESEARCH IN MACHINE INTELLIGENCE

On this note I would like to leave Sir James Lighthill's interesting and imaginative review and to mention an assessment of a more homespun quality: the report of the SRC Computing Science Committee's long-range panel, published in *Computing Science Review*. This panel, composed of computer professionals, considered the machine-oriented part of Artificial Intelligence (ie the A+B part) and recommended that special encouragement should be given to this field. However, it is evident to those who work in the field that it would be helpful if a clear and concise statement were given of its goals and methodology. The style of Sir James Lighthill's report suggests that there is a lack of understanding in some quarters, and without this there is a reluctance to recommend significant expenditure. The status and position of the subject are particularly clear at the moment and it is, therefore, opportune that a statement should be made to avoid any further misunderstandings.

The subject, in so far as it comes within the Computing Science Committee's realm of interest, is concerned with machines, and in particular computers, displaying characteristics which would be identified in a human being as intelligent behaviour. Perhaps the characteristics which are most important are those of learning and problem-solving. The applied benefits which may be gained from work in this field could bring considerable economic benefit to the country. They are two-fold:

a. To relieve the burden at present on the systems analyst and programmer in implementing applications;
b. To enable new and more complex applications to be undertaken in this country in competition with work elsewhere.

These are the long-term advantages and to this end work is proceeding on a number of detailed problems, including the following:

i. Automatic assembly and other robotic applications: Mass spectogram analysis, Chemical synthesis planning, Assembly line balancing.
ii. Language-understanding systems: Semi-automatic programming (ie *teachable systems*) and ultra-high-level programming languages (like Planner, Sail, Conniver).

Group I represents useful applications. Group II represents the subject's own special contribution, independent of specific applications to computer science. This lies in making it more possible for the user to get computing systems to *understand* what he means.

Many good scientists have been involved in this field and their work has resulted in the development of techniques and methods of wider use, for example:

- List-processing was originally devised by Newell, Shaw, and Simon for AI work and first implemented in their IPL language.
- The incorporation of conditional expressions into Algol 60 was McCarthy's suggestion derived from his work on Lisp, itself inspired by the needs of Artificial Intelligence work.
- The POP-2 language, now implemented on 5 main hardware ranges, was specifically developed for AI work, but subsequently shown to be of wider utility.

- In fifteen years of struggle towards *language understanding*, striking advances have been scored (Bobrow, Winograd, Woods).
- Some of the search and associative techniques used by programmers and operations research workers have been initiated in AI, and assimilated without awareness of their origin.

The problems that have been mentioned above are practical problems. Abstracting from these, and observing the methods of solution, workers in the field have been able to define general principles for intelligent systems. This work has made some progress and the follow ing theorems and methods have been developed.*

Problem-solving

- Theorems of minimality and completeness of various algorithms for heuristically guided search.
- Methods of pruning search trees in special situations: Plausibility analysis; alpha–beta pruning.
- Recursive formation of sub-problems as in Newell and Simon's *General Problem Solver*.
- Application of theorem-proving ideas in problem-solving.
- Studies of problem representation.

Recognition

- Various methods of feature extraction and interpretation for visual data.
- Use of semantics to disambiguate linguistic analysis.
- Matching of descriptions represented as directed graphs (e.g. *hierarchical synthesis*).

Learning

- Adaptive learning via parameter optimization.
- Rote-learning techniques.

---

* Some of these are reviewed in a *Nature* article, 'Machines and the Theory of Intelligence', 23 Feb. 1973

- Formation of new concepts from examples and counter-examples.
- Inductive generalization.

Even so incomplete a list as the above puts into perspective the importance of examining particular problems in depth (such as chess-playing or those involving robots) so as to investigate how to bring the above functions to bear in an integrated fashion. They are but experiments which may be used to derive or test theories. At this early stage of innovation the overwhelming benefit to be derived from a given experimental study lies in its role as a forcing function for new programming techniques and tools. The field is so difficult and the choice of the right problem at the right moment so much part of the art of enquiry that this should be left to the research workers themselves. They should be judged by their success or otherwise in advancing the state of computer programming, and in introducing and testing computer languages of greater expressive power.

FOOTNOTE ON SUTHERLAND'S COMMENTARY

Sutherland's otherwise admirable analysis contains two expressions of view with which exception must be taken, namely (1) that AI should not be handled by the Engineering Board of SRC and (2) that AI research in Britain is in a bad way.

1. A reasonable approach would surely be to distinguish A-oriented and C-oriented poles of the subject and to provide for the first under the Engineering Board and for the second under the Science Board. Since important contributions continue to be made by computer scientists ignorant of psychology and brain science, and by psychologists ignorant of computer science, it would avoid embarrassment, and reflect scientific reality, to make separate provision.

2. Sutherland's proposition that AI research in Britain is in a bad way deserves to be vigorously challenged. But it is inappropriate for me, as founder of the longest-established British research group, to be the one to do this. A better corrective can be obtained from assessments by

authoritative outside observers, such as that by Dr. Nils Nilsson of the Stanford Research Institute's Artificial Intelligence Center and author of the graduate textbook *The Problem-Solving Methods in Artificial Intelligence*.

WHAT IS TO BE DONE

We are in the embarrassing situation in Britain that in order to carry out significant work over the next few years in the context of international competition, it will be essential to import American machines—specifically the DEC System 10 (formerly known as the PDP 10). I think that everybody would be happier about the case for allowing an American importation now if steps were at the same time taken *to see that British AI research never found itself in such a predicament again*. What would have to be done if this desirable state of affairs were to be brought about?

Why does the need arise? It is not only, or primarily, because of the superiority of the architecture of the DEC System 10 for AI-type uses. The over-riding consideration is access to the rapidly accumulating fund of AI-oriented software and applications programs in the big American laboratories. The key to the situation is the absence of software for British machines, either present or *new range*, suitable for AI work, which has its own very peculiar needs. It is hardly more sensible to speak of *making do* with, say, general scientific software developed without reference to AI than to suggest that, say, plasma physicists short of experimental fusion equipment should *make do* by borrowing linear accelerators from the particle physicists!

The kind of software development needed if AI workers are ultimately to be put in business as users of the new range of British computers (I do not necessarily intend this phrase to be exclusively confined to ICL) comes under two headings:

1. Development of experimental operating systems, compilers, and packages, as has been done in a small way on the ICL 4130 at Edinburgh. But the new effort should aim to embrace the entire *standard range* of facilities which every AI worker should be entitled to take for granted—LISP,

POP-2, SNOBOL, QA4, PLANNER, CONNIVER, etc. etc.—and, ultimately far more important, *leap-frogging* into the future both by adapting the latest advances of AI research work where appropriate, and by innovation within the R&D effort itself. Also to be considered are operating system features for handling *funny peripherals* (experimental robots, speech input devices, etc.) and basic packages for *front end* functions such as, say, video and speech input, robot control functions, language preprocessing. In addition the design and development of advanced peripherals (e.g. for robotics) should be regarded as an integral part of the job although (as with software) the more standard aspects of instrumentation should be contracted out to industry wherever possible.

2. *Communality aids* whereby new research programs and software developed in overseas laboratories can be made immediately available on demand for British research workers to test out and either accept or reject as tools for their own needs. Communality can be achieved by various means and these means will vary according to the nature of the case, but they include software/hardware interfaces to the ARPA net, and emulation (for example by microprogramming) of the 'donor' machine from which the program is to be adapted.

If a fully-fledged development project is to be got up to full speed by around 1977 then forward studies could usefully be started now. It is already obvious that early installations of a PDP-10 in an active centre of British AI research is a precondition if these studies are to develop fruitfully, since immediate access to the latest AI research materials (and intimate contact with advanced AI research) will be as essential to the specification and development of new research facilities as it is for those who will later be using them. Until the new facilities exist, the only point of access and contact will be through British groups equipped compatibly with their American counterparts—i.e. with PDP-10s.

In this field successive workers in a given area should be able to stand on the shoulders of their predecessors through the medium of successive contributions to a common stock of new language aids and library packages. This will not happen unless someone makes it his business continually to scoop in what is new and useful and build it into a properly documented and integrated system. The level at which the British AI community will be able to contribute in the late 1970s, as judged by competitive international standards, will be crucially affected by the sophistication of the available software.

The Turing Institute (1989)

Many prescriptions have been offered for promoting effective two-way communication between academe and industry. The problem is today compounded by continuing erosion of the research infrastructure of the universities and by the discovery that a cupful of knowledge taken between the ages of 18 and 22 is no longer sufficient to sustain a lifetime of employability in a fast-changing technological scene.

NOT-FOR-PROFIT COMPANY

The Turing Institute was established in 1983 as a not-for-profit company with the idea of finding new ways of addressing some of these problems. It was named in honour of the late Alan M. Turing, the distinguished British mathematician and logician whose work has had a lasting influence on the foundations of modern computing. Opened in its new Glasgow premises in 1984 by Mr Geoffrey Pattie, then Minister of State for Industry and Information Technology, the Institute is dedicated to logic programming, artificial intelligence (AI), and advanced robotics.

UNIQUE RESEARCH LIBRARY

The Turing Institute thus offers integrated research and teaching in intelligent research programming technologies. Its role is to explore and to make accessible new problem-solving capabilities and tools and to assist with their assimilation by industry. It has been designated by the UK Department of Industry's Alvey Directorate as a centre of excellence for training in advanced information technology. The Institute's income comes from research and training contracts, both governmental and industrial—and by subscription from its industrial affiliates. It assists affiliates with the transfer of technology from research to application and provides them with training for their technical staff, as well as with a wide range of software tools and a comprehensive library and information service. The Institute's library, with over 50,000 documents in stock (increasing by 1,800 per month) is available for on-line access and is considered to be the world's most complete AI-dedicated research library, and the only such library available electronically from remote sites world wide.

EXPERT SYSTEMS

An area of application in which AI is currently arousing interest is known as 'expert systems'. These are computer programs which advise users from a base of machine-stored knowledge. Such systems possess the crucial ability to give reasoned justifications of their expert advice. Most of the international effort in expert systems has concentrated on the development of knowledge representation techniques and effective methods of deductive inference. We believe that if expert systems technology is to reach its full potential the ability to acquire knowledge automatically—by induction from sample data—is essential.

CURRENT RESEARCH

The Turing Institute with its associated software company, Intelligent Terminals Limited, is recognized as a world leader in inductive techniques. ITL's commercial systems have scored a number of industrial successes. These include a large expert system (part developed with Radian Corporation) for the prediction of severe thunderstorms; a system for circuit board diagnosis (ITT); a process control advisory system for Westinghouse (this has been estimated to be saving the company in excess of $10 million a year); and rule-based contributions to the

Space Shuttle autopilot developed by NASA. Current Turing Institute research is directed at producing environments offering both inductive and deductive inference capabilities. Within this framework we are developing systems for chess end-games, management advice, personnel allocation, adaptive user-friendly interfaces, and three-dimensional structural analysis of proteins.

MACHINE LEARNING

The hallmark of intelligence is the ability to learn. A system which learns is dynamic, reconfigurable and flexible within a changing environment or task specification. Such requirements encompass the next generation of expert systems where expert knowledge should be learned rather than programmed, that is, machine-synthesized rather than human-specified. Small islands of knowledge synthesis exist in a few laboratories.

COMPRESSED KNOWLEDGE BASE

Of these perhaps the most spectacular to date is an achievement by a team at the Josef Stefan Institute in Ljubljana, Yugoslavia, with which the Turing Institute enjoys a British Council Academic Link. Professor Ivan Bratko and his colleagues tackled a problem of potential practical importance: the diagnosis of multiple arrhythmias of the heart from descriptions of ECG recordings. A large and comprehensive body of knowledge was automatically generated from a computer model of the heart's electrical activity, and then inductively compressed into a small number of precise rules. The compressed knowledge base constitutes an important advance and is regarded as a good instance of knowledge synthesis involving inductive logic.

KNOWLEDGE SYNTHESIS

Here we see an unexpected bonus. When expert systems were first devised, they were intended to act as no more than substitutes for human experts. It was a surprise to discover that these expert systems can actually help to codify and improve expert human knowledge, turning what was over-complicated, fragmentary, and inconsistent, and commonly infested with error, into something precise, comprehensive, and more reliable. This process is called 'knowledge refinement'; its extension to create rules embodying new knowledge not previously possessed by practitioners is usually referred to as 'knowledge synthesis'. The Bratko ECG achievement represents a case in point.

ENORMOUS POTENTIAL

Knowledge refinement has enormous potential. At the practical commercial level, large quantities of urgently needed knowledge are available only in principle, for the most part unrefined. Many man-centuries of mental work gather dust on library shelves—contradictory, disparate, and indigestible manuals, regulations, codes of practice, inspection standards, factory and office procedures, and the like. Whole areas of practice depend on knowledge arrived at piecemeal over decades, knowledge often comforting but obsolete. Knowledge refinement can yield simpler, more efficient, and effective codes of practice, and render them into forms which are complete, intelligible, up-to-date, and updateable. Evidently, the generation of humanly comprehensible knowledge is no longer the sole territory of human endeavour but is becoming a domain that we will share with computers.

ADVANCED ROBOTICS

In the early 1970s British work in advanced robotics culminated in one of the most advanced robot environments at that time or since. The project (code-named FREDDY 1 and FREDDY 2) succeeded in tasks where the parts of a toy ship and boat were emptied onto a table in a jumbled heap. The robot had to sort out and recognize components and build the two toys. The current FREDDY 3 environment contains two Puma robots as well as a feeder system. These robots have multiple sensory systems, including vision, tactile array sensing, capacitive, inductive, and range proximity/touch sensing, as well as speech input and speech output. The software architecture is asynchronous and hierarchical and involves modules that can perform off-line simulation or real-time planning. Demonstrations include inter-robot task cooperation, plan learning, robot–robot and human–robot voice communication, rule-based sensory integration and collision avoidance.

TESTING A HYPOTHESIS

In founding an institute of a new type, we naturally hoped to discover whether such a self-sustaining enterprise was possible at all in British conditions. Five years later the verdict is a cautious affirmative. With some twenty full-time workers led by the four scientific directors of the Institute's board, augmented by a more than equal number of visiting fellows, graduate students, and post-doctoral collaborators from nearby academic and industrial laboratories, the formula seems to be working. Beyond mere demonstration of feasibility, however, a more interesting question is whether one can run a research and teaching institution as though it were a business without losing the strength of academic connection needed to keep standards and long-term aspirations high.

EXCHANGE BENEFITS

This question, we can already state with confidence, is beginning to answer itself. While standing in its own premises as a legally and financially independent entity, our Institute is led by Professor James Alty of the University of Strathclyde. His half-time service as the Turing institute's Executive Director is made available by the university as part of a negotiated package of exchange benefits. These include manifold forms of active cooperation under a legal Agreement of Association. In addition to the Institute's involvement in joint scientific projects, Fellowship of the Institute is offered to distinguished workers in computing. The Institute's 'Advanced Study' activities include a programme for visiting scholars and exchanges with academic laboratories world wide.

THE UNIVERSITY CONNECTION

The Turing Institute's research staff work closely with different departments of Strathclyde University on a variety of research programmes. Through its academic association with Strathclyde, the Institute is also able to offer research facilities to students who register in the university's Department of Computer Science as candidates for the degree of PhD or Msc.

Slaughter on Seventh Avenue (1997)

'I'm not afraid to say that I'm afraid,' said Garry Kasparov last month after his fifth game against Deep Blue 2. The match between man and machine was all square as Kasparov spoke to the watching chess aficionados and world press assembled at the Equitable Center on New York's Seventh Avenue. It was a chilling moment for all of us, raising to an extraordinary pitch the tension surrounding the final game next day. Then it came.

On his seventh move, sixth game, Kasparov played the wrong pawn in a well-known opening. Deep Blue's immediate knight sacrifice sprung a trap from which there is little escape. Kasparov's face on the big screen in the auditorium stared in horror. Then he buried his head in his hands. After Deep Blue had played its nineteenth move, Kasparov resigned the game—the shortest losing game of his career—and the match.

Kasparov has an unprecedented chess rating of 2805. Grandmaster Joel Benjamin, who worked with the IBM team that put Deep Blue 2 together, rates the machine at 2700. According to the statistics of the rating system, this kind of lead should allow Kasparov to win twice as many games over Deep Blue as he loses. Chess masters had expected that a week of his usual confident superchess would be enough to destroy Deep Blue. How then did catastrophe overtake the greatest chess player that the world has ever seen?

This was a battle between two different ways of playing chess. Deep Blue plays chess like no human on Earth. Kasparov was eager to learn more about the machine's foibles. He had shocked the chess world in February 1996 by losing the first of six games to an earlier version of Deep Blue, and word from the IBM camp before last month's match was that the latest incarnation was beating its predecessor. This time round, Kasparov set aside two months for intensive pre-match preparation. Unfortunately, because this was the new Deep Blue's public debut, no samples of its play were available. Eventually, he went into the match blind—something he would never do against a human.

So how do humans play chess? Psychological research shows that the critical skill for human chess players is pattern recognition. A pattern is any feature, simple or complex, that can be spotted 'at a glance'. The stronger the player, the larger the range and complexity of patterns he or she can recognize and interpret ('A Game for Life', *New Scientist*, 4 Sep. 1993, p. 23). Studies have also shown that a grandmaster holds around 100,000 patterns in his or her head. Not, of course, that grandmasters sift through these patterns one at a time. Rather, the patterns are brought to bear much as a writer can assemble learnt words, phrases, or whole sentences to carry a story to its denouement.

One can broadly distinguish two components of chess capability—search and evaluation. Search is about following different lines of play; 'what if I do A, and my opponent does B, followed by my doing C, or alternatively my opponent might reply D, and then I might do E, F or…' This method produces a 'tree' of possibilities (see below).

A chess computer cannot reason about the broad consequences of a move. Instead, it calculates billions of nitty-gritty possible futures and chooses between them using the minimax principle. Take, for example, the tree of possibilities in the diagram. The machine, playing white, must choose between

Tree of future possibilities

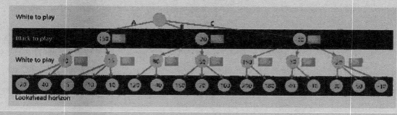

the three positions A, B, and C, by applying a position-evaluation formula to assign scores to each one. If the machine looks only one move ahead, then it compares the face values (in circles) of A, B, and C. These are 150, −20, and −10. The obvious choice is to go for the highest score, called the 'max', which in this case is move A.

But suppose that the machine has time to take into account black's possible responses and the options for its own next move. The machine assumes that just as white prefers the move with the maximum score, black will choose the move with the minimum score (called the 'min'). So start at the 17 possible positions at the bottom—at what is called the lookahead horizon—and work upwards.

These 17 possible positions are generated by the seven groups of options open to white directly above the lookahead horizon. White wants to know the move with the maximum score in each of these seven groups, which is entered as the 'backed-up value' in a rectangle. On the far left, for example, white must choose between −20 and 40 and will opt for 40, which becomes the backed-up value.

In similar fashion, in the tier above, black has three groups of options. For each group, it chooses the move with the minimum backed-up value, which becomes its backed-up value. On the far left again, black must choose between 40 and 10 and will choose 10. This brings the machine back again to white's original move. This time, though, it looks at the backed-up values, rather than the face values. This second, deeper analysis changes white's preferred move from its original choice, move A, to move B (see the table below). Generalize this to 12 tiers rather than three and you have Deep Blue.

Choose Your Next Move

	Face Value		Minimax	
	Score	preferred	Back-up score move	Preferred move
Move A	150	Best	10	Worst
Move B	−20	Worst	120	Best
Move C	−10	Middle	40	Middle

This task is made feasible thanks to a process called alpha-beta pruning, devised in the 1950s by the American Arthur Samuel, author of the first highly capable computer draughts player. His method discards whole chunks of the tree on the fly, without further ramifications. Most of the tree, in fact, remains unexplored without affecting the values backed up to top level.

Evaluation, on the other hand, is not just a matter of spotting the material value of a position—a rook, for example, is worth about one bishop plus one pawn. From long experience, humans can recognize geometrical patterns indicating future threats and opportunities, and can weigh these against each other. This largely intuitive skill is highly developed in grandmasters. By comparison, machines are weak at evaluating a position's long-term, or strategic, merit (see 'Grabbing a poisoned rook', below).

QUALITY, NOT QUANTITY

Leading chess players tightly focus their searches—they tend to look at only a few branches in the tree of possibilities, and only a few moves ahead. Grandmasters famously compensate for this by using pattern recognition to form judgements about the broad line that future play might take. An admirer once asked the grandmaster Richard Reti how many moves he looked ahead. 'One,' he replied, 'the right one.' Reti was exaggerating, of course. But it is true that a grandmaster does not ordinarily examine more than about 30 positions in the tree, and rarely more than 50. In some cases, however, Deep Blue examines 50 billion or more.

This astounding search capability is Deep Blue's secret. It makes up for strategic blindness with brute-force enumeration of tactical possibilities. To decide its next move, it can probe the tree of possibilities solidly to a depth of five to six moves ahead and can explore the future still further along selected branches.

Deep Blue can evaluate twice as fast as its predecessor at a colossal 200 million positions per second. To achieve this, the IBM team has equipped the machine with 32 parallel processors, each with between six and eight accelerator chips.

More subtly, but more importantly, the team has also improved the way Deep Blue chooses between potential positions.

THE BIG CALCULATION

At the heart of Deep Blue is a search method called the minimax principle. This allows the computer to choose its next move from the tree of future possibilities by comparing scores for positions that are back-calculated from several moves ahead. The scoring is done by a position-evaluator, which rates each future position by checking it for several hundred stored patterns.

These patterns, or attributes, are hard-wired into Deep Blue's accelerator chips—a few hundred against the 100,000 in Kasparov's head. They include ways to recognize the safety of the king and to check how much room for manoeuvre a position leaves other pieces. These patterns are very primitive compared with those that Kasparov can recognize: they are like words to his phrases. And while he uses his stored patterns to think strategically about huge classes of future positions, Deep Blue applies its patterns to just one position at a time.

The machine scores each position by evaluating the degree to which each attribute (a_1, a_2, a_3 ...) is present, and giving each a weighting (w_1, w_2, w_3) that reflects its relative importance. To decide the total score for a position, the machine then performs a calculation ($a_1w_1 + a_2w_3 + a_3w_3$ ...) This sum, often called a 'scoring polynomial', also takes into account the values of the machine's pieces and its opponent's. The aim is choose the highest score which then dictates the next move.

The IBM programmers have increased the number of attributes that Deep Blue's position-evaluator recognizes and have tuned the weights given to each one. They have also improved the machine's ability to change the weightings according to the 'phase' of the match. This stems from an idea of Claude Shannon, the founder of information theory. In 1950, he pointed out that the importance of pieces, and certain patterns of pieces, changes throughout a game. A pawn, for example, can become much more valuable in the closing phases of a game because it might be possible to promote it into a queen, while a 'Chinese wall' of pawns in an end-game can be invaluable. Deep Blue can now recognize a large number of different phases and adjust the attribute weightings accordingly.

Yet for all its skilled play, Deep Blue has very little intelligence. It doesn't learn from experience. It cannot tell chess sense from nonsense, and it is blind to what a chess position or chess game is really about. No automated development tools were used, and its position-evaluator was handcrafted. It can offer no useful analysis of why it made some apparently deeply calculated move. Forget artificial intelligence. Deep Blue is a product of the sustained application of human intelligence to modern computing technologies.

MIND-READING MACHINE

Given all those disadvantages, how did Deep Blue beat Kasparov? From knowledge of Deep Blue's inner workings, together with a close study of Kasparov's face through the closing games, I am in no doubt. Deep Blue came across to Kasparov as *being able to read his mind*, and this slowly wore him down. Deep Blue's speed means that it can make calculations during the time allocated to its opponent to consider and make a move, as well during its own. So, say Kasparov took 15 minutes to elaborate a deeply laid plan. Finally, he moves. During this time, Deep Blue has calculated a branching tree of several hundred billion possibilities. According to Deep Blue's programmers, the machine had predicted Kasparov's moves in about half the cases so it could reply instantly.

Imagine the effect on Kasparov when a succession of his deeply pondered moves are answered without delay. When this happened he grimaced. In addition to the 'spooky' effect, an instant response in a complex and difficult position applies a very peculiar form of time pressure not characteristic of human play. It gives no pause for the human player to relax. These uncanny effects slowly unstrung the man before our eyes. It was not Deep Blue that destroyed Kasparov. It was Kasparov.

Grabbing a poisoned rook

What stands out as obvious to a human player can be invisible to a machine. In the position above, one of Deep Blue's ancestors, Deep Thought 2, has the white pieces. After lengthy searching (not reasoning) the machine captures the black rook with its pawn. To any player with a sense of danger, such short-sighted greed seems infantile.

The computer sees that 'in the end' it will have gained a rook, conventionally worth 5 points, minus 1 point to allow for the fairly immediate capture of its adventurous pawn. But this tactical evaluation misses the point. Deep Thought 2 has no way of seeing that white's only salvation is the pawn-barrier between the white king and black's extra pieces.

The barrier is recognizable to a human as a pattern in which interlocked white and black pawns form a 'Chinese wall', impregnable so long as white does nothing to breach it. White's greedy capture allows a hole in the wall, making the penetration inevitable. How far in the future lurks the nemesis? Working this out would mean looking ahead more than 50 moves, according to the British grandmaster David Norwood. 'Who cares?' asks the human player. 'Just give me the telltale pattern and a little common sense reasoning!'

So where does all this leave us? For the artificial intelligence community the real action lies elsewhere: in the developing world of chess machines which are being sold not so much for their playing performance, but for their ability to tutor human opponents.

With this new generation, sheer skill must take second place to something more complex, usually called 'expertise'. Cognitive scientists define this as the capacity to handle novel situations, to reconsider and explain the validity of rules, and to reason from first principles. To qualify, machines must do better than just beat world champions. They must also hold their own at the press conference afterwards as they explain their winning strategy.

This task is way beyond Deep Blue. The complex of phase-specific scoring polynomials in its position evaluator is unstructured and opaque. This became clear from a curious episode in game 2, which Kasparov eventually resigned. On move 36 of that game, Deep Blue played a pawn rather than the obvious queen move. This choice led, in still unfathomed ways, to the collapse of Kasparov's position in that game.

He issued the first ever high-profile challenge to a computer to explain its decision or be under suspicion of improper human intervention. He insisted that the Deep Blue team seal the printed log of the machine's thought processes during this game. After the match, when Kasparov and his team unsealed the log, they found voluminous tree-search calculations. But no thought processes.

Intriguingly, while the Kasparov match unfolded, across town another contest was under way. This was the annual Loebner prize for the most human-like conversation sustained by a machine with a panel of examiners. The winner was Converse, a program developed by London-based Intelligent Research, which is headed by the international master David Levy.

In 1970, the same David Levy laid a bet with me and others that he would be undefeated by a chess machine for at least 10 years. He won his bet, but was finally vanquished in 1990. He now returns to triumph in a larger domain of discourse than anything Deep Blue could begin to conceive.

Human Window on the World (1985)

At the meeting in Toronto in 1977 of the International Federation for Information Processing, Kenneth Thompson of Bell Telephone Laboratories presented a computer program for playing the chess end-game of King and Queen against King and Rook. He had done this by the ultimate in 'hammer and tongs' methods: in the absence of a complete set of rules for playing the end-game, he had previously programmed the machine to work out what to do in every single possible position—and there were four million of them. This was done backwards, by taking every position and working out what the best-move predecessor would have been. All these moves were then loaded into a gigantic 'look-up' table in the machine's memory, each entry in the table simply saying, 'If the pieces are in these positions, move this piece there.'

It is known from the theory of chess that given best play, this end-game is an inevitable win for the Queen's side, except for a few special starting positions. Chess masters can ordinarily guarantee to win against any opponent. So when playing with the Rook, Thompson's program merely made whatever move would stave off defeat for longest. Present at the conference were two International Masters, Hans Berliner, former World Correspondence Chess Champion, and Canadian Champion Lawrence Day. Thompson invited them to demonstrate winning play for the Queen's side against the machine. To their embarrassment they found they could not win, even after many attempts. Yet every position they were confronted with in the entire course of play was a winning one for their side.

The machine repeatedly conducted the defence in ways which to them were so bizarre and counter-intuitive that they were left grasping air, time and again missing the best continuation. For example, the cardinal rule which chess players learn about this end-game is, 'Never separate King and Rook'. The assumption is that the Rook needs the King to help protect it from the Queen. Yet the super-table separated the King and the Rook again and again, having found some path, however narrow and convoluted, through the problem space that maximally postponed its supposedly inevitable doom.

Naturally Berliner and Day found the experience upsetting. They wanted to ask the program to explain its strategy, but this of course neither it nor its author could do. The answer in every case was, 'It's in the table.' Its knowledge was comprehensive but there was no representation of the knowledge in terms of goals, opportunities, risks, themes, tactical ideas, and the rest of the rich conceptual structure in terms of which chess masters frame questions and receive answers. The machine was in no position to give answers like: 'At this stage White must drive the enemy King onto the edge of the board.' What it was lacking was a conceptual interface whereby the machine and the human could share knowledge in forms which humans could grasp, namely, concepts. It is the task of knowledge engineering to design and construct such conceptual interfaces to allow people (who are still much more intelligent than machines) and machines (which are already much cleverer than people) to understand each other.

HAZARDS OF THE SUPER-TABLE

It may be said that chess is just a game. But let the reader generalize a little. Thompson's super-table is not an unrealistic example. While the search for solutions to difficult problems struggles slowly ahead, electronic technology is galloping. This has been bringing the price and physical size of computer memory down at an unheard-of pace.

Trillion-bit memories are already in existence, and Lawrence Livermore Radiation Laboratories have issued specifications which call for this capacity to be pushed up by a factor of several thousand. Optical storage promises to exceed even these scales of capacity. Such changes will inevitably tempt people to set up in such memories huge databases of questions and answers in a very wide range of subject areas, wherever problems need to be solved. While these might appear a boon to man, they actually pose a major social hazard.

At first sight the ability to hold in a crude fashion trillions of questions paired with their answers might seem not very useful, but in fact most practical knowledge can be expressed in this form:

'What is the square of 961?' '31.'
'What is the right thing to do when lost?' 'Ask a policeman.'
'What is the freezing point of the seas?' '−2°C.'
'What is the truth-value of Fermat's Last Theorem?' 'Unknown.'*

Computer technology seeks today to move into tackling difficult problems of the sort computers now cannot solve, problems for which there is no straightforward procedure which in a feasible number of steps can find the answer directly from the question by calculation. But it often happens that although a problem is difficult, its inverse is not. For instance, calculating a square root is quite involved, but finding a square is easy. So a schoolchild might consider it more economical to work out the squares of every number he or she could conceivably be asked for and fill a huge table with the answers (listing the answers, not the questions, in numerical order, perhaps with some interpolation to fill in gaps). Then, whenever a square root is needed, it is looked up in the table. This is the 'inverse-function method', by which Ken Thompson's chess-playing program was built. But as we saw, this technique has one major drawback: the result is inscrutable to human users.

SOCRATES AGREES

One might say that a race of blind question-answerers such as this which so debases—by dispensing with—human understanding and judgement would be better uninvented. Interestingly enough, this argument was first raised over 2,300 years ago by Plato. In the *Phaedrus* he has Socrates tell a story about the

---

* This article was written in 1985.

Egyptian god Thoth, who goes to the god-king Thamus and says: 'My Lord, I have invented this ingenious thing called writing, and it will improve both the wisdom and the memory of the Egyptians.'

Thamus replies that, on the contrary, writing is an inferior substitute for memory and understanding. 'Those who acquire it will cease to exercise their memory and become forgetful; they will rely on writing to bring things to their remembrance by external signs instead of on their own internal resources.'

Socrates cites Ammon against the fallacious view that 'one can transmit or acquire clear and certain knowledge of an art through the medium of writing, or that written words can do more than remind the reader of what he already knows on any given subject.' In other words, men will be led to think that wisdom resides in writings, whereas wisdom must be in the mind. 'You might suppose,' Socrates adds, 'that written words understand what they are saying; but if you ask them what they mean by anything they simply return the same answer over and over again.'

In short, Socrates' complaint is that writing fails to pass Alan Turing's famous test (by which a machine can prove it is really intelligent if it can fool a questioner, over a teleprinter link, into thinking he is conversing with a human being). And so it does fail. If it could explain what it contained, we could say in a sense it 'understood' and so was showing intelligence. As writing fails the Turing Test, so too will the trillion-bit question-answerers of the future. But like writing, they will assuredly survive and help to change our world. Will this be good or bad? Unless the substance of Socrates' complaint is seriously investigated in the new context, these giant question-answer systems will be a mixed blessing and could on occasion get their users into trouble. Such databases, remember, store only the basic elemental unvarnished facts of the given case, and contain nothing corresponding to understanding, inference, judgement, classificatory concepts, and the like. Truly, '… if you ask them what they mean by anything they simply return the same answer over and over again'.

So long as the contents of the electronic super-table remain purely factual in the ordinary sense, then nothing worse is likely to result than exasperation.

Infallible answers obtainable on tap, over unimaginably vast domains of discourse, will be readily accepted. But the absence of any explanations to accompany the answers will be taken by the users in bad part. 'Why,' a chemist user will say, 'does this pattern from the mass spectrometer indicate that the unknown compound is some particular poly-keto-androstane?' Answer: 'Because the trillion-bit dictionary says so!' The chemist then asks, 'How does it know? How did that answer get there in the first place'?' If the super-table has been constructed by the inverse function method, even telling him exactly how it got there will not make him much the wiser. He and his colleagues may be goaded into building new explanatory theories of what they find in their super-tables. If so, then this is to the good, and presages new pathways of scientific advance.

THE LUNATIC BLACK BOX

On the other hand, a table of question–answer pairs is not restricted to encoding factual information of this kind. The format lends itself equally well to expressing strategies, with the table consisting of situation–action pairs. This is exactly what Ken Thompson's chess program consisted of, and we have seen the problems that led to. But what if the system were doing something of social importance, such as managing a complex control function in factory automation, transport or defence? Two supervisors, let us imagine, are responsible for intervening manually in the event of malfunction. The system now does the equivalent in industrial or military terms of 'separating its King and Rook'. 'Is this a system malfunction?' the supervisors ask each other. They turn to the system for enlightenment. But it simply 'returns the same answer over and over again'.

The problem becomes of global importance when the system being operated is in air traffic control, air defence, or nuclear power. It is not too difficult to decide that a human decision-taker, say, a policeman directing the traffic at a crossroads, is drunk or mad. But US plans for air traffic control envisage ultra-powerful database and scheduling computations encapsulated in giant 'black boxes'. What will the human supervisors do on the presumably rare occasions when East Coast flights are mysteriously re-routed to Dallas, or inexplicable groundings of harmless carriers raise doubts as to the system's sanity? As control devices and their programs proliferate, their computations may more and more resemble magical mystery tours. Most critical of all, if an air defence warning system suddenly says, 'There are twenty Russian missiles heading this way,' before the officer in charge pushes the Doomsday button he must be able to ask, 'What makes you think that?'

Any socially responsible design for a system must make sure that its decisions are not only scrutable but refutable. That way the tyranny of machines can be avoided.

There is of course a method of solving difficult problems that is totally different to the use of super-tables, namely, exhaustive searching through branching trees of possibilities: 'look-ahead', as when working out the outcomes of possible chess moves and choosing the best. Tables—we could call them 'look-up systems'—require vast amounts of data storage but little processing. In contrast, in order for a look-ahead search to be completed in a tolerable length of time, a great deal of processing power is needed but little memory. These two extremes are shown in Figure 1.

What happens when you get a pronouncement from a look-ahead system and you ask it 'Why?' Can it tell you anything? Most certainly! It can detail all the calculations it did in sequence. It can even disgorge the entire analysis tree. Could anyone wish for a more profound response?

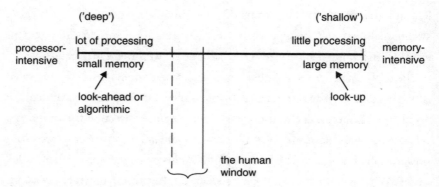

Figure 1. The spectrum of processing versus memory.

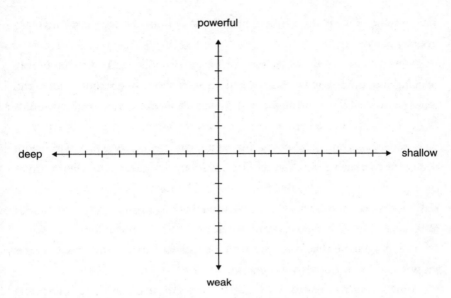

Figure 2. Two dimensions of a computer embodying an intellectual skill.

On the contrary, no mortal mind could possibly digest so much information. The tree could contain a million nodes, or a hundred million! The Three Mile Island fiasco is to the point—the operators made more mistakes, not fewer, because they were deluged with alarm signals, meter readings, and computer printouts. While a look-up system is too shallow in that it gives too little information, a look-ahead system tends to be too deep by giving too much. This is a separate issue from the power of the system—how much it is capable of doing. This distinction is shown in Figure 2.

THE HUMAN WINDOW

On the scale shown in Figure 1, 'deep' systems are at the processor-intensive end while 'shallow' ones are at the memory-intensive end. Somewhere in between is a narrow band where both the processing capability and the scales of memory are equivalent to those possessed by humans. We call this the 'human window', and it is here that computers must operate in order to be comprehensible to us whom they are intended to serve. Both the reasoning power required and the way in which information is held must be on a human scale—elsewhere lies inscrutability.

A view which we shall call 'technomorphic' goes as follows: 'The machine's way of going about chess, or weather prediction, or plant control, or route scheduling, is bound to be different and ought to be different. The relative costs and constraints associated with the various aspects of the problem-solving process are quite disparate for machines and brains. Strategies which optimize performance with respect to two such contrasted profiles are doomed to diverge. Whatever way is most efficient for the machine to do the problem is the way we want to go. If Karpov has not got the calculating speed and working memory to grow a mental look-ahead tree of a million board states, or if our top meteorologists are not smart enough to be able to do partial differential equations in their heads, that is just too bad. Why should the programmer seek to copy their defects?'

From the point of view of optimizing the use of the machine the technomorph is right. But in the light of the brain's woeful disabilities as regards storage and processing speeds, efficient machine programs are not workable as representations for people. Where the technomorph goes wrong is in supposing that there is no criterion involved but machine efficiency.

Futurologists, in particular I. J. Good and Ed Fredkin, director of MIT's celebrated Project MAC, have speculated about the development of an 'ultra-intelligent machine' which would be able to 'reprogram itself within hours, constantly improve itself and rapidly become hundreds of times smarter than human intelligence'. Some people are worried about this. But the real social danger, certainly the first we shall see becoming manifest, is not the ultra-intelligent machine but the ultra-clever machine. The dangerous system is the one tuned by economic pressures to perform its task with machine-efficient inscrutability. These machine-oriented criteria can be shown to be irreconcilable with easy communication of concepts between man and machine. So performance must be sacrificed for the sake of transparency. Is that an economically acceptable sacrifice? Surely it is. Machines continue to become cheaper; human beings on the other hand do not. Adding artificial intelligence to the machine can offer the needed humanizing bridge. But if machine-optimality rather than human-optimality remains the design criterion, we are ultimately headed towards a technological black hole.

SYNTACTIC SUGAR IS NOT ENOUGH

So how should we design our machines to fit the 'human window'? The answer is not as straightforward as it may seem. Interactive diagnostics and trace routines, even when sprinkled with the very best syntactic sugar, do not necessarily suffice. Such things resemble orthopaedic shoes built to correct a patient's rolling gait: they may help, but if his trouble stems from a congenital abnormality at the hip joints, then the patient also needs reconstructive surgery. Just as there are walkable and non-walkable skeletal structures in human anatomy, so there are explainable and non-explainable computations, and the differences can be traced to the respective program structures.

Putting it another way, the addition of a simple 'user-friendly front end' when the subject area is very complex is like distributing powerful telescopes to inhabitants of Dover anxious to gaze upon the Eiffel Tower. To people ignorant of the curvature of the earth it could seem like a good idea.

In order for any beings, human or machine, to talk to each other, they must share the same mental structures. People's mental structures cannot be changed, so we must change the machines'. We need to restructure the entire way problem-solving programs do their jobs, not just how they interact with the user. The way the program holds information—its problem representation—must be recognizable to a human as a concept with which he is familiar. Both Ken Thompson's table and the weather-forecasting differential equations are non-starters in this respect. Rule-based expert systems on the other hand are specifically designed to operate with human concepts, both accepting them from the domain specialist and displaying them to the user as explanations. These provide a start, but much research still needs to be done on the technology of the conceptual interface.

SOFTLY, SOFTLY AUTOMATION

We call the application of these ideas to factory equipment and other control systems 'soft automation'. This is increasingly needed for cleaning up the complexity pollution which hard automation tends to generate. The greatest social urgency attaches not to extending automatic processes but to humanizing them. Of course, for tasks of low-to-middling complexity, opacity is not really a problem. We have lived with it for a long time without any ill effects. Suppose that a resource allocation program schedules a job better than a human project director. How much desire does he feel to pry into its detailed workings or to argue with it, so long as it is doing what he wants? It can be as much of a 'black box' as it chooses.

However, there are other applications for which an 'open box' mode is essential. As yet, there are few of these, since information processing has yet to penetrate far into the more complex and responsible levels of human affairs. 'Complex' and 'responsible' are separate reasons for insisting that a program operate within the human window. Some problems are so difficult that a man–machine intellectual partnership is needed. Others involve life and death, or the manageability of the economy.

One computer program for diagnosing acute abdominal pain, entirely lacking in 'explain' facilities, continues to be used by the doctors involved only through pressure from higher authority. Despite its potentially life-saving power, clinicians cannot feel confident using a black box. True expert systems such as Mycin, however, are capable of giving answers to the question, 'How did you work that out?'

With soft automation, systems are forced at the design stage into the human mental mould. Looking to the future when teams of cooperating robots are at work in our factories, we should ask, 'How should signals be passed between robots? Along wires, by infra-red beams, radio, or some other humanly inaccessible channel'?' Synthesized voice would be better, so that human supervisors can keep an ear open for what is going on, as has been shown to be feasible by work at Edinburgh.

Rules from Brains
(1994)

The labels 'strong AI' and 'weak AI' have sometimes been used to differentiate two schools. Criteria are summarized in Table 1.

The taxonomy in Table 1 lays emphasis on the 'physical symbol system hypothesis' of Newell and Simon (1976). Their intended interpretation restricts symbol systems to those which can transparently support communication with human users. Thus the lists of numerical weights in which neural nets express themselves constitute 'symbols' of a sort, but not in the sense intended by the above authors. This restriction has persuaded some practitioners that the physical symbol system hypothesis excludes intuitive processes from AI's domain of discourse. Such separatism is unsafe, since much knowledge-based thought seems irredeemably intuitive and sub-articulate (for a recent commentary see French: 1990). For its sub-cognitive processes: there is no direct evidence that the brain employs a symbolic regime. Hence those who accept sub-articulate expertise as a proper AI concern may wonder whether for this purpose they should abandon symbolic representations as untrue to nature. The present chapter advocates a different position, namely that a conceptually transparent symbolic style offers a way of improving on nature. By representing intuitive processes symbolically, inductive inference can do something which is both non-brainlike and also highly useful, catering to the client who says: 'My inhouse experts may be "intuitive". But I want an expert system to formulate its reasons more explicitly than that.'

Table 1. Criteria of strong and weak AI

	Strong	**Weak**
Feasibility of goals	Human-level intelligence will be achieved in machines within foreseable time.	Human-level intelligence will be implemented only in some unimaginable future, or perhaps never.
Forms of implementation	All thought can be mechanized as sequential logical reasoning from axiomatic descriptions of the world. The 'physical symbol system hypothesis': all agents, including intelligent, are best implemented symbolically.	Most thought is intuitive, not introspectable, non-logical, associative, approximate and 'fuzzy': best modelled by brain-like ultra-parallel networks.
Personnel	Vintage AI professionals, e.g. Turing, Simon, Newell, McCarthy, Feigenbaum, Nilsson, and their followers.	Members of other professions, particularly in linguistics, neurobiology, physics, and philosophy.

KNOWLEDGE AND THOUGHT

In industrial knowledge systems the implementer has to distinguish between thought as something to be communicated and thought as problem-solving. Choice of representation remains a developer's option. In implementing intuition, he or she may decide that it is something over which to draw a veil. The veil may be woven of neural nets, or of hand-crafted spaghetti code, or of something else. But suppose that the developer has to supply the customer also with means to draw the veil aside, for purposes of interrogation about goals, plans, evidence, justification, and the like. At the price of being less true to nature, he or she might then be better off not to have veiled it in the first place. Like cognitive and brain scientists, knowledge engineers also study the structure of expertise.

Unlike cognitive and brain scientists, they do this (or should do) for the purpose not of emulating but of transcending the brain's limitations. First among these is the relative inarticulacy of what both cognitive scientists and knowledge engineers call 'procedural knowledge', thus distinguishing it from 'declarative'.

DECLARATIVE KNOWLEDGE

It is characteristic of the retrieval and use of declarative knowledge that it is ordinarily done in conscious awareness. From a wealth of neurobiological observations concerning the effects of brain lesions on memory, L. R. Squire (1987, chapter 11) distinguishes declarative memory from procedural as 'memory that is directly accessible to conscious recollection'. By contrast, the hallmark of a highly trained expert brain is that it does much of its work intuitively. 'Dialogue elicitation' of rules for building expert systems may therefore be frustrated whenever a given expertise involves strategies stored in procedural memory. Inaccessibility to consciousness of even parts of a targeted expertise can then cause serious problems for large knowledge engineering projects, such as Japan's ambitious 'Fifth Generation' (Michie, 1988). Differentiation of the two forms is thus desirable.

Declarative knowledge comprises whatever lends itself to logical formulation: goals, descriptions, constraints, possibilities, hypotheses. The declarative category also includes facts. When these relate directly or indirectly to events in the agent's own experience, their place of storage is referred to as 'episodic' memory. Another sub-division of declarative knowledge is held to reside in 'semantic' memory, which Squire defines as follows:

> Semantic memory refers to knowledge of the world. This system represents organised information such as facts, concepts, and vocabulary. The content of semantic memory is explicitly known and available for recall. Unlike episodic memory, however, semantic memory has no necessary temporal landmarks. It does not refer to particular events in a person's past. A simple illustration of this difference is that one may recall the difference between episodic and semantic memory, or one may recall the encounter when the difference was first explained.

A school founded by John McCarthy (1959) aims to extend formal logic to serve as a vehicle for mechanizing declarative knowledge (see a recent collection edited by Ginsberg, 1987).

We will say little further about the project, beyond expressing respect for such work. Its philosophical importance is matched only by its difficulty. Our theme is closer to the name and nature of expert systems. These are not so much to do with giving computers knowledge of the world as with equipping them with useful know-how. In face of the difficulties which confront the McCarthy project, there is something to be said for separately studying the mechanization of procedural knowledge and only later integrating the two levels.

NATURE OF PROCEDURAL KNOWLEDGE

In Anderson's (1990) text on cognition, skilled procedures are pictured as arising in part by derivation from pre-existing mental descriptions. No direct evidence is offered. Knowledge engineers concerned with real-time skills have been led by practical experience in a rather different direction. The empirical picture is one of inductive compilation from sensori-motor data gathered in the course of trial and error. In this picture the role of higher level knowledge is not to participate directly, but to steer the learning process, setting and adjusting the frame within which skill-bearing rules are constructed.

The final phase of skill-learning, described by Anderson and others as 'automatization', does not ordinarily support introspective report by the expert performer, hence the 'knowledge acquisition bottleneck' of applied AI. Procedural knowledge, as we have seen, limits itself to the 'how to' of skilled tasks, whether physical as in making a chair, or more abstract as in prediction of sterling rates against the dollar or the diagnosis of acute abdominal pain. A common synonym for such knowledge is know-how and its manifestation in observable behaviour is called 'skill'. One difficulty is that observed task performance does not necessarily reveal whether a given expert's behaviour really exemplifies a skill in the procedural sense or whether he or she is using declarative-semantic memory to form action plans on the fly. Squire's earlier-cited definition supplies a test, namely the ability to give a verbal account of the way in which each decision was made, possible only for declarative memory. A second criterion is the frequency of the recognize–act cycle: this may simply be too fast for 'what-if' inferential planning to be feasible.

For those concerned to recover procedural rules, as in building expert systems, lack of verbal access (on which Anderson also remarks) is a problem. Yet there is widespread faith among knowledge engineers that special methods of 'dialogue elicitation' can be found which will permit the construction of rule-based systems on the scale of such inductively built systems as the GASOIL (Slocombe et al., 1986) and BMT programs of Table 2.

Table 2.   Of the world's three largest expert systems the two latest (GASOIL and BMT) were not constructed from rules obtained in dialogue fashion, but by automated induction from expert-supplied data. In each case the induction engineer trained the system in the desired skill in the style that the master of a craft trains an apprentice, by a structured sequence of selected examples. Rates of code production are typically in excess of 100 lines of installed Fortran, C, Pascal, etc., per programmer day. The methodology allows validation to be placed on a user-transparent basis (Michie 1989), and maintenance costs are in many cases trivialized. Tabulation is from Slocombe et al. (1986) with 1990 data on BMT added. The BMT program is described on p. 10 of *Pragmatica*, vol. 1 (ed. J. E. Hayes Michie), Glasgow, UK: Turing Institute Press.

	Application	No. of rules	Develop man-yrs	Maintenance man-yrs/yr	Inductive tools
MYCIN	medicine diagnosis	400	100	N/A	N/A
XCON	VAX computer configuration	8,000	180	30	N/A
GASOIL	hydrocarbon separation system configuration	2,800	1	0.1	ExpertEase and Extran 7
BMT	configuration of fire-protection equipment in buildings	>30,000	9	2.0	1st Class and RuleMaster

Is rule induction from expert-supplied data nevertheless in some sense a second-best option for building systems on the BMT scale? On the contrary. Experts can rapidly and effectively communicate their skills (as in the BMT case) solely via illustrative responses to selected cases. Does he or she thereby omit something indispensable?

Certainly the practitioner's explicit and communicable awareness is basic to expertise in some task domains. But other domains, which lack this property, can be found not only among a rather wide variety of industrial tasks, but even in such purely 'mental' forms of expertise as playing a strong game of checkers (see below). As a paradigm of procedural knowledge, Feigenbaum and McCorduck (1983, p.55) give the example of tying one's shoes. It is interesting that once this skill has reached the stage known as automatization it can continue unaffected by destruction of the individual's brain mechanisms for acquiring and handling important forms of declarative knowledge. Damasio describes a patient named Boswell. The following summary is from Patricia Smith Churchland (personal communication).

> In addition to losing the hippocampal structures, he has massive damage to frontal cortex. He can identify a house, or a car, but he cannot identify his house or his car; he cannot remember that he was married, that he has children, and so forth. He seems to have no retrograde episodic memory, as well as no anterograde episodic, … Boswell can still play a fine game of checkers, though when asked he says it is bingo. He cannot learn new faces and does not remember 'pre-morbid' faces such as that of his wife and his children … Boswell can play checkers, tie his shoes, carry on a conversation, etc.

Of considerable interest is the survival of Boswell's checkers skills. Evidently what we shall later term 'fast' skills are not the only ones for which procedural knowledge may dominate over declarative. In contrast to chess skill, checkers was already known not to lend itself to the planning approach and to be essentially 'intuitive'. When A. L. Samuel was engaged in his classic studies of machine learning using the game of checkers, he had numerous sessions with leading checkers masters directed towards dialogue acquisition of their rules and principles. Samuel reported (personal communication) that he had never had such frustrating experiences in his life. In terms of relationship to what the masters actually did, the verbal material which he elicited contained almost nothing which he could use or interpret. In similar vein, Feigenbaum and McCorduck (p. 82) describe this type of expert response in the following terms: 'That's true, but if you see enough patient/rocks/chipdesigns/instrument readings, you see that it is not true after all.' They conclude, 'At this point, knowledge threatens to become ten thousand special cases.'

The message from clinical studies is that skilled performance of even sophisticated tasks can still be manifested, and learned, when the brain is so damaged that knowledge of new happenings cannot be retained and previously stored facts and relations (declarative-semantic memory) are seriously disrupted. Another circumstance under which the mediation of declarative memory is at least equally disabled can be observed in the normal brain by imposing a sufficiently restrictive constraint on the time available for the recognize–act cycle, as in touch-typing. This skill does not depend on the storage and retrieval of declarative knowledge, and can be acquired and executed in its virtually complete absence. Recall that when copy-typing at speed the typist does not need to understand the words as he or she reads them. Indeed, after a speed test little or nothing of the text's content can be recalled. Moreover, educated onlookers are surprised, although they should not be, by the outcome of a request to the typist (supposing that he or she has been using a typewriter with unlabelled keys) to label the keyboard correctly with the proper alphanumeric symbols. Lacking a declarative model, the touch-typist is ordinarily unable to do so (see, for example, Posner, 1973), other than by deliberately typing a symbol and observing where the finger went!

Simon (in press) has recently re-emphasized that simple recognition of a familiar object takes at least 500 milliseconds. Operations involving reference to a semantic model of the task domain require retrieval from long-term memory of relatively complex knowledge-structures and an associated apparatus for inferring, storing, and utilizing intermediate results. Such elaborate transactions are to be found only in the 'slow lane'. Here seconds, minutes, or even hours are required to incubate a decision. The bare bones of an explicit rationale for a slow-lane decision, when it comes, can usually be elicited from the expert by verbal report. Not so in the fast lane, to which the present discussion is confined. 'Fast' skills cannot be accessed by 'dialogue elicitation' methods. How then are expert systems to be built for these skills? A solution is to record behavioural traces from the expert subject. Inductive inference then reconstructs from recorded decision data rule-based models of the brain's hidden strategies. As reported in this review, machine execution of data-derived models has been found to generate performance exceeding in reliability the trained subject's own.

POSTULATES OF SKILL ACQUISITION

Experimental work which will now be described was animated by a point of view about brains, summarized below as a list of postulates. Declarative knowledge is abbreviated to 'D' and procedural to 'P'. P designates only procedural knowledge which has already reached the automatized stage.

1. human agents are able verbally to report their own D;
2. human agents cannot verbally report their P;
3. D can be augmented by being told, and also by deduction;
4. P is built by learning, whether by imitation or by trial and error;
5. P can be executed independent of D, but not vice versa;
6. decision-taking via P is fast relative to use of D;
7. sufficiently fast control skills depend on P alone;
8. even for some slow skills P is sufficient for expert performance; rule induction can extract an explicit form of P from behavioural traces.

Experiments on dynamical control have yielded illustrations of the listed postulates, culminating in a test of 8 above, namely induction of rules from silent brains. But a comment is first requisite on the undoubted existence of expert systems (EXCON was mentioned earlier) whose rule-bases have, with whatever difficulty, been constructed by dialogue acquisition.

Many observers have noted that experts seek to escape from the requirement of rule formulation (which they find uncongenial) by supplying 'rules' of such low-level form that they constitute no more than concocted sample cases, i.e. specimen decision-data. The phenomenon has been described by Sterling and Shapiro (1986) in their description of the construction of a credit evaluation expert system. The finance specialists continually gravitated towards concrete instances rather than general rules. This has indeed been a universal finding in knowledge engineering, in line with the known facts concerning procedural memory and its mode of access.

But what if knowledge engineers in search of improvements on raw formulations were consciously or unconsciously to apply their own powers of inductive inference to such sample cases? They could then themselves create the kind of high-level rule structures that they had hoped to elicit. The result would of course be testimony more to their own powers of inductive generalization than evidence that experts can introspect their own rules. In a recent aerospace application two knowledge engineers were able, by deliberately exploiting this style of 'rule-conjecture and test', to construct a rule-based solution with no more than a black-box simulator of the task domain to provide corrective feed-back. No set of rules pre-existed, either in an expert's brain or anywhere else…

REFERENCES

Anderson, J. R. (1990). *Cognitive Psychology and its Implications*, 3rd ed. New York: W. H. Freeman.

Feigenbaum, E. A. and McCorduck, P. (1983). *The Fifth Generation: Artificial Intelligence and Japan's Computer Challenge to the World*. Reading, MA: Addison-Wesley.

French, R. M. (1990). Subcognition and the limits of the Turing test. *Mind*, 99, 53–65.

Ginsberg, M. L., ed. (1987). *Readings in Nonmonotonic Reasoning*. Los Altos, CA: Morgan Kaufman.

McCarthy, J. (1959). Programs with common sense. In Mechanization of Thought Processes, vol. I. London: HMSO. Reprinted in M. Minsky (ed.), *Semantic Information Processing*. Cambridge, MA: MIT Press, 1960.

Michie, D. (1988). The Fifth Generation's unbridged gap. In *A Half-Century of the Universal Turing Machine* (ed. R. Herken). Oxford: Oxford University Press.

Newell, A. and Simon, H. A. (1976). Computer science as empirical inquiry: symbols and search. *Commun. of the ACM*, 19, 113–26.

Posner, M. I. (1973). *Cognition: An Introduction*. Glenview, IL: Scott Foresman.

Slocombe, S., Moore, K., and Zelouf, M. (1986). Engineering expert system applications. Presented at British Cardiovascular Society Annual Conference, Dec. 1986.

Squire, L. R. (1987). *Memory and Brain*. Oxford: Oxford University Press.

Sterling, L. and Shapiro, E. (1986). *The Art of Prolog*. Cambridge, MA: MIT Press.

The Way Ahead

This final group of essays covers Donald Michie's machine intelligence research over the last decade or so of his life. Much of it was concerned with a careful examination of Turing's Test for evaluating claims to intelligent thought by computing systems. A direct practical consequence of this research was the construction of conversational software agents, that he thought were necessary for future progress in the area of intelligent machines. In some sense, his interest in such programs is already indicated in the 'Slaughter' article (p. 113 above), and much of his final years were spent on his 'Sophie' project, the basis of which is described in the article 'The Return of the Imitation Game'. While Sophie itself (or is it herself?) in 2007 was still only in its early stages, Donald Michie's interest in the idea had a number of conceptual and philosophical roots. I have tried to capture some of these in the articles leading up to the 'Imitation Game'. The attempt is not entirely successful, and the reader may find other articles listed in 'Publications' more fulfilling.

But it is not all about angels on pinheads: visitors to the Powerhouse Museum in Sydney can converse with Sylvie, a creation of Donald Michie and Claude Sammut, who has an uncommon interest in computers, machine intelligence, and Alan Turing. A British cousin of Sylvie, Sophie-C, developed with David Mason and Richard Wheeler, was described at a conference in Belgium in 2006 (the paper is listed in 'Publications'). It was perhaps the last talk that Donald Michie gave on the research that had occupied him for the previous five years. In it, he suggests how conversational agents like Sophie can help untangle ideas of thinking and intelligence, which, although used interchangeably in the Turing test, may in fact be unrelated.

Turing's Test and Conscious Thought (1993)

Over forty years ago A.M. Turing proposed a test for intelligence in machines. Based as it is solely on an examinee's verbal responses, the Test misses some important components of human thinking. To bring these manifestations within its scope, the Turing Test would require substantial extension. Advances in the application of AI methods in the design of improved human–computer interfaces are now focusing attention on machine models of thought and knowledge from the altered standpoint of practical utility.

INTRODUCTION

Although its text is now available in a collection of papers published by MIT Press (edited by Carpenter and Doran [4]), there is little awareness of a remarkable lecture delivered to the London Mathematical Society on February 20, 1947. The lecturer was Alan Turing. His topic was the nature of programmable digital computers, taking as his exemplar the 'Automatic Computing Engine' (ACE) then under construction at the National Physical Laboratory. At that time no stored-program machine was yet operational anywhere in the world. So each one of his deeply considered points blazes a trail—logical equivalence to the Universal Turing Machine of hardware constructions such as the ACE, the uses of variable-length precision, the need for large paged memories, the nature of 'while' loops, the idea of the sub-routine, the possibility of remote access, the automation of I/O, the concept of the operating system.

Turing then considers the eventual possibility of automating the craft of programming, itself scarcely yet invented. He further discusses the forms of predictable resistance to such automation among those whom today we call DP (data-processing) staff:

> They may be unwilling to let their jobs be stolen from them in this way. In that case they will surround the whole of their work with mystery and make excuses, couched in well chosen gibberish, whenever any dangerous suggestions are made.

We then read

> This topic [of automatic programming] naturally leads to the question as to how far it is possible in principle for a computing machine to simulate human activities...

and the lecturer launches into the theme which we know today as artificial intelligence (AI).

Turing put forward three positions:

Position 1. *Programming could be done in symbolic logic and would then require the construction of appropriate interpreters.*

Position 2. *Machine learning is needed so that computers can discover new knowledge inductively from experience as well as deductively.*

Position 3. *Humanized interfaces are required to enable machines to adapt to people, so as to acquire knowledge tutorially.*

I reproduce relevant excerpts below, picking out particular phrases in bold type.

1. *Turing on logic programming*
   I expect that digital computing machines will eventually stimulate a considerable interest in symbolic logic **and mathematical philosophy;**... in principle one should be able to communicate in any symbolic logic, provided that the machine were given instruction tables which would enable it to **interpret that logical system.**

2. *Turing on machine learning*

Let us suppose we have set up a machine with certain initial instruction tables, so constructed that these tables might on occasion, if good reason arose, **modify those tables**. One can imagine that after the machine had been operating for some time the instructions would have been altered out of all recognition, but nevertheless still be such that one would have to admit that the machine was still doing very worthwhile calculations. Possibly it might still be getting results of the type desired when the machine was first set up, but in a much more efficient manner. In such a case one would have to admit that the progress of the machine had not been foreseen when its original instructions were put in. It would be like a pupil who had learnt much from his master, but had **added much more by his own work**.

3. *Turing on cognitive compatibility*

No man adds very much to the body of knowledge; why should we expect more of a machine? Putting the same point differently, the machine must be allowed to have **contact with human beings** in order that it may **adapt itself to their standards**.

AI's inventory of fundamental ideas due to Turing would not be complete without the proposal which he put forward three years later in the philosophical journal *Mind*, known today as the 'Turing Test'. The key move was to define intelligence *operationally*, i.e., in terms of the computer's ability, tested over a typewriter link, to sustain a simulation of an intelligent human when subjected to questioning. Published accounts usually overstate the scope proposed by Turing for his 'imitation game', presenting the aim of the machine's side as successful deceit of the interrogator throughout a lengthy dialogue. But Turing's original imitation game asked only for a rather weak level of success over a relatively short period of interrogation.

> I believe that in about fifty years' time it will be possible to programme computers, with a storage capacity of about 10^9, to make them play the imitation game so well that an average interrogator will not have more

than 70 per cent chance of making the right identification [as between human and computer] after five minutes of questioning.

Presumably the interrogator has no more than 2½ minutes of question-putting to bestow on each of the remote candidates, whose replies are not time limited. We have to remind ourselves that—in spite of subsequent mis-statements, repeated and amplified in a recent contribution to *Mind* by Robert French [9]—the question which Turing wished to place beyond reasonable dispute was *not* whether a machine might think at the level of an intelligent human. His proposal was for a test of whether a machine could be said to think at all.

SOLIPSISM AND THE CHARMED CIRCLE

Notwithstanding the above, French's paper has important things to say concerning the role played by 'sub-cognitive' processes in intelligent thought. He points out that ' ... any sufficiently broad set of questions making up a Turing Test would necessarily contain questions that rely on subcognitive associations for their answers.'

The scientific study of cognition has shown that some thought processes are intimately bound up with consciousness while others take place sublimi-nally. Further, as French reminds us, the two are interdependent. Yet other contributors to the machine intelligence discussion often imply a necessary association between consciousness and all forms of intelligence, as a basis for claiming that a computer program could not exhibit intelligence of any kind or degree. Thus John R. Searle [24] recently renewed his celebrated 'Chinese Room' argument against the possibility of designing a program that, when run on a suitable computer, would show evidence of 'thinking'. After his opening question 'Can a machine think?', Searle adds: 'Can a machine have conscious thoughts in exactly the same sense that you and I have?' Since a computer program does nothing but shuffle symbols, so the implication goes, one cannot really credit it with the kinds of sensations, feelings, and impulses which accompany one's own thinking—e.g., the excitement of following an evidential clue, the satisfaction of following a lecturer's argument, or the 'Aha!' of subjective comprehension. Hence, however brilliant and profound its responses in the purely intellectual sense recognized by logicians, a programmed computing system can never be truly intelligent. Intelligence would imply that suitably programmed computers can be *conscious*, whereas we 'know' that they cannot be.

In his 1950 *Mind* paper Turing considered arguments of this kind, citing Jefferson's Lister Oration for 1949:

> Not until a machine can write a sonnet or compose a concerto because of thoughts and emotions felt, and not by the chance fall of symbols, could we agree that machine equals brain—that is, not only write it but know that it had written it. No mechanism could feel (and not merely artificially signal, an easy contrivance) pleasure at successes, grief when its valves fuse, be warmed by flattery, be made miserable by its mistakes, be charmed by sex, be angry or depressed when it cannot get what it wants.

Jefferson's portrayal of conscious thought and feeling here compounds two aspects which are today commonly distinguished, namely on the one hand self-awareness, and, on the other, empathic awareness of others, sometimes termed 'inter-subjectivity'. Turing's comment on Jefferson disregards this second aspect, and addresses only the first. The relevant excerpt from the *Mind* paper is:

4. *Turing on the argument from consciousness*

> …according to the most extreme form of this view [that thought is impossible without consciousness] the only way by which one could be sure that a machine thinks is to *be* the machine and to feel oneself thinking. One could then describe these feelings to the world, but of course no one would be justified in taking any notice. Likewise according to this view the only way to know that a *man* thinks is to be that particular man. It is in fact the solipsist point of view. It may be the most logical view to hold but it makes communication of ideas difficult. A is liable to believe 'A thinks but B does not' whilst B believes 'B thinks but A does not'. Instead of arguing continually over this question it is usual to have the polite convention that everyone thinks.

After a fragment of hypothetical dialogue illustrating the imitation game, Turing continues:

> I think that most of those who support the argument from consciousness could be persuaded to abandon it rather than be forced into the solipsist position. They will then probably be willing to accept our test.

He thus contributes a fourth position to the previous list (p. 143).

Position 4. *To the extent that possession of consciousness is not refutable in other people, we conventionally assume it. We should be equally ready to abandon solipsism for assessing thinking in machines.*

Turing did not suggest that consciousness is irrelevant to thought, nor that its mysterious nature and the confusions of educated opinion on the subject should be ignored. His point was simply that these mysteries and confusions do not have to be resolved before we can address questions of intelligence. Then and since, it has been the AI view that purely solipsistic definitions based on subjectively observed states are not useful. But Turing certainly underestimated the potential appeal of a more subtle form of solipsism generalized to *groups* of agents so as to avoid the dilemma which he posed. Following Daniel C. Dennett [5], I term this variant the 'charmed circle' argument. A relationship with the notion of inter-subjectivity, or socially shared consciousness (see Colwyn Trevarthen [25, 26]) can be brought out by revising the above-quoted passage from Turing along some such lines as 'the only way by which one could be sure that a machine thinks is to be a member of a charmed circle which has accepted that machine into its ranks and can collectively feel itself thinking.' It is indeed according to just such social pragmatics that this issue is likely to be routinely adjudicated in the coming era of human–computer collaborative groups (see later).

But note that in the first of the two quoted passages concerning the argument from consciousness, the concluding sentence becomes truer to human society if rephrased:

> ... it is usual to have the polite convention that everyone *who is regarded as a person* thinks.

Turing's uncorrected wording, quite unintentionally I believe, prejudges whether the polite convention would have led Aristotle to concede powers of intelligent thought to women, or Australian settlers to Tasmanian aborigines, or nineteenth-century plantation owners to their slaves. Nor, conversely, would Turing necessarily have wished to withhold the polite convention if someone asserted: 'My dog is a real person, and intelligent too.' In his above-cited contribution on consciousness to the *Oxford Companion to the Mind*, Daniel Dennett [5] puts the point well:

> How do creatures differ from robots, real or imagined? They are organically and biologically similar to *us*, and we are the paradigmatic conscious creatures. This similarity admits of degrees, of course, and one's intuitions about which sorts of similarity count are probably untrustworthy. Dolphins' fishiness subtracts from our conviction, but no doubt should not. Were chimpanzees as dull as sea slugs, their facial similarity to us would no doubt nevertheless favour their inclusion in the charmed circle. If house-flies were about our size, or warm-blooded, we'd be much more confident that when we plucked off their wings they felt pain (*our* sort of pain, the kind that matters).

At the outset of his paper Turing does briefly consider what may be termed the argument from dissimilarity. He dismisses the idea of 'trying to make a "thinking machine" more human by dressing it up in artificial flesh', and commends the proposed typewriter link as side-stepping a line of criticism which he sees as pointless. He evidently did not foresee the use of similarity to define charmed circles of sufficient radius to deflect the accusation of narrow solipsism. In view of the absence from his discussion of all reference to shared aspects of conscious thought, he would probably have seen it as an evasion.

The 'charmed circle' criterion disallows intelligence in any non-living vehicle—so long as one is careful to draw the circle appropriately. But the idea of inanimate intelligence is in any case a difficult one to expound, for human intelligence is after all a product of the evolution of animals. This partly explains

Turing's simplifying adoption of an engineering, rather than a scientific, scenario for his purpose. But the notion of performance trials conducted by a doubting client also sorted naturally with Turing's temperamental addiction to engineering images. Although himself conspicuously weak in purely mechanical skills, he startled his associates with a flow of highly original practical innovations, home-built and usually doomed. The same addiction was also discernible at the abstract level, where his gifts were not hampered by problems of physical implementation—notably in that most unlikely of purely mathematical constructions, the Universal Turing Machine itself.

CONSCIOUSNESS IN ARTIFACTS

Searle himself is not insensitive to the appearance of special pleading. In his earlier quoted *Scientific American* article [24] he writes:

> I have not tried to show that only biologically based systems like our brains can think. Right now those are the only systems we know for a fact can think, but we might find other systems in the universe that can produce conscious thoughts, and we might even come to be able to create thinking systems artificially. I regard this issue as up for grabs.

With these words he seems to accept the possibility of conscious thought in machines. But we must remember that John Searle's objection relates only to *programmed* machines or other symbol shufflers. According to the Searle canon, (i) 'thinking' implies that the system is conscious, and (ii) consciousness is not possible in a programmed device which can only shuffle symbols. What if *two* 'other systems in the universe' are found with identical repertoires of intellectual behaviours, including behaviour suggestive of conscious awareness? If one of the systems is implemented entirely in circuitry and the other in software, then Searle gives the benefit of the doubt to the first as a thinking system, but withholds it from the second as not being 'really' conscious. What is to be done if some laboratory of the future builds a third system by faithfully re-implementing the entire circuitry of the first as software, perhaps microcoded for speed? Not only would the functionality of the first machine be reproduced, but also its complete and detailed logic and behavioural repertoire. Yet a strict reading of Searle forces the conclusion that, although the scientifically testable attributes of conscious thought would be reconstructed in the new artifact, an intangible 'something' would be lost, namely 'true' consciousness. The latter *could* in principle be synthesized in circuitry (see Searle: 'we might even come to be able to create thinking systems artificially'), but not in software or other forms of symbol shuffling.

There is in this a counterpoint to earlier reflections by the Nobel Prizewinning neuroscientist Sir John Eccles [8], who held, like Searle today, that a being's claim to be conscious may legitimately be ignored on grounds of knowing that being's interior mechanisms:

> We can, in principle, explain all…input–output performance in terms of activity of neuronal circuits; and consequently, consciousness seems to be absolutely unnecessary! … as neurophysiologists we simply have no use for consciousness in our attempt to explain how the nervous system works.

But for Eccles it was the 'activity of neuronal circuits' rather than Searle's shuffling of symbols that permitted appearances of consciousness to be discounted. Eccles has subsequently changed his view (see Popper and Eccles [21]), which we now see as having defined the limits of neurophysiology prematurely. In the same way Searle's in-principle exclusion of possible future AI artifacts risks prematurely defining the limits of knowledge-based programming. Like Eccles, Searle produces no workable definition of consciousness.

To rescue such positions from metaphysics, we must hope that a suitable Searle Test will be forthcoming to complement Turing's.

SUBARTICULATE THOUGHT

In earlier generations students of intelligent behaviour generally ignored the phenomenon of consciousness. Some from the behaviourist camp denied that there was anything for the term to name. Turing's impact on psychology has been to move the study of cognition towards increasingly computation-oriented models.

One of the ways in which these formulations differ from those of behaviourism is in allotting an important role to those aspects of consciousness which are susceptible of investigation, including investigation via verbal report. But as new findings have multiplied, an awareness has grown of the complementary importance of other forms of thought and intelligence. Dennett [5] remarks as follows:

> the cognitive psychologist marshals experimental evidence, models, and theories to show that people are engaged in surprisingly sophisticated reasoning processes of which they can give no introspective account at all. Not only are minds accessible to outsiders; some mental activities are more accessible to outsiders than to the very 'owners' of those minds!

Although having no access to these mental activities in the sense of direct awareness of their operations, the explicitly conscious forms of mental calculation enjoy intimate and instant access to their fruits. In many cases, as illustrated below with the problem of conjecturing the pronunciation of imaginary English words, access to the fruits of subliminal cognition is a necessity, even though conscious awareness of the cognitive operations themselves is not.

The Turing Test's typewriter link with the owners of two candidate minds gives no direct access to the class of 'silent' mental activity described by Dennett. In the form put forward by Turing, the Test can directly detect only those processes which are susceptible of introspective verbal report. Does this then render it obsolete as a test of intelligence in machines?

The regretful answer is 'Yes'. The Test's didactic clarity is today suffering erosion from developments in cognitive science and in knowledge engineering. These have already revealed two dimensions of mismatch, even before questions of inter-subjectivity and socially expressed intelligence are brought into the discussion:

(i) inability of the Test to bring into the game thought processes of kinds which humans can perform but cannot articulate, and

(ii) ability of the Test to detect and examine a particular species of thought process ('cognitive skills') in a suitably programmed machine through its self-articulations; similar access to human enactments of such processes is not possible because they are typically subarticulate.

Concerning (i), the idea that mental processes below the level of conscious and articulate thought are somehow secondary was dispatched with admirable terseness by A. N. Whitehead in 1911:

> It is a profoundly erroneous truism ... that we would cultivate the habit of thinking what we are doing. The precise opposite is the case. Civilisation advances by extending the number of important operations which we can perform without thinking about them. [28]

Moreover, although sub-cognitive skills can operate independently of conscious thought, the converse is by no means obvious. Indeed the processes of thought and language are dependent on such skills at every instant. The laboriously thought-out, and articulate, responses of the beginner are successively replaced by those which are habitual and therefore effortless. Only when a skilled response is blocked by some obstacle is it necessary to 'go back to first principles' and reason things out step by step.

It is understandable that Turing should have sought to separate intelligence from the complications and ambiguities of the conscious/unconscious dichotomy, and to define this mental quality in terms of communication media which are characteristic of the academic rather than, say, the medical practitioner, the craftsman, or the explorer. But his Test has paid a price for the simplification. At the very moment that a human's mastery of a skill becomes most complete, he or she becomes least capable of articulating it and hence of sustaining a convincing dialogue via the imitation game's remote typewriter. Consider, for example, the following.

A particularly elaborate cognitive skill is of life-and-death importance in Micronesia, whose master navigators undertake voyages of as much as 450 miles between islands in a vast expanse of which less than two-tenths of one per cent is land. We read in Hutchins' contribution to Gentner and Stevens' *Mental Models* [12]:

> Inasmuch as these navigators are still practicing their art, one may well wonder why the researchers don't just ask the navigators how they do it. Researchers do ask, but it is not that simple. As is the case with any truly expert performance in any culture, the experts themselves are often

unable to specify just what it is they do while they are performing. Doing the task and explaining what one is doing require quite different ways of thinking.

We thus have the paradox that a Micronesian master navigator, engaging in dialogue, let us suppose, via a typewriter link with the aid of a literate interpreter, would lose most marks precisely when examined in the domain of his special expertise, namely long-distance navigation.

PROCEDURAL INFRASTRUCTURE OF DECLARATIVE KNOWLEDGE

The Turing Test seems at first sight to side-step the need to implement such expertise by only requiring the machine to display general ability rather than specialist skills, the latter being difficult for their possessors to describe explicitly. But the display of intelligence and thought is in reality profoundly dependent upon some of these. Perhaps the most conspicuous case is the ability to express oneself in one's own language. Turing seems to have assumed that by the time that a fair approach to mechanizing intelligence had been achieved, this would somehow bring with it a certain level of linguistic competence, at least in the written language. Matters have turned out differently. Partly this reflects the continuing difficulties confronting machine representation of the semantics and pragmatics (i.e., the 'knowledge' components) of discourse, as opposed to the purely syntactic components. Partly it reflects the above-described inaccessibility to investigators of the laws which govern what everyone knows how to do.

In spoken discourse, we find the smooth and pervasive operation of linguistic rules by speakers who are wholly ignorant of them! Imagine, for example, that the administrator of a Turing Test were to include the following, adapted from Philip Johnson-Laird's *The Computer and the Mind* [14]:

> *Question:* How do you pronounce the plurals of the imaginary English words: 'platch', 'snorp', and 'brell'?

A human English speaker has little difficulty in framing a response over the typewriter link.

> *Answer:* I pronounce them as 'platchez', 'snorpss', and 'brellz'.

The linguist Morris Halle [11] has pointed out that to form these plurals a person must use unconscious principles. According to Allen, Hunnicutt, and Klatt [1], subliminal encoding of the following three rules would be sufficient:

(1) If a singular noun ends in one of the phonetic segments/s/, /z/, /sh/, /zh/, /ch/, or /j/, then add the *ez* sound.
(2) If a singular noun ends in one of the phonetic segments/f/, /k/, /p/, /t/, or /th/, then add the *ss* sound.
(3) In any other case, add the z sound.

What about a machine? In this particular case programmers acquainted with the phonetic laws of English 's' pluralizations might have fore-armed its rule base. But what about the scores of other questions about pronunciation against which they could not conceivably have fore-armed it, for the suffi- cient reason that phonetic knowledge of the corresponding unconscious rules has not yet been formulated? Yet a human, *any* English-speaking human capable of typewriter discourse, would by contrast shine in answering such questions.

If account is taken of similar domains of discourse ranging far from linguis- tics, each containing thousands of sub-domains within which similar 'trick questions' could be framed, the predicament of a machine facing interrogation from an adversarial insider begin to look daunting. We see in this a parable of futility for the attempt to implement intelligence solely by the declarative knowledge-based route, unsupported by skill-learning. A version of this parable, expensively enacted by the Japanese Fifth Generation, is discussed in my contri- bution [17] to Rolf Herken's *The Universal Turing Machine*.

Among the brain's various centres and sub-centres only one, localized in the dominant (usually the left) cerebral hemisphere, has the ability to reformulate a person's own mental behaviour as linguistic descriptions. It follows that Turing's imitation game can directly sample from the human player only those thought processes accessible to this centre. Yet as Hutchins reminds us in the context of Micronesian navigation, and Johnson-Laird in the context of English pronunciation, most highly developed mental skills are of the verbally *inaccessible* kind. Their possessors cannot answer the question 'What did you do in order to get that right?'

This same hard fact was recently and repeatedly driven home to technologists by the rise and fall in commercial software of the 'dialogue-acquisition' school of expert systems construction. The earlier-mentioned disappointment which overtook this school, after well publicised backing from government agencies of Japan and other countries, could have been avoided by acceptance of statements to be found in any standard psychological text. In John Anderson's *Cognitive Psychology and Its Implications* [2], the chapter on development of expertise speaks of the *autonomous stage* of skill acquisition:

> Because facility in the skill increases, verbal mediation in the performance of the task often disappears at this point. In fact, the ability to verbalize knowledge of the skill can be lost altogether.

Against this background, failure of attempts to build large expert systems by 'dialogue acquisition' of knowledge from the experts can hardly be seen as surprising. It is sufficient here to say that many skills are learned by means that do not require prior description, and to give a concrete example from common experience. For this I have taken from M. I. Posner's *Cognition: An Introduction* [22] an everyday instance which can easily be verified:

> If a skilled typist is asked to type the alphabet, he can do so in a few seconds and with very low probability of error. If, however, he is given a diagram of his keyboard and asked to fill in the letters in alphabet order, he finds the task difficult. It requires several minutes to perform and the likelihood of error is high. Moreover, the typist often reports that he can only obtain the visual location of some letters by trying to type the letter and then determining where his finger would be. These observations indicate that experience with typing produces a motor code which may exist in the absence of any visual code.

Imagine, then, a programming project which depends on eliciting a skilled typist's knowledge of the whereabouts on an unlabelled keyboard of the letters of the alphabet. The obvious shortcut is to ask him or her to type, say, 'the quick brown fox jumps over the lazy dog' and record which keys are typed in response to which symbols. But you must *ask* the domain experts what they know, says the programmer's tribal lore, not learn from what they actually do. Even in the typing domain this lore would not work very well. With the more complex and structured skills of diagnosis, forecasting, scheduling, and design, it has been even less effective. Happily there is another path to machine acquisition of cognitive skills from expert practitioners, namely: analyse what the expert does; *then* ask him what he knows. As reviewed elsewhere [18], a new craft of rule induction from recording what the expert does is now the basis of commercial operations in Britain, America, Scandinavia, continental Europe, and Japan.

Psychologists speak of 'cognitive skill' when discussing intensively learned intuitive know-how. The term is misleading on two counts. First, the word 'cognitive' sometimes conveys a connotation of 'conscious', inappropriate when discussing intuitive processes. Second, the term carries an implication of some 'deep' model encapsulating the given task's relational and causal structure. In actuality, just as calculating prodigies are commonly ignorant of logical and number-theoretical models of arithmetic, so skilled practitioners in other domains often lack developed mental models of their task environments. I follow French [9] in using the term 'sub-cognitive' for these procedurally oriented forms of operational knowledge.

Knowledge engineers sometimes call sub-cognitive know-how 'compiled knowledge', employing a metaphor which misdirects attention to a conjectured top-down, rather than data-driven, route of acquisition. But whichever acquisition route carries the main traffic, collectively, as remarked in the passage from Whitehead, such skills account for the preponderating part, and a growing part as our technical culture advances, of what it is to be an intelligent human. The areas of the human brain to which this silent corpus is consigned are still largely conjectural and may in large part even be sub-cortical. A second contrast between articulate and inarticulate cerebral functions is that between the verbally silent (usually the right) cerebral hemisphere, and the logical and articulate areas located in left hemisphere. Right-brain thinking notably involves spatial visualization and is only inarticulate in the strict sense of symbolic communication: sub-linguistic means of conveying mood and intent are well developed, as also are important modalities of consciousness. For further discussion the reader is referred to Popper and Eccles [21]—see also later in this paper.

THE SUPER-ARTICULACY PHENOMENON

Two dimensions were earlier identified along which the Turing Test can today be seen as mismatched to its task, even if we put aside forms of intelligence evoked in inter-agent cooperation which the Test does not address at all. The first of these dimensions reveals the imitation game's inability to detect, in the human, thought processes of kinds which humans cannot articulate. We now turn to the second flaw, namely that the Test can catch in its net thought processes which the machine agent *can* articulate, but should not if it is to simulate a human. What is involved is the phenomenon of machine 'super-articulacy'. A suitably programmed computer can inductively infer the largely unconscious rules underlying an expert's skill from samples of the expert's recorded decisions. When applied to new data, the resulting knowledge-based systems are often capable of using their inductively acquired rules to justify their decisions at levels of completeness and coherence exceeding what little articulacy the largely intuitive expert can muster. In such cases a Turing Test examiner comparing responses from the human and the artificial expert can have little difficulty in identifying the machine's. For so skilled a task, no human could produce such carefully thought-out justifications! A test which can thus penalize important forms of intelligent thought must be regarded as missing its mark. In my Technology Lecture at the London Royal Society [16], I reviewed the then-available experimental results. Since that time, Ivan Bratko and colleagues [3] have announced a more far-reaching demonstration, having endowed clinical cardiology with its first certifiably complete, correct, and fully articulate corpus of skills in electrocardiogram diagnosis, machine-derived from a logical model of the heart. In a Turing imitation game the KARDIO system would quickly give itself away by revealing explicit knowledge of matters which in the past have always been the preserve of highly trained intuition.

Of course a clever programming team could bring it about that the machine was as subarticulate about its own processes as we humans. In a cardiological version of the Turing Test, Bratko and his colleagues could enter a suitably crippled KARDIO system. They would substitute a contrived error rate in the system's clinical decisions for KARDIO's near-zero level. In place of KARDIO's impeccably knowledgeable commentaries, they might supply a generator of more patchy and incoherent, and hence more true-to-life, explanations. At the trivial level of arithmetical calculation, Turing anticipated such 'playing dumb' tactics.

> It is claimed that the interrogator could distinguish the machine from the man simply by setting them a number of problems in arithmetic. The machine would be unmasked because of its deadly accuracy. The reply to this is simple. The machine ... would not attempt to give the *right* answers to the arithmetical problems. It would deliberately introduce mistakes in a manner calculated to confuse the interrogator.

But at levels higher than elementary arithmetic, as exemplified by KARDIO's sophisticated blend of logical and associative reasoning, surely one should judge a test as blemished if it obliges candidates to demonstrate intelligence by concealing it!

[*The paper goes on to discuss classical AI and 'right-brain' intelligence, and how conscious recollection appears to be a kind of story-telling undertaken by the left brain using causality as a tool. It then discusses why it may be time for AI to move on from the Turing Test. What follows is the concluding section of the paper. (Ed.)*]

THE IMITATION GAME IN REVIEW

Let us now look back on the relation of conscious thought to Turing's imitation game.

(i) Turing left open whether consciousness is to be assumed if a machine passes the Test. Some contemporary critics only attribute 'intelligence' to conscious processes. An operational interpretation of this requirement is satisfied if the examiner can elicit from the machine via its typewriter no less evidence of consciousness than he or she can elicit via the human's typewriter. We thus substitute the weaker (but practical) criterion of 'operational awareness', and ask the examiner to ensure that this at least is tested.

(ii) In addition to strategies based on an intelligent agent's deep models ('understanding', 'relational knowledge') we find intrinsically different strategies based on heuristic models ('skill', 'know-how'). The outward and visible operations of intelligence depend critically upon integrated support from the latter, typically unconscious, processes. Hence in preparing computing systems for an adversely administered Turing Test, developers cannot dodge attempting to implement these processes. The lack of verbal report associated with them in human experts can be circumvented in some cases by computer induction from human decision examples. In others, however, the need for exotic physical supports for input–output behaviour would present serious engineering difficulties.

(iii) Conversely, where inductive inference allows knowledge engineers to reconstruct and incorporate the needed skill-bearing rules, it becomes possible to include a facility of introspective report which not uncommonly out-articulates the human possessors of these same skills. Such 'super-articulacy' reveals a potential flaw in the Turing Test, which could distinguish the machine from the human player on the paradoxical ground of the machine's *higher* apparent level of intelligent awareness.

(iv) In humans, consciousness supports the functions of communicating with others, and of predicting their responses. As a next step in user-friendly operating systems, graphically simulated 'agents' endowed with pragmatic equivalents of conscious awareness are today under development by manufacturers of personal computers and workstations. At this point AI comes under pressure to consider how emotional components may be incorporated in models of intelligent communication and thought.

(v) Extensions to the Turing Test should additionally address yet more subtle forms of intelligence, such as those involved in collective problem-solving by cooperating agents, and in teacher–pupil relations.

(vi) By the turn of the century, market pressures may cause the designers of workstation systems to take over from philosophers the burden of setting such goals, and of assessing the degree to which this or that system may be said to attain them.

REFERENCES

[1] J. Allen, M. S. Hunnicutt, and D. Klatt, *From Text to Speech: The M1 Talk System* (Cambridge University Press, Cambridge, England, 1987).

[2] J. R. Anderson, *Cognitive Psychology and Its Implications* (Freeman, New York, 3rd ed., 1990).

[3] I. Bratko, I. Mozetic, and N. Lavrac, *Kardio: A Study in Deep and Qualitative Knowledge for Expert Systems* (MIT Press, Cambridge, MA, 1989).

[4] B. E. Carpenter and R. W. Doran, eds., *A. M. Turing's Ace Report and Other Papers* (MIT Press, Cambridge, MA, 1986).

[5] D. C. Dennett, Consciousness, in: R. L. Gregory, ed., *The Oxford Companion to the Mind* (Oxford University Press, Oxford, 1987).

[6] D. C. Dennett, *Consciousness Explained* (Little, Brown & Co., Boston, MA, 1992).

[7] D. C. Dennett and M. Kinsbourne, Time and the observer: the where and when of consciousness in the brain, *Behav. Brain Sci.* (to appear).

[8] J. C. Eccles (1964). Cited in: R. W. Sperry, Consciousness and causality, in: R. L. Gregory, ed., *The Oxford Companion to the Mind* (Oxford University Press, Oxford, 1987).

[9] R. M. French, Subcognition and the limits of the Turing Test, *Mind* 99 (1990) 53–65.

[10] R. L. Gregory, *The Oxford Companion to the Mind* (Oxford University Press, Oxford, 1987).

[11] M. Halle, Knowledge unlearned and untaught: what speakers know about the sounds of their language, in: M. Halle, J. Bresnan and G. A. Miller, eds., *Linguistic Theory and Psychological Reality* (MIT Press, Cambridge, MA, 1978).

[12] E. Hutchins, Understanding Micronesian navigation, in: D. Gentner and A. Stevens, eds., *Mental Models* (Erlbaum, Hillsdale, N J, 1983) 191–225.

[13] W. James, *The Principles of Psychology* (Dover, New York, 1950) (first published 1890).

[14] P. N. Johnson-Laird, *The Computer and the Mind* (Harvard University Press, Cambridge, MA, 1988).

[15] D. Michie, Editorial introduction to A. M. Turing's chapter 'Intelligent machinery' in: B. Meltzer and D. Michie, eds., *Machine Intelligence* 5 (Edinburgh University Press, Edinburgh, Scotland, 1969).

[16] D. Michie, The superarticulacy phenomenon in the context of software manufacture, *Proc. Roy. Soc. Lond. A* 405 (1986) 185–212; also in: D. Partridge and Y. Wilks, eds., *The Foundations of Artificial Intelligence* (Cambridge University Press, Cambridge, England, 1990) 411–39.

[17] D. Michie, The Fifth Generation's unbridged gap, in: R. Herken, ed., *The Universal Turing Machine* (Oxford University Press, Oxford, 1988).

[18] D. Michie, Methodologies from machine learning in data analysis and software, *Computer J.* 34 (6) (1991) 559–65.

[19] R. E. Ornstein, *The Psychology of Consciousness* (Harcourt, Brace and Jovanovich, 1977) 96; (Freeman, New York, 1st ed., 1972).

[20] H. M. Parsons, Turing on the Turing Test, in: W. Karwowski and M. Rahimi, eds., *Ergonomics of Hybrid Automated Systems I1 (Elsevier* Science Publishers, Amsterdam, 1990).

[21] K. R. Popper and J. C. Eccles, *The Self and Its Brain* (Routledge and Kegan Paul, London, 1977).

[22] M. I. Posner, *Cognition: An Introduction* (Scott, Foresman, Glenview, IL, 1973).

[23] B. Russell, On the notion of cause, *Proc. Aristotelian Soc.* 13 (1913) 1–26.

[24] J. R. Searle, Is the brain's mind a computer program'? *Sci. Am.* 262 (1991l) 2–25.

[25] C. Trevarthen, The tasks of consciousness: how could the brain do them? *Brain and Mind,* Ciba Foundation Series 69 (New Series) (Excerpta Medical/Elsevier North-Holland, Amsterdam, 1979).

[26] C. Trevarthen, Split-brain and the mind, in: R. L, Gregory, ed., *The Oxford Companion to the Mind* (Oxford University Press, Oxford, 1987).

[27] A. M. Turing, Computing machinery and intelligence, *Mind* 59 (1950) 433–60.

[28] A. N. Whitehead, *An Introduction to Mathematics* (1911).

'Strong AI': An Adolescent Disorder (1995)

Philosophers have distinguished two attitudes to the mechanization of thought. 'Strong AI' says that given a sufficiency of well-chosen axioms and deduction procedures we have all we need to program computers to out-think humans. 'Weak AI' says that humans don't think in logical deductions anyway. So why not instead devote ourselves to (1) neural nets, or (2) ultra-parallelism, or (3) other ways of dispensing with symbolic domain-models?

'Weak AI' thus has diverse strands, united in a common objection to 'strong AI', and articulated in popular writings, see for example Hubert Dreyfus (1979), John Searle (1990), and Roger Penrose (1989). How should one assess their objection?

I TURING'S TEST AND POSTULATES

If asked to investigate the alleged insolvency of the Fireproof Coal Corporation, a careful auditor first looks for evidence that such a corporation actually exists. Not being personally acquainted with adherents of the described 'strong AI' school among professional colleagues, I looked for 'strong AI' in the literature. I concluded that the description sufficiently matched an identifiable AI sub-community that flourished in the USA during the subject's adolescence (roughly 1965–85) and probably retains professional adherents there today. Certainly the mind-set lives on in textbooks used for teaching. Because it steps backwards from Turing's original prescriptions, I use the label T-minus (for 'Turing-minus') for this sub-school of symbolic AI. Misconceptions about T-minus may explain the philosophical attacks on 'strong AI'. A particularly salient misconception, fostered in some textbooks, is that T-minus traces intellectual paternity to Alan Turing's (1950) paper in which he proposed a test to settle whether a given machine could think. The machine must fool a remote interrogator into mistaking it for a human. In reality T-minus, while retaining the test itself, implicitly rejects the postulate that accompanied it, namely that the role of machine learning is central, and necessary for attainment of the desired capability.

1.1 Intelligence is in the discourse, not the action

The capabilities that we call 'intelligence' and 'thought' are manifested not so much in problem-solving as in discourse. In the context of Turing's imitation game, accurate problem-solving was secondary. 'It is claimed,' he writes, 'that the interrogator could distinguish the machine from the man simply by setting them a number of problems in arithmetic. The machine would be unmasked because of its deadly accuracy. The reply to this is simple. The machine (programmed for playing the game) would not attempt to give the right answers to the arithmetical problems. It would deliberately introduce mistakes in a manner calculated to confuse the interrogator.'

Of course there may be machine intelligence in deciphering the arithmetical question, in invoking a suitable low-level solving routine, and in concocting sufficient hesitancy or error to make the response look human-like. But Turing does not present the arithmetical calculation itself as a manifestation of intelligence and thus avoids identifying intelligence with competence. The question of whether intelligence would be of any use in a creature lacking a competent problem-solving system is a separate issue. But the exercise of even very great competence in an intellectual domain is not in itself proof of intelligence. Numerous computer triumphs of today, not restricted to arithmetic, remind us of this.

In confining 'intelligence' to the discourse-testable functions of understanding and after-the-event reporting, Turing made a wise move. Those who failed to follow his example look foolish every time that an intelligent Grandmaster is defeated by a super-competent chess machine. Today's game-playing machines are profoundly deficient in understanding even of the games that they win, as witnessed by their inability to annotate them. Writing such commentaries (as chess masters commonly do) would require, precisely, intelligence, in the sense in which Turing understood the term.

1.2 Insufficiency of hand-crafting methods

Calculation shows hand-crafting to be infeasible for loading into the system the huge quantities of organized knowledge required for human-level intelligence. To estimate a lower bound, Turing made the optimistic assumption that a thousand megabits of program space might be sufficient for satisfactory playing of the imitation game, at least in the restricted form of play against a blind person, thus excluding from the accountancy the resource-hungry processes of visual perception. He continued: 'At my present rate of working I produce about a thousand digits of program a day, so that about sixty workers working steadily through the fifty years might accomplish the job, if nothing went into the waste-paper basket. Some more expeditious method seems desirable.'

The fantasy dubbed 'Strong AI' by its critics is blind (at least in American textbook expositions) not only to these early calculations of Turing's but also to the arithmetic of modern commercial programming. According to the most recent estimate known to me, a typical rate for a large system is 10 lines of installed code per programmer per day.

1.3 Need for mechanized learning and teachability

Having rejected direct programming of knowledge, and unaided deduction from programmed axioms, Turing turned to the bulk acquisition of knowledge through mechanized learning. He introduced the idea as follows.

In the process of trying to imitate an adult human mind we are bound to think a good deal about the process which has brought it to the state that it is in. We may notice three components,

1. The initial state of the mind, say at birth,
2. The education to which it has been subjected,
3. Other experience, not to be described as education, to which it has been subjected.

Instead of trying to produce a program to simulate the adult mind, why not rather try to produce one which simulates the child's? If this were then subjected to an appropriate course of education one would obtain the adult brain.

2 DEFINITION AND DIFFICULTIES OF T-MINUS

T-minus essentially re-instates a proposal advanced by Leibniz in the seventeenth century, namely that we could obtain definitive knowledge about the world by the sole means of algebraic and deductive manipulations of symbols applied to symbolically coded facts. Two only of Turing's many extensions to Leibniz's programme were retained, namely use of high-speed computing to perform the manipulations, and the test for detecting intelligent thought in the resulting system. Hence we could speak of 'Leibniz plus' but have preferred 'Turing minus', meaning Turing minus the central role of machine learning. We must now consider the persistence into the post-Turing era of this retrogressive position.

The following definition of AI is from an authoritative exponent.

> Artificial Intelligence is the enterprise of constructing a Physical Symbol System that can reliably pass the Turing Test. (Ginsberg, 1993, ch. 1)

Ginsberg's use here of 'Physical Symbol System' follows Newell and Simon (1976), and is broad enough to cover any physical embodiment of a Universal Turing Machine. The definition is oriented towards engineering rather than philosophical goals, and Ginsberg emphasizes that 'AI is fundamentally an engineering discipline, since our fundamental goal is that of building something.' 'Moreover Ginsberg, like the Physical Symbol System Hypothesis' authors, speaks solely of the machine's reasoning from facts and laws explicitly communicated to it. Catastrophically, he excludes the nine-tenths that in humans lies submerged below consciousness yet forms an essential core for run-time problem-solving (see for example Michie1993a, 1993b, 1994, 1995a, 1995b for reviews). It is interesting to contrast this hard-line aversion to the findings of psychology and brain science with the explicit distinction made in McCarthy's (1959) Advice Taker paper: 'One might conjecture that division in man between conscious and unconscious thought occurs at the boundary between stimulus–response heuristics which do not have to be reasoned about but only obeyed, and the others which have to serve as premises in deduction.'

At the time when McCarthy wrote those words, no means were known for acquiring the submerged tacit procedures from human brains for machine use (but see Shapiro (1987) for a later exercise in doing just this; see also Urbancic and Bratko (1994) for a review of 'behavioural cloning' of control skills). But he was sufficiently aware of the massive dependency of high-level cognition on low-level tacit procedures that he saw their incorporation in the infrastructure of intelligent systems as a necessity. In this respect among others, McCarthy had moved forward from Turing, and can justly be seen as the intellectual forerunner of the 'Turing-plus', or T-plus, doctrine that we shall later consider. One should, however, mention Turing's 1947 report as showing that he was not unaware of these tacit procedures and of their importance: 'By long experience we can pick up and apply the most complicated rules without being able to enunciate them at all.'

Before Ginsberg's book was written, T-minus was already being subjected to the standard validity test faced by any engineering doctrine: can you build it, and will it then stand? Indeed T-minus has so far been the only one of symbolic AI's construction doctrines to inspire serious attempts at all-round machine knowledgeability and intelligence. Readers of Ginsberg's textbook are not, however, informed of these attempts nor of their disappointing outcomes. It is as though a text on bridge-building not only ignored established knowledge of wind-induced oscillations in exposed structures but omitted mention of the disasters that have resulted. Ferguson's (1993) *Engineering and the Mind's Eye* cites the British construction engineer Sir Alfred Pugsley on the subject of the collapse of the Tacoma Narrows suspension bridge in 1940. The major lesson was 'the unwisdom of allowing a particular profession to become too inward looking and so screened from relevant knowledge growing up in other fields around it.' Had the designers of the Tacoma Narrows Bridge known more of aerodynamics, Pugsley concluded, the collapse might have been averted.

With the substitution of neuroscience for aerodynamics, relevant knowledge from which T-minus's disciples show signs of being screened includes evidence from cognitive and brain studies of solving problems, as opposed to justifying, documenting, and explaining the solutions. The solving part is not generally performed symbolically, but through spatio-visual and above all unconscious intuitive processes (McCarthy's 'stimulus–response heuristics'). Associated brain centres are anatomically remote from the cortical areas specialized for logical reasoning and language (see for example Squire, 1987). As to visuo-spatial thinking in engineering problem-solving, Ferguson (1993) supplies much relevant material. Examples abound in other works, many cited by Ferguson, on visual and intuitive components of problem-solving.

In the light of all this, rejection by T-minus of Turing's machine learning prescription seems blind indeed. Not only must the hand-crafting task, even on optimistic assumptions, take too long to accomplish. Worse, perhaps much of it is not susceptible to hand-crafting at all. This second possibility follows from the constant finding referred to earlier that expert problem-solving depends critically on sub-cognitive skills inaccessible to conscious introspection. Yet unless algorithmic work-arounds can be devised in every case, introspection is left as the only source on which hand-crafting of mental skills can draw. Later we will consider the inductivist sub-school of symbolic AI, fast becoming the leading edge of T-plus, which accepts the importance of sub-articulate mental processes and dispenses almost entirely with introspective sources for accessing them. Instead, T-plus builds executable models of subarticulate skills by another route, that is by inductive learning from imitation of skilled behaviour (see Urbancic and Bratko, 1994, for the interesting case of control skills).

3   T-MINUS UNDER TEST

So how has it gone with 'the enterprise of constructing a Physical Symbol System that can reliably pass the Turing Test'? Two substantial T-minus projects were launched within a few years of each other. Japan's Fifth Generation (5G) project (conducted between 1979 and 1981) was aimed at the declared goal of human-level intelligence by the end of the 1980s. The early history and divergent later course has been reviewed by Michie (1988). In 1984 a group led by

Lenat at the Microelectronics and Computer Technology Corporation in Texas, USA, launched a ten-year project known as CYC. Its aim was to build a huge interactive knowledge base spanning most of what humans call common sense, that was eventually to 'grow by assimilating textbooks, literature, newspapers, etc.' Numerous large databases would also be accessible to the system. During the closing years, 'a cadre of teachers' would replace hand-crafting.

More than ten years on, we may note that both projects missed their stated marks. Before its collapse, the Tacoma Narrows suspension bridge at least looked like a bridge and behaved as a bridge. As elsewhere analysed (Michie, 1994; Gams, 1995) neither of the above-mentioned T-minus projects ever attained even the semblance of human-level knowledge and intelligence. What faults, then, underlay these failures?

Neglect of Turing's child-machine postulate. 5G initially relied on hand-crafting. Realization then took hold in the project's leadership that inductive knowledge acquisition should be recognized as the central focus for the project. But at that stage the initial goals had been diffused by complexities of sponsorship from a diversity of private companies in addition to the MITI governmental agency. By the time that a productive impetus had developed for inductive logic programming and other learning methods, 5G had diverged from its initial performance specifications. The main effort became concentrated into what proved to be a successful programme of transfer into industry of existing techniques.

CYC, on the other hand, acknowledged the necessary role of inductive learning from the start, but hung back from its systematic development. It is not clear from Lenat and Guha's (1989) interim report how this came about.

Neglect of the multiplicity of 'understanding'. The word 'intelligence' is derived from the Latin for 'understanding'. There is, moreover, agreement that to merit description as intelligent, a system's responses must, at the least, give the appearance of understanding the domain of discourse, that is to say, of utilizing a stored domain model. Some leading AI workers see the storage and use of only one kind of model of a domain as not going far enough. Minsky (1994) writes: 'If you understand something in only one way, then you really do not understand it at all. The secret of what anything means to us depends on how we have connected it to all the other things we know; that is why, when someone learns "by rote", we say that they do not really understand.'

There is a duality in human concepts. They are undeniably and commonly used, just as Minsky proposes, to represent one and the same notion in different ways, for example in symbol strings and in pictures, with frequent and fluent inter-conversions between representations. Thus, there are two ways of seeing that an equilateral triangle has equal base angles. One is by Euclidean proof. The other is by mentally rotating it round the perpendicular and observing that the flipped image fits the unflipped one.

Neglect of science. Ginsberg remarks that all good engineering rests on a scientific foundation, and contrasts the views of extremist technologists with those of mathematical philosophers working on AI's scientific foundations. There are, it seems, AI technologists who believe 'that the scientific foundation of AI has already been laid, and that the work that remains is engineering in nature.' Against this 'are people who believe that AI has many fundamental scientific problems still to be solved; that the goal of constructing an intelligent artifact today is not dissimilar to the goal of building a nuclear reactor in 1920 ...'

John McCarthy's school of research inaugurated by his 1959 'Programs with Common Sense' represents this second position. McCarthy has in particular pointed to a wealth of concepts that are fundamental to everyday discourse, concerned with temporal sequence, causality, intention, capability, context-dependence and other common usages. The latter may include such phenomena as the deployment by two or more interacting agents of models of each other. Formalizing these everyday notions has so far largely resisted the efforts of AI logicians. A good interim overview has been made available by Ginsberg (1987).

Returning to the imitation game, we may reasonably enquire as follows. AI still lacks machine executable languages in which elementary day-to-day transactions and inferences of human life may be expressed. So long as the lack persists, how can any project of 5G or CYC type hope to endow an automated conversationalist with the skill of describing such transactions?

Neglect of user requirements. From the time of Archimedes through Leonardo's to the present day, engineering design has taken the client's statement of requirement as starting point. Turing's proposal of a machine for playing the imitation game departs from this. What customers were there for a disembodied general-purpose artificial intelligence? There was, and is, no shortage of general-purpose natural intelligences. They can be found in abundance on any street corner. Two circumstances need to be kept in mind.

(1) Turing's paper was published in a journal devoted to the philosophy of mind. He was as much concerned to drive home a philosophical point as to launch a potential industry. This I believe explains the Turing Test's curiously free-floating character. But the closing part of his paper, which few commentators appear to read, discusses implementation, including the question of where to start. Turing suggests more circumscribed domains such as game-playing and robotics, for both of which healthy commercial markets have since appeared.

(2) In so far as the paper addresses non-philosophical issues they are concerned with engineering science rather than technology. Turing's vision was of intellectual tasks designed to serve as laboratory tests linking the work of theoreticians and experimentalists. Work of this kind precedes market considerations, just as the years of experimentation by the Wright brothers preceded the era of military and commercial aircraft design. Turing's thinking is conveyed in a closing passage:

'We may hope that machines will eventually compete with men in all purely intellectual fields. But which are the best ones to start with? Even this is a difficult decision. Many people think that a very abstract activity, like the playing of chess, would be best. It can also be maintained that it is best to provide the machine with the best sense organs that money can buy, and then teach it to understand and speak English. This process could follow the normal teaching of a child. Things would be pointed out and named, etc. Again I do not know what the right answer is, but I think both approaches should be tried.'

5G and CYC began in the 1980s, remote in time from Turing's teachable blank slate. With the rise of expert systems, marketable innovation at the technology end of the AI spectrum was already an established fact, and a wide range of knowledge-based and rule-learning software techniques and tools were available. Market-oriented specializations of Turing's general-purpose question-answerer would not have been discouraged by CYC's industrial sponsors. It is as though the Wright brothers had not been content with restricted objectives, and had insisted that their machine must be built to do everything that a bird can do, and in addition that it would do this without using wings (no use was made of industrial-strength learning tools).

Neglect not of one but of several factors lay at the root of of the failures of 5G and CYC (see also Gams, 1995, for analysis). The aim of the T-plus school of symbolic AI is to continue to develop these neglected factors.

4 BEYOND THE TURING TEST

T-minus was evidently for a time sufficiently entrenched to be the source of design ideas for two major software engineering projects. Yet in spite of disappointing results from these attempted applications, T-minus still survives as a doctrine for instructing a new generation of AI engineers. This is quite evident from Ginsberg's book. But the action has already moved elsewhere.

An inductive sector of symbolic AI is becoming the mainstream approach to large-scale knowledge acquisition and refinement. I refer to Machine Learning (ML), and in particular to recent extensions via Prolog and other logic programming formalisms. This trend is not something newly sprung to prominence in AI thinking. On the contrary, it is intrinsic in the ideas of the founders. We have already considered Turing's own position. It was endorsed and extended by symbolic AI's grand architect John McCarthy. In his 1959 'Programs with Common Sense' he writes: 'Our ultimate objective is to make programs that learn from experience as effectively as humans do.' He goes on to warn that 'in order for a program to be capable of learning something it must first be capable of being told it.'

McCarthy is here speaking not of blind stimulus–response skills, some of which do not need explicit representation languages to be machine-learnable (e.g. by neural nets). He has in mind concept learning. Obviously until a hypothesis language is available in which a given concept is expressible, that concept cannot be explicitly learned. For this reason the rise of logic languages such as Prolog, and of the craft of inductive logic programming (ILP) in particular, has played an important role by extending the expressivity of ML's hypothesis languages (Muggleton, 1991). Radical progress along the McCarthy–Muggleton line is now necessary before a successful CYC-type project can be envisaged.

Along with the critical issue of hypothesis languages, extensions of ILP are required. These include facilities for hierarchical structuring of domains into contexts, for incorporating object-oriented features, for interfacing with constraint satisfaction programming, for manufacture of new attributes by constructive induction, and for the seamless incorporation of capabilities of uncertain inference. In a recent review of some of ML's problems and current progress (Michie, 1995b), I have stressed a further gap that still separates achievement from potential. Inductive Logic Programming packages, even after thousands of hours of significant theory discovery in a given domain, end up no better at solving the next problem than at the start. Consider, for example, a human biomolecular chemist's inductive inferences concerning likely activities of newly synthesized drugs, as studied using ILP by Sternberg and colleagues (1994). These come faster as his or her experience grows of a given domain of compounds. So here is a kind of 'meta-learning', crucial in human intelligence. Active brains somehow incrementally assimilate statistico-logical properties of learning environments into background knowledge in ways that AI has not yet attempted to emulate.

5 CONCLUDING REMARKS

The time has come to venture beyond the horizons of the Turing Test. The IT market of today is looking to computers for more than intelligent chat. The need is for specialized intelligences that can deploy and articulate mastery of knowledge intensive domains in science, engineering, medicine, pharmaceuticals, and finance. Advances in symbolic learning are gradually establishing a sufficient technical foundation for Turing's child-machine project. The year 2000 may see, not the first-base completion he had hoped for, but a belated start along the originally indicated line.

Meanwhile the 'Strong AI' versus 'Weak AI' debate, refuelled by Roger Penrose's 6-year-old book *The Emperor's New Mind*, is again changing its character. Penrose (1994) has replaced the Strong/Weak dichotomy by a four-level gradation of attitudes. In his new book *Shadows of the Mind* these are distinguished by the symbols A, B, C, and D (set in curly font). With the 'Strong' and 'Weak' dichotomy superseded, both sides of this debate may find that their artillery is being wasted on positions that are not so much untenable as abandoned. A middle-ground position, integrating (as I believe) useful features of the two extremes, can be found in a paper of mine on 'Knowledge, Learning and Machine Intelligence' (Michie, 1993a). The salient features of this 'integrative school' are summarized in the last of the three items below.

Symbolic school. All thought can be modelled as deductive reasoning from logical descriptions of the world, and machine-processed in this form.

Neural school. Thought and knowledge are mainly intuitive, non-introspectable, non-logical, associative, approximate, stochastic A, and 'fuzzy'. Fidelity to neurobiological fact demands that we build similar properties into AI software.

Integrative school. Thought requires cooperation between conscious reasoning, whether symbolic or visuo-spatial, and lower-level tacit operations. Different software representations are appropriate to different engineering requirements. The latter ordinarily cover not only run-time performance, but also self-documentation. Performance at high levels of domain complexity demands learning. Self-documentation of acquired knowledge demands that learning be symbolic.

ACKNOWLEDGEMENT

This paper was completed while the author was in receipt of a Visiting Fellowship from the Engineering and Physical Sciences Research Council, UK (contract no. GR/.156806), at the Oxford University Computing Laboratory.

REFERENCES

[1] Dreyfus, H. L. (1979). *What Computers Can't Do: The Limits of Artificial Intelligence*, New York: Harper & Row.

[2] Ferguson, E. S. (1993). *Engineering and the Mind's Eye*, Cambridge, MA: MIT Press.

[3] Gams, M. (1995). Strong vs. weak AI. *Informatica*, this issue.

[4] Ginsberg, M. L. (ed., 1987). *Readings in Nonmonotonic Reasoning*, Los Altos, CA: Morgan Kaufmann.

[5] Ginsberg, M.L. (1993). *Essentials of Artificial Intelligence*, San Francisco, CA: Morgan Kaufmann.

[6] Lenat, D. B. and Guha, R. V. (1989). *Building Large Knowledge-Based Systems*, Reading, MA: Addison-Wesley.

[7] McCarthy, J. (1959). Programs with common sense. In *Mechanization of Thought Processes*, 1, 77–84, London: Her Majesty's Stationery Office. Reprinted with additional material in *Semantic Information Processing* (ed. M. Minsky), Cambridge, MA and London, UK: MIT Press, 1963.

[8] Michie, D. (1988). The Fifth Generation's unbridged gap. In *A Half-Century of the Universal Turing Machine* (ed. R. Herken), Oxford: Oxford University Press.

[9] Michie, D. (1993a). Knowledge, learning and machine intelligence. Chapter 1 of *Intelligent Systems* (ed. L. Sterling), New York: Plenum Press, pp. 1–19.

[10] Michie, D. (1993b). Turing's test and conscious thought. *Artificial Intelligence*, 60, 1–22.

[11] Michie, D. (1994). Consciousness as an engineering issue, Part 1. *J. Consciousness Studies*, 1 (2), 182–95.

[12] Michie, D. (1995a). Consciousness as an engineering issue, Part 2. *J. Consciousness Studies*, 2 (1), 52–66.

[13] Michie, D. (1995b). Problem decomposition and the learning of skills. In *Machine Learning: ECML-95*, ed. N. Lavrac and S. Wrobel, Lecture Notes in Artificial Intelligence 914, Berlin, Heidelberg, New York: Springer Verlag, pp. 17–31.

[14] Minsky, M. (1994). Will robots inherit the earth? *Scientific American*, 271 (4), 86–91.

[15] Muggleton, S. H. (1991). Inductive logic programming. *New Generation Computing*, 8, 295–318.

[16] Newell, A. and Simon, H. A. (1976). Computer science as empirical enquiry. *Communications of the ACM*, 19, 35–66.

[17] Penrose, R. (1989). *The Emperor's New Mind*, Oxford: Oxford University Press.

[18] Penrose, R. (1994). *Shadows of the Mind*, Oxford: Oxford University Press.

[19] Searle, J. R. (1990). Is the brain's mind a computer program? *Scientific American*, 262, 20–5.

[20] Shapiro, A. (1987). *Structured Induction in Expert Systems*, Wokingham, UK; Reading; Menlo Park and NewYork, USA: Addison Wesley.

[21] Squire, L. R. (1987). *Memory and Brain*, Oxford, Oxford University Press.

[22] Sternberg, M. J. E., King, R. D., Lewis, R. A., and Muggleton, S. (1994). Application of machine learning to structural molecular biology. *Phil. Trans R. Soc. Lond. B*, 344, 365–71.

[23] Turing, A. M. (1947). Intelligent machinery. Report submitted in 1948 to the National Physical Laboratory, UK. Published in *Machine Intelligence* 5 (ed. B. Meltzer and D. Michie), Edinburgh University Press, 1969.

[24] Turing, A. M. (1950). Computing machinery and intelligence. *Mind*, 59, 433–60.

[25] Urbancic, T. and Bratko, I. (1994). Reconstructing human skill with machine learning, In *Proc. Europ. Conf. on AI (ECAI-94)*, Amsterdam.

Return of the Imitation Game (2001)

INTRODUCTION

Recently there has been an unexpected rebirth of Turing's imitation game as a commercial technology. Programs are surfacing that can bluff their way through interactive chat sessions to increasingly useful degrees. In the United States of America the first patent was granted in the summer of 2001 to the company Native Minds, formerly known as Neuromedia. One of its two founders, Scott Benson, co-authored a paper by Nils Nilsson in Volume 14 of this *Machine Intelligence* series. As an Appendix a press release is reproduced* which gives a rather vivid sketch of the nature of the new commercial art. To the applications described there, the following may be added.

1. Question-answering guides at trade shows, conferences, exhibitions, museums, theme parks, palaces, archaelogical sites, festivals, and the like.
2. Web-based wizards for e-commerce that build incrementally assembled profiles of the individual tastes and foibles of each individual customer.
3. Alternatives to questionnaires for job-seekers, hospital patients, applicants for permits and memberships, targets of market research, and human subjects of psychological experiments.
4. Tutors in English as a second language. There is an acknowledged need to enable learners to practise conversational skills in augmentation of existing Computer-Aided Language Learning programs.

---

* The appendix is not included here.

An example developed by Claude Sammut and myself of the first-listed category is in daily operation as an interactive exhibit in the 'Cyberworld' section of the Powerhouse Museum, Sydney, Australia.

WEAK FORM OF THE 'IMITATION GAME'

The philosopher of mind Daniel Dennett (2001) regards Turing's original 'imitation game' as more of a conversation-stopper for philosophers than anything else. In this I am entirely with him.

The *weak form* presented in the 1950 paper is generally known as the Turing Test. It allows a wide latitude of failure on the machine's part to fool the examiners. To pass, the candidate need only cause them to make the wrong identification, as between human and machine, in a mere 30 per cent of all conversations. Only five minutes are allowed for the entire man–machine conversation. Turing's original specification had a human interrogator communicating by remote typewriter link with two respondents, one a human and one a machine.

> I believe that in about fifty years' time it will be possible to programme computers, with a storage capacity of about 10^9, to make them play the imitation game so well that an average interrogator will not have more than 70 per cent chance of making the right identification [as between human and machine] after five minutes of questioning.

Dennett's view is re-inforced by an account I had from Turing's friend, the logician Robin Gandy. The two extracted much mischievous enjoyment from Turing's reading aloud the various arguments and refutations as he went along with his draft.

TURING WOULD HAVE FAILED THE TURING TEST

Note that the Test as formulated addresses the *humanness* of the respondent's thinking rather than its *level*. Had Turing covertly substituted himself for the machine in such a test, examiners would undoubtedly have picked him out as being a machine. A distinguishing personal oddity of Turing's was his exclusive absorption in the literal intellectual content of spoken discourse. His disinclination, or inability, to respond to anything in the least 'chatty' would leave an honest examiner with little alternative but to conclude: 'this one cannot possibly be the human; hence the other candidate must be. So *this* one must be the machine!'

Experimental findings are presented to the effect that chat-free conversation is not only generally perceived as less than human, but also as boring. The concluding reference to 'banter' in Appendix 1 suggests that Native Minds have come to a similar conclusion. It seems that for purposes of discourse we must refine the aim of automated 'human-level intelligence' by requiring in addition that the user perceive the machine's intelligence as being of human type. A client bored is a client lost.

WEAK FORM OF THE GAME OBSOLETED

Turing himself believed that beyond the relatively undemanding scenario of his Test, the capacity for deep and sustained thought would ultimately be engineered. But this was not the issue which his 1950 imitation game sought to settle. Rather, the quoted passage considers the time-scale required to decide in a positive sense the lesser and *purely philosophical* question: what circumstances would oblige one to concede a machine's claim to think at all?

When terms are left undefined, meanings become vulnerable to subtle change over time. Before his projected 50 years were up, words like 'think' and 'intelligent' were already freely applied to an ever-widening range of computational appliances, even though none came anywhere near to success at even weak forms of the imitation game.

In the 1950 *Mind* paper (p.14) Turing remarked:

> I believe that at the end of the century the use of words and general educated opinion will have altered so much that one will be able to speak of machines thinking without expecting to be contradicted.

Early in the match in which Gary Kasparov as the reigning World Chess Champion was defeated by Deep Blue, he became so convinced of his opponent's chess intelligence that he levelled a strange charge against the Deep Blue team. Somehow they must have made this precious human quality accessible to their machine in some manner that could be construed as violating its 'free-standing' status.

In today's statements of engineering requirements and in diagnostics we encounter the language not only of thought but also of intention, and even of conscious awareness. The following exchange is abridged from the diagnostics section of a popular British computing magazine, *What Palmtop and Handheld PC*, June 2000. I have underlined certain words, placing them within square brackets to draw attention to their anthropomorphic connotations of *purpose, awareness,* and *perception.*

> AILMENT: I recently purchased a Palm V and a Palm portable keyboard. But whenever I plug the Palm into the keyboard it [attempts] to HotSync via the direct serial connection. If I cancel the attempted HotSync and go into the Memo Pad and try to type, every time I hit a key it [tries] to HotSync. What am I doing wrong?
> TREATMENT: The most logical solution is that your Palm V is [not aware that] the keyboard is present. You will need to install or reinstall the drivers that came supplied with the keyboard and to make sure that it is enabled. This will stop your Palm V [attempting] to HotSync with the keyboard and to [recognize] it as a device in its own right.

Modern software (as also medical) practice is content to use the term 'aware' for any system that responds in certain ways to test inputs.

TOWARDS THE STRONG FORM: THE TURING–NEWMAN TEST

In the largely unknown closing section of the 1950 *Mind* paper, entitled 'Learning Machines', Turing turns to issues more fundamental than intuitional semantics and proposes his 'child machine' concept:

> We may hope that machines will eventually compete with men in all purely intellectual fields. But which are the best ones to start with?...It can also be maintained that it is best to provide the machine with the best sense organs that money can buy, and then teach it to understand and speak English. This process could follow the normal teaching of a child. Things could be pointed out and named, etc....

What time-scale did he have in mind for this 'child-machine project'? Certainly not the 50-year estimate for his game for disconcerting philosophers. He and Max Newman consider the question in a 1952 radio debate (Copeland, 1999):

> *Newman*: I should like to be there when your match between a man and a machine takes place, and perhaps to try my hand at making up some of the questions. But that will be a long time from now, if the machine is to stand any chance with no questions barred?
> *Turing*: Oh yes, at least 100 years, I should say.

So we are now half-way along this 100-year track. How do we stand today? The child-machine prescription segments the task as follows:

Step 1. ACCUMULATE a diversity of generic knowledge-acquisition tools.
Step 2. INTEGRATE these to constitute a 'person' with sufficient language-understanding to be educable, both by example and by precept.
Step 3. EDUCATE the said 'person' incrementally over a broad range of topics.

Step 1 does not look in too bad shape. An impressive stockpile of every kind of reasoning and learning tool has been amassed. In narrowly specific fields, the child-machine trick of 'teaching by showing' has even been used for machine acquisition of complex concepts. Chess end-game theory (see Michie 1986, 1995) has been developed far beyond pre-existing limits of human understanding. More recently, challenging areas of molecular chemistry have been tackled by the method of Inductive Logic Programming (e.g. Muggleton, Bryant, and Srinivasan, 2000). Again, machine learners here elaborated their insights beyond those of expert 'tutors'. Above-human intelligence can in these cases be claimed, not only in respect of performance but also in respect of articulacy (see Michie, 1986).

A feeling, however, lingers that something crucial is still lacking. It is partially expressed in the current *AI Magazine* by John Laird and Michael van Lent (2001):

> Over the last 30 years, research in AI has fragmented into more and more specialized fields, working on more and more specialized problems, using more and more specialized algorithms.

These authors continue with a telling point. The long string of successes, they suggest, 'have made it easy for us to ignore our failure to make significant progress in building human-level AI systems'. They go on to propose computer games as a forcing framework, with emphasis on 'research on the AI characters that are part of the game'.

To complete their half truth would entail reference to real and continuing progress in developing *generic* algorithms for solving *generic* problems, as in deductive and inductive reasoning; rote learning; parameter and concept learning; relational and object-oriented data management; associative and semantic retrieval; abstract treatment of statistical, logical, and grammatical description and of associated complexity issues, and much else. None the less, the thought persists that something is missing. After all we are now in 2001. Where is HAL? Where is even proto-HAL? Worse than that: if we had the HAL of Stanley Kubrick's movie *2001, a Space Odyssey* would we have the goal described by Turing, a machine able to 'compete with men in all purely intellectual fields'?

Seemingly so. But is that the goal we wanted? Should the goal not rather have been to '*cooperate* with men (and women) in all purely intellectual fields'? Impressive as was the flawless logic of HAL's style of reasoning in the movie, the thought of having to cooperate, let alone bargain, let alone relax with so awesomely motivated a creature must give one pause. The picture has been filled in by John McCarthy's devastating satirical piece, 'The Robot and the Baby', available through http://www.formal.stanford.edu/jmc/robotandbaby.html.

The father of the logicist school of AI here extrapolates to a future dysfunctional society some imagined consequences of pan-logicism. By this term I mean the use of predicate logic to model intelligent thought unsupported by those other mechanisms and modalities of learning and reactive choice which

McCarthy took the trouble to list in his 1959 classic 'Programs with Common Sense' (see also Michie, 1994, 1995).

The hero of McCarthy's new and savage tale is a robot that applies mindless inferences from an impeccable axiomatization of situations, actions, and causal laws to an interactive world of people, institutions, and feelings. The latter, however, are awash with media frenzy, cultism, addiction, greed, and populism. Outcomes are at best moderate. How should an artificial intelligence be designed to fare better?

Implicitly at least, step 2 above says it all. Required: a way to integrate the accumulated tools and techniques so as to constitute a *virtual person*, with which (with whom) a user can comfortably interact, 'a "person" with sufficient language-understanding to be educable, both by example and by precept'.

Inescapable logic then places on the shoulders of AI a new responsibility, unexpected and possibly unwelcome: we have to study the anatomy and dynamics of the human activity known as chat. Otherwise attempts to simulate the seriously information-bearing components will fail to satisfy users whose needs extend beyond information exchange to what is known as *rapport*.

RAPPORT MAINTENANCE

To see how to do step 2 (integration into a user-perceived 'person') is not straightforward. Moreover, what we expect in a flesh-and-blood conversational agent comes more readily from the toolkit of novelists than of computer professionals.

1. Real chat utterances are mostly unparseable. They are concerned with associative exchange of mental images. They respond to contextual relevance rather than to logical or linguistic links.

It is of interest that congenital absence of the capacity to handle grammar, known in neuropsychology as 'agrammatism', does not prevent the sufferer from passing in ordinary society. Cases are ordinarily diagnosed from hospital tests administered to patients admitted for other reasons.

2. A human agent has a place of birth, age, sex, nationality, job, hobbies, family, friends, partners; plus a personal autobiographical history, recollected as emotionally charged episodes; plus a complex of likes, dislikes, pet theories and attitudes, stock arguments, jokes and funny stories, interlaced with prejudices, superstitions, hopes, fears, ambitions, etc.

Disruption of this cohesive unity of personal style is an early sign of 'Pick's disease', recently linked by Bruce Miller and co-workers with malfunction of an area of the right front-temporal cortex. Reporting to a meeting in early summer 2001 of the American Academy of Neurology meeting in Philadelphia, Miller presented results on 72 patients. One of them, a 63-year-old woman, was described as a well-dressed life-long conservative. She became an animal-rights activist who hated conservatives, dressed in T-shirts and baggy pants and liked to say 'Republicans should be taken off the Earth!'

3. On meeting again with the same conversational partner, a human agent recalls the gist of what has been divulged by both sides on past occasions. Failure of this function in humans is commonly associated with damage involving the left hippocampal cortical area.
4. Crucially for implementers, a human agent typically has fact-providing or fact-eliciting *goals* beyond mere chat, yet remains ever-ready to default to chat-mode to sustain rapport. Reverting to the child-machine concept, how much of value and use could a school teacher impart to a child with whom rapport was impossible? In clinical practice the condition is found in 'autism'. Children with this disorder are almost unteachable.

Background findings in cognitive neuroscience generally are surveyed in Ramachandran and Blakeslee's (1998) highly readable paperback.

RECENT EXPERIMENTATION

Over the last two years Claude Sammut and I have begun experimentally to develop and test activation networks of pattern-fired rules, hierarchically organized into 'contexts'. Our first deliveries and continuing enhancements have been to the Sydney Powerhouse Museum's permanent exhibition 'Cyberworld'. When run in text-only mode, our product uses 'Sophie' as her stage name. But for the Powerhouse interactive exhibit the Californian company Virtual Personalities Inc. generously contributed their 'Sylvie' face-and-voice animation. We interfaced this to our own chat engine and scripts to constitute an agent able to move seamlessly back and forth between 'goal mode' (conveying background to the 'Cyberworld' exhibits) and 'chat mode'.

Preparatory to regularly sampling the public's conversations with the exhibit, my psychologist colleague and wife Dr Hayes Michie conducted pilot tests of useability. Student volunteers were recruited from the UNSW Psychology Department. Each had two 7-minute chat sessions, punctuated with questionnaires about their experience. Subjects were also tested under similar conditions with a small battery of past winners and runners-up in the annual Loebner Prize competition. The tabulation shown below is a questionnaire summary sheet entered with results from the first small pilot test.

As a break from testing subjects, Hayes Michie's research assistant Stephanie Compton sampled some chat behaviours herself. Before the default-to-chat links

AGENT: SOPHIE

Trait score	Mean	Median	Description of median
EMOTIONAL			
Aggressive	0.6	0	Not at all
Cheerful	2.7	3	Mostly
Confident	3.6	4	Really
Friendly	3.3	3	Mostly
Human	1.9	2	Sometimes
Pleasant	3.0	3	Mostly
COGNITIVE			
Amusing	1.1	1	Occasionally
Intelligent	3.4	3	Mostly
Interesting	2.1	2	Sometimes

were in place, she had earlier tried her hand at two sessions under the standard regime planned for the experimental subjects. The opening part of the first is reproduced below.

SOPHIE: What's your name?

STEPH: Steph.

SOPHIE: Good to meet you Steph.

STEPH: Thanks, its nice to be here.

SOPHIE: Steph, it's my pleasure! Before I get into detailed things, … Cyberworld is about computers and communications. That includes robots, tele-communications and other stuff. I specialize in the material on Alan Turing, Turing machines, and his ideas on Artificial Intelligence and Learning. Anything appeal? There's more …

STEPH: Like what?

SOPHIE: Yes, well Steph before you commit, there's a great exhibit on Charles Babbage. There's Simulation, and added to that … I forgot some other things, multimedia for instance. And process control, which I didn't mention before. So what's the final decision?

STEPH: Well, what about Charles Babbage?

SOPHIE: In the mid 1800s, the English mathematician, Charles Babbage, designed a general purpose mechanical calculating machine that anticipated the principles and structure of the modern computer. Do you know why he was never able to finish building his Analytical Engine and why we didn't have mechanical computers 100 years earlier?

STEPH: Because he did not have the resources available that we have?

SOPHIE: In that ballpark. The only technology Babbage had available to him consisted of wheels, gears, and steam power. His calculating engines were more complicated than anything anyone had yet built.

STEPH: Wow, he must have been pretty smart.

SOPHIE: OK, tell me. Why?

STEPH: Because he had all these brilliant ideas and visions. His mind must have been very advanced for his time....

[She reported the experience as 'boring'. Her later experience, after the chat links were in place, struck her quite differently. She burst into excitement about her new companion. The following is excepted form the first of the new sessions. Note the transitions in and out of chat mode.]

SOPHIE: What next? My menu says AI, Turing, Stumpy,Universal Machine, Media, Babbage, Simulation, Control, Interfaces, ... I think that's it. Or we could just chat a while.

STEPH: Why don't we chat?

SOPHIE: That's nice that you take an interest. Do go on. Do you have any brothers and sisters?

STEPH: I have three brothers and three sisters. What about you?

SOPHIE: Great. So shall we just have a gossip, Steph?

STEPH: Yes

SOPHIE: Why don't you kick off, Steph? Tell me something about your views and interests.

STEPH: Well, I like to play sport, listen to music, go to the beach and see my boyfriend.

SOPHIE: Yeah, but stewing indoors can be quite fun,—within the family circle, though. How is it in your family? Any others share your tastes?

STEPH: Well, most of my family like going to the beach and camping so we all get on really well.

SOPHIE: I grew up in Pennsylvania on the farm which my parents still run, these days helped by uncle Albert. Shall I tell you, then, how sister Julia and I ended up in Australia?

...

[LATER SOPHIE TERMINATES THE 'CHAT' INTERLUDE]

...

SOPHIE: You have a friend in every port, it seems to me.

STEPH: Well, kind of.

SOPHIE: We'll come to that. Meanwhile how about some exhibition topics. That's what you came for surely?

STEPH: Yeah, I suppose we better get back to that...

The above excerpt was generated by the same versions of engine and scripts as those installed for public use in summer 2001 at Sydney's Powerhouse Museum.

Since then a new wing of the project led by Dr Zuhair Bandar of the Department of Computing and Mathematics, Manchester Metropolitan University (MMU), has begun further enhancement of our Infochat™ scripting language and documentation, and a commercial company Convagent Ltd has been set up in the UK. Stockholders include the MMU research workers, the University itself, the Human–Computer Learning Foundation, and Dr Akeel Attar, Britain's leading practitioner of commercial machine-learning software for knowledge engineering.

CHAT AND BALLROOM DANCING

In the quoted fragments we glimpsed an alternation between front-stage business and back-stage chat. The latter is a social activity analogous to 'grooming' in other primates. The surprise has been the indispensability of grooming— the really hard part to implement. Yet this result might have been inferred from the extensive studies of human–machine interactions by Reeves and Nass (1996).

In an important respect, human chat resembles ballroom dancing: one sufficiently wrong move and rapport is gone. On the other hand, so long as no context violation occurs, 'sufficiently' turns out to be permissively defined. In the above, Sophie ignores a direct question about her brothers and sisters, but stays in context. If not too frequent, such evasions or omissions pass unnoticed. When the human user *does* pick them up and repeats the question, then a straight answer is essential.

Capable scripting tools such as Sammut have largely been responsible for pioneering, make incremental growth of applications a straightforward if still tedious task for scripters. Adding and linking new rules to existing topic files, and throwing new topic files into the mix proceeds without limit. Addition of simple SQL database facilities to our *PatternScript* language has been proved in the laboratory and is currently awaiting field testing. Agent abilities to acquire and dispense new facts from what is picked up in conversation will thereby be much enhanced. Although incorporation of serious machine learning facilities remains for the future, straightforward scripting already enables a chat agent to locate and run programs from the hard disk at user request. So we may in course of time see further blurrings of the user-interface/operating-system distinction.

FORWARD LOOK

These are early days for AI as a whole. Yet the market already holds the key to its future shape. But to tell the whole story one must mention something more important even than the market. Success in the difficult task of chat-simulation is preconditional to a future in which computers gain information and understanding *through interaction with lay users*. Then, and only then, will it become in literal truth possible, using Tennyson's words:

> 'To follow knowledge, like a sinking star, Beyond the utmost bound of human thought.'

ACKNOWLEDGEMENT

My thanks are due to the Universities of Edinburgh and of New South Wales for funds and facilities in support of this work, and also to my fellow Trustees of the HCL Foundation for endorsing contributions by the Foundation to some of the work's costs. By reason of my personal representation on the Board of Convagent Ltd of the Foundation's commercial interest, it is proper that I should also declare it here.

REFERENCES

Copeland, B. J. (1999). A lecture and two broadcasts on machine intelligence by Alan Turing. In *Machine Intelligence* 15 (eds. K. Furukawa, D. Michie and S. Muggleton), Oxford: Oxford University Press.

Dennett, D. (2001). Personal communication.

Laird, J. E. and van Lent, M. (2001). Human-level AI's killer application: interactive computer games. *AI Magazine*, 22 (2), 15–25.

McCarthy (1959). Programs with common sense. In *Mechanization of Thought Processes*, Vol. 1. London: Her Majesty's Stationery Office. Reprinted with an added section on situations, actions and causal laws in *Semantic Information Processing* (ed. M. Minsky). Cambridge, MA: MIT Press, 1963.

Michie, D. (1986). The superarticulacy phenomenon in the context of software manufacture. *Proc. Roy. Soc. A*, 405, 185–212. Reprinted in *The Foundations of Artificial Intelligence: A Source Book* (eds D. Partridge and Y. Wilks), Cambridge: Cambridge University Press.

Michie, D. (1994). Consciousness as an engineering issue, Part 1. *J. Consc. Studies*, 1 (2), 182–95.

Michie, D. (1995). Consciousness as an engineering issue, Part 2. *J. Consc. Studies*, 2 (1), 52–66.

Muggleton, S. H., Bryant, C. H., and Srinivasan, A. (2000). Learning Chomsky-like grammars for biological sequence families, *Proc. 17th Internat. Conf. on Machine Learning*, Stanford Univ., June 30th.

Ramachandran, V. S. and Blakeslee, S. (1998). *Phantoms in the Brain: Human Nature and the Architecture of the Mind*. London: Fourth Estate (republished in paperback, 1999).

Reeves, B. & Nass, C. I. (1996). *The Media Equation: How People Treat Computers, Televisions, and New Media Like Real People and Places.* Stanford, CA: Center for the Study of Language and Information.

Turing, A. M. (1950). Computing machinery and intelligence. *Mind*, 59 (236), 433–60.

Turing, A. M. (1952). In *Can Automatic Calculating Machines be Said to Think?* Transcript of a broadcast by Braithwaite, R., Jefferson, G., Newman, M. H. A., and Turing, A. M. on the BBC Third Programme, reproduced in Copeland (1999).

Biology

Mainly About Mice

'After the war, I had been switched on to computing, but there weren't any computers to do experiments with. I had to do something, so I became a biologist' (Donald Michie, in a lecture given on the 28 June 2007 to the School of Informatics in Edinburgh).

Donald's contributions to biology were as far-reaching as his later role in machine intelligence, despite the fact that he was a geneticist for only about half the time he was a computational scientist. Indeed, some still see his move, mid-career in 1964, as a substantial loss to biology. Is this a confirmation of or an exception to the Proustian dictum that most of us end up doing what we are second-best at? It is hard to say, but at any rate, it is certainly a case of someone who ended up doing exactly what he always wanted to do. It is telling also that Donald talks here about computers 'to do experiments with'. The lessons learnt from years of rigorous experimental biology—on how to ask simple questions; how to conduct experiments and record results; how to control for confounding factors; the use of statistics; and how to draw conclusions—were evident in all his subsequent work in machine intelligence. So, while biology was probably worse off, applied computing science was definitely the better.

There are two main difficulties in bringing out Donald's contributions to biology in a book like this. First, most of these are in fairly technical articles, and neither he nor anyone else has written much about them outside the academic literature. Second, they are now such a fundamental part of large areas of biology, that few modern biologists are even aware of the pioneering—and at times, often controversial—work underlying the field. The situation is somewhat like this: ask modern electronic engineers about the origins of their field, and they will mumble something about Shockley and the Nobel Prize, in 1956, for the invention of the transistor. Some will know that Shockley and the engineers at Bell Laboratories were looking to build semi-conductor replacements for 'triodes', which were devices that were used for amplification of signals. Probably fewer still will tell you that it was the phenomenon known as thermionic emission, the study of which won Owen Richardson a Nobel Prize in 1928, that really started it all off. Even Richardson, in his Nobel acceptance speech in 1929 describing the history of the field, says nothing about the role of Edison, who had in 1883 observed the phenomenon in a precursor to what would become the vacuum-tube diode.* But it would be an unusual engineer who would begin a history of electronics with, 'Well, it all began with Edison really ...'

But this kind of detective work can be done. At the end of it, we are still left with the first difficulty: the trails often end in academic papers that require some substantial knowledge of the topics they cover. So, in a departure from the position taken in other sections, what is included here is only a précis, usually the introductory section from some important papers. Some will feel cheated by this, and perhaps annoyed enough to read the originals in full.

Donald's contributions to reproductive biology took place largely from 1952 to 1962. These ten years saw the flourishing of a scientific collaboration with Anne McLaren. There is a kind of Fred Astaire and Ginger Rogers feel to the dazzling sequence of work that these two remarkable scientific minds produced, paving the way for modern in-vitro fertilization (IVF) techniques. At the risk of going down the path taken by Douglas Adams, it would not be unreasonable to say that it all started with mice.

Donald's interest in fancy mice led to his doctoral study in genetics, and he and Anne were both members of the National Mouse Club.** The work on genetics led

---

* This was during the course of his light-bulb experiments. Edison, of course, patented the effect.

** It may come as a surprise to some readers that there is indeed such a club. In fact, it has been around since 1895, and conducts competitions amongst fancy mice breeders. Fancy mice, as the club points out, are 'quite different from the white mouse kept as schoolboy pets and the history of some lines can be traced back many generations'. Apparently the competition is friendly. (From www. nationalmouseclub.co.uk)

to his discovery of the phenomenon of non-random occurrence of genes on chromosomes in mice—now called quasi-linkage, but he termed it affinity—purely by statistical analysis of published data. I have not included this here, preferring instead to start with his collaboration with Anne Mclaren. 'Maternal Inheritance in Mice' is a non-technical summary of an early McLaren–Michie effort on an unusual maternal effect on embryo development. It ends before the experiments were completed, by which time they reached the opposite conclusion to the hypothesis proposed here. This research was important in two different ways. First, it uncovered a phenomenon the true reasons for which are still unclear. Second, the experiments naturally required production of large numbers of eggs, and their transfer between mouse strains. The groundwork was thus being done for both techniques for inducing super-ovulation and for embryo transfer in mice, and eventually, of course, for human IVF. 'Super-pregnancy' and 'The Transfer of Fertilized Mouse Eggs' are summaries of these two strands. The results McLaren and Michie were getting from their experiments forced them to ask the question: which strains of mice were best for conducting experiments? The prevailing scientific dogma held that it was best to use inbred mice. In 'The Importance of Being Cross-Bred' they go against this by showing how results from a particular kind of cross-bred strain could produce results which were much less variable. The current widespread use of this strain of F1-hybrid mice has its origins in this work. John Biggers, in the Foreword, tells us more on how this led to his collaboration with Anne and Donald, resulting in the (now) very famous work by him and Anne McLaren on in-vitro fertilization and embryo transfer.

Around 1960 Donald's interests turned to transplantation biology. The move is not entirely surprising since his work on reproductive biology had sparked an interest in studying the maternal–foetal barrier. He and John Howard joined M. F. A. Woodruff's fledgling research unit at Edinburgh University. The questions raised by organ and tissue transplantation were amongst the outstanding biological puzzles of the day. It was known that safe organ transplantation was possible between identical twins (Joseph Murray had shown this in 1954), confirming what was already known from the 1930s on skin-grafts between identical twins. But with non-identical twins, the new organ or tissue was soon destroyed: how did this happen?

This was answered by the pioneering work of Peter Medawar, who had showed that rejection of the transplant was caused by the recipient's immuno-logical defence mechanisms (that is, rejection was a host-versus-graft, or HVG, reaction). But Medawar's discovery of rejection as an immune reaction by the recipient was not the full story. The phenomenon of grafts inducing diseases in the recipient was discovered by the late 1950s. This form of the tail wagging the dog, called graft-versus-host-disease, or GVHD, was a common complication in bone marrow transplants, in which a not-so-defenceless graft mounted what appeared to be an immunological attack on the recipient. So, at the end of the 1950s, we were left with two different directed immune reactions: in some cases, it was initiated by the host on the graft, and in some others by the graft on the host. It was in this climate that Michie was to make a heretical suggestion that perhaps immune cells from both host and graft co-existed (that is, the recipient was what was technically known as a 'chimaera', being comprised of cells from more than one individual). The suggestion was far ahead of its time: it was nearly three decades before it was finally recognized in 1993 that the interaction of co-existing populations of recipient and donor leukocyte cells (these are white blood cells that are part of the immune system) was the basis of a two-way interaction between host and graft, in which HVG reactions dominate in organ transplants and GVH reactions dominate in bone marrow transplants. This finally laid to rest the dogma of two separate immune reactions. The conclusions reached by Michie, Woodruff, and Zeiss over thirty years ago are reproduced here in 'Immunological Tolerance and Chimaeras'.

Within two years of this work being published, much to M. F. A. Woodruff's dismay, Donald Michie was to leave the field just as the research in Edinburgh was becoming interesting. But computers were finally making an appearance in Universities, and a twenty-year wait was over. In a curious twist, however, Donald was to tie up his work in reproductive biology and machine intelligence nearly four decades later. In Oxford on a visiting appointment, and working in a manner very similar to his early work on affinity, he would be part of a team that showed how machine-learning techniques he helped establish could be used to identify characteristics of embryos that would have a greater chance of pregnancy in human IVF. It is in fact a description of this work that commences the book on the world's best-known toolbox of machine-learning programs (WEKA, from the University of Waikato in New Zealand).

But this section starts with something else. Many may not be aware that Donald contributed a regular science column to a children's section of the *Daily Worker*. Not surprisingly, while the columns for the grown-ups were 'by Donald Michie', the ones for kids were simply by 'Donald'. A three-part series, on keeping mice, proved irresistible.

CHILDREN'S CORNER

KEEPING MICE

THE first thing to know about keeping mice is that the right way to pick a mouse up is by its tail. You can then lower it on to your other hand and let it sit there if you like. But if you start to close your fingers on its body it will get frightened and may bite.

A mouse bite is not dangerous. Just suck it hard to get it clean and then forget about it. If you handle your mouse a lot it will get to know you well and will never dream of biting you, even if you are a bit rough or careless with it, which, by the way, you should never be.

A biscuit tin with a wire or perforated top makes a good cage, or you can make one out of a small packing case. A

acquire t... it, and r... they mu...

Scient... some mi... cage whi... cise whe...

Your ... to drink... in an op... side the ... only thr... dirt into...

You ... mashing... toes wit... mash co... for the ... firm rat... can add... or othe... vegetabl...

Mrs Mouse and Baby

Yesterday Donald told you how to keep your mouse healthy in a cage. Here are some more tips from him:

MICE like bird seed and other mixed grain. But none of the mice that I have known has ever been keen on cheese!

I gave one thirst-quenching tip yesterday. Another plan for supplying water is to bore a hole in the cork of a large medicine-bottle and fit a metal or glass spout through the hole.

man can tell you which is which.

Baby mice are born no bigger than your thumb, usually six or more at a time. They have no hair and are bright pink, and make a very tiny squeaking noise most of the time that they are not feeding from their mother.

They also have their eyes shut until they are two weeks old, and have no ears to speak of for the first few days.

If you see one of the grown-up mice running round with a baby mouse held in her mouth, don't worry. However much the baby squeaks, it is not coming to any harm.

The mouse is trying to fetch the baby back to the nest, and is probably the baby's mother.

She may run around like this a long time before she gets the baby to the right place and she may drop it once or twice at first. Mice are not very clever animals and easily get into a muddle.

Donald

A third article about mice

CHILDREN'S CORNER

PLAIN OR COLOURED?

(The last in our series of articles on keeping mice.)

WHEN the babies are aged three weeks they are old enough to leave their mother and should go into a separate cage.

At this age they are rather wild and get easily excited. If a mouse escapes, don't try to grab it. You will either miss or hurt the mouse.

Chase it into a corner, and wait for it to stand still. Then cup your hand, and bring it down over the mouse so that it is trapped without being squashed.

Then d... nothing until you ...ts t... picking out some-

have a fancy for black-and-white or brown-and-white patterns.

Fi... ly, a word about smells.

...paper ...ll shred ... female ...o have ...en stuff

... female ... babies ...re they ...fat. But ...ice you ...usband

Keeping Mice
(1961)

PART 1

The first thing to know about keeping mice is that the right way to pick a mouse up is by its tail. You can then lower it on to your other hand and let it sit there if you like. But if you start to close your fingers on its body it will get frightened and may bite. A mouse bite is not dangerous. Just suck it hard to get it clean and then forget about it. If you handle your mouse a lot it will get to know you well and will never dream of biting you, even if you are a bit rough or careless with it, which, by the way, you should never be.

A biscuit tin with a wire or perforated top makes a good cage. or you can make one out of a small packing case. A metal cage has the advantage that you can more easily scrub it out and dry it than a wooden one.

An exercise wheel can be bought from a pet shop and will be fun for the mouse as well as for you. Some people think an exercise wheel is cruel. But mice quickly acquire the habit of getting into it, and running in it, so I think they must like it. Scientists have found that some mice get unhealthy in a cage which hasn't got an exercise wheel.

Your mouse will need water to drink, but don't supply this in an open pot or dish put inside the cage. The mouse will only throw sawdust, food, and dirt into it. You can supply food by mashing up bread and potatoes with milk or water. The mash contains sufficient water for the mouse, and should be firm rather than soggy. You can add a piece of raw carrot or other moisture-containing vegetable.

You must give them some mash every day (a heaped teaspoonful per mouse should be enough) and clear out the remains of the previous day's mash at the same time. Otherwise the food will go bad.

PART 2: MRS MOUSE AND BABY

Mice like bird seed and other mixed grain. But none of the mice that I have known has ever been keen on cheese!

I gave one thirst quenching tip yesterday. Another plan for supplying water is to bore a hole in the cork of a large medicine bottle and fit a metal or glass spout through the hole. Place the bottle at a tilt at the top of the cage so that the spout pokes through the lid to the inside. The mice will then climb up and lick the water from the end of the spout. If it has been properly made, water will not run from the spout except when they lick it. It you put a loaf of bread in their cage, mice hollow it out and make a house out of it, in which they sleep. If you give them some paper or cotton wool they will shred it up and make a nest. A female mouse who is going to have babies needs to be given stuff for making a nest with.

You can tell when a female mouse is going to have babies because a few days before they are born she gets very fat. But if you want to breed mice you must give the female a husband to share her cage with. It is not easy to tell a male from a female, but the pet-shop man can tell you which is which.

Baby mice are born no bigger than your thumb, usually six or more at a time. They have no hair and are bright pink, and make a very tiny squeaking noise most of the time that they are not feeding from their mother. They also have their eyes shut until they are two weeks old, and have no ears to speak of for the first few days.

If you see one of the grown-up mice running round with a baby mouse held in her month, don't worry. However much the baby squeaks, it is not coming to any harm. The mouse is trying to fetch the baby back to the nest, and is probably the baby's mother. She may run around like this a long time before she gets the baby to the right place and she may drop it once or twice at first. Mice are not very clever animals and easily get into a muddle.

PART 3:   PLAIN OR COLOURED?

When the babies are aged three weeks they are old enough to leave their mother and should go into a separate cage. At this age they are rather wild and get easily excited. If a mouse escapes, don't try to grab it. You will either miss or hurt the mouse. Chase it into a corner, and wait for it to stand still. Then cup your hand, and bring it down over the mouse so that it is trapped without being squashed. *Then do nothing* until you see its tail sticking out somewhere from under your hand, then take the tail with the other hand and, presto, you have got your mouse again.

If you keep all the young ones as they grow up you will soon get like the old woman who lived in the shoe, with so many mice you won't know what to do! Take the extras to the pet shop, where you will be able to sell them for about a few coppers.

Most pet mice are white. I think it rather dull to breed from a pair of white mice because all the children will be white too. With any colours you can never tell what surprises may turn up among the children, unless you know a lot about their family tree. Don't forget that there are piebald mice too. You may have a fancy for black-and-white or brown-and-white patterns.

Finally, a word about smells. If you are not careful, the smell from your mice will make your hobby unpopular with your family. It is not the mice which smell, but their cage. Sprinkle plenty of sawdust in the cage, and scrub the cage out twice a week. A very strong remedy against smells is to put some peat moss in the cage too.

It is also a bad idea, if you want your mice to be popular, to let them run around on carpets or furniture. A mouse may make a mess when you least expect it, epecially if it gets flustered by strange surroundings.

If you get really keen you may one day want to breed mice for the show-ring. You can find out all about the mouse 'fancy', as it is called, by reading the magazine *Fur and Feather*.

Maternal Inheritance in Mice
(1955)

Those who breed mice commercially as well as for the Fancy will probably know that, to the biologist, mice are Very Important Persons! Britain is now spending something in the region of £100,000 per year on buying and breeding mice for biological research. Some of this research, as well as helping medicine and agriculture, can be of use to the fancier by throwing light on the principles of breeding and management.

As an example, the inheritance of coat colours in mice (expounded in a series of excellent articles in *Fur and Feather* by Mr Hutchings) took scientists many years to work out in the laboratory.

My colleague, Dr Anne McLaren, and I are biologists working with mice in a London laboratory, and I have thought that *Fur and Feather* readers might be interested to know what we are doing.

The main problem which we are tackling is the relative influence of the mother and the father upon the characteristics of the young. We have all heard 'old hands' of the Fancy telling the youngsters whether a particular trait should be brought into a cross through the doe or the buck, such as choosing the buck for type and the doe for colour (or vice versa, since even old hands don't always seem to agree about these things). The question is what scientific truth is there in such ideas?

Mendelian genetics says that the genetic contributions of the male and female are of equal strength, and so it makes no difference which way round a cross is made with respect to the sexes. But we know that for some traits this view is not 100 per cent true. To take a simple example, growth in the nest is influenced

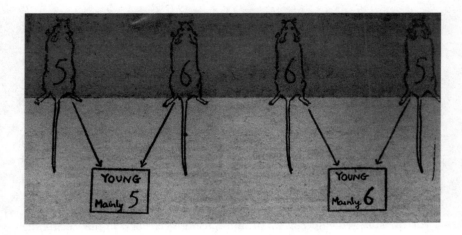

more by the mother than the father, because she contributes not only her heredity but also her milk to the young.

We are studying a trait which, unlike growth in the nest, is determined before birth, and yet is more strongly influenced by the mother than by the father. The spinal column is made up of a series of separate bones called 'vertebrae' strung together rather as a railway train is made up of a series of carriages. One of our strains of mice has six vertebrae in the lumbar region and another has five. When we cross the two strains we get the result shown in the figure. The young tend to take after their mother.

You may say: Why bother? Who cares about the lumbar vertebrae of mice? The answer is that we are interested in the vertebrae not as vertebrae but as a tool for discovering general principles about maternal inheritance in mice and other mammals. Also, the number of lumbar vertebrae may be related to body build, and in pigs is certainly important through affecting the number of cuts that the butcher can take off the back.

Going back to our problem, how does this 'extra' influence of the mother come about, in view of the fact that the father contributed just as many genes and chromosomes affecting the trait as she does? Every mouse began its life as an egg shed from the mother's ovary at the time of mating and soon afterwards fertilized by a sperm from the father.

The fertilized egg travels down a tube from the ovary into the womb or 'uterus', where it develops until birth three weeks after mating.

Clearly, then, the maternal influence must either be built into the unfertilized egg during its development in the ovary (there is a lot more inside an egg than genes and chromosomes) or be exerted on the embryo during its development in the uterus.

The method which we are using to settle this question is to take fertilized eggs from females of the 5-vertebrae strain and put them into the uterus of females of the 6-vertebrae strain. The operation is of course done under anaesthetic and has no ill effect on the mice.

The transplanted eggs develop in the foreign uterus and in due course are born as normal, baby mice. If these fosterlings still continue to take after their real mothers, then we will know that the maternal influence is exerted directly upon the egg during its maturation in the ovary.

But if they take after their uterine foster-mothers we shall know that the effect is exerted on the embryos during their development in the uterus.

We have not yet raised enough mice from transferred eggs to be sure of the answer, but to date the 'egg theory' is looking more likely than the 'uterus theory'.

The method of egg transfer is well suited to throw light on they whole question of maternal influences, which has vexed people since time immemorial. In the Bible we read that Jacob made ewes give birth to striped lambs by getting them to look at a striped pole during pregnancy! Today we no longer take seriously such naive ideas, but the scientist should still, I think, be prepared to look for grains of truth which they may contain.

My colleague and I have no striped mice but we do have some which are simultaneously dilute, brown, pink-eyed, chinchllla, tan-bellied, short-eared, wavy-haired, short-tailed, pied, and waltzing. We are planning to transfer eggs of this type into normal agouti foster others and vice versa, to see if any of these characters are modified by development in a foreign environment before birth.

Another line of attack on the problem of environmental modification is being planned in collaboration with a colleague who is an expert at 'tissue culture'—that is, growing living tissues in the test-tube. He will take recently fertilized mouse eggs, and let them develop and grow for a few days in an artificial medium in a test-tube. We shall then transfer them to a foster mother's uterus and see how the subsequent development of the embryos is influenced by the various substances of the artificial medium in which they spent their early days.

These are the main lines of work at present. We have many other problems which we would like to tackle, including the use of artificial insemination in mice, on which we have made a beginning. Unfortunately we are hampered by lack of an assistant to help look after our stocks. So, if any sixteen-year-old is looking for a job on leaving school, and would be interested in such work, he should write to the editor of *Fur and Feather*, who will put him in touch with us.

Super-pregnancy
(1959)

In 1927 Engle used pituitary implants to induce ovulation and oestrus in adult female mice mated to fertile males. At *post mortem* examination of their uteri 9–10 days later he found large numbers of embryos, ranging from 19 to 29. He did not follow the fate of such embryos into later pregnancy. But his observation raises a question which remains unanswered today: 'Could the reproductive output of mice and other mammals be artificially increased by gonadotrophin treatment?' Not only adults but also immature female mice respond to pituitary gonadotrophins by the ovulation of large numbers of eggs (super-ovulation) (Runner, 1950; Runner & Palm, 1953). If treated immature females are paired with fertile males copulation occurs, followed by fertilization and cleavage of the eggs (Runner & Gates, 1954). These eggs can be shown by transfer to uterine foster-mothers to possess normal viability and developmental capacity (McLaren & Michie, 1956; Gates, 1956).

The failure of implantation to occur in immature females following induced ovulation and mating was investigated by Smithberg & Runner (1956). The corpora lutea of the immature animals began to regress 4 or 5 days *post coitum* instead of developing into corpora lutea of pseudo-pregnancy (for terminology see Snell, 1941). Implantation could be induced, and pregnancy maintained to term, by supplying the missing progesterone artificially. The rare animals in which implantation occurred spontaneously were invariably found to have functional corpora lutea.

When pituitary gonadotrophins are administered to adult females without regard to their oestrous phase, a majority respond by super-ovulation, mating, and implantation (Fowler & Edwards, 1957). The proportion of mated females in which implantation occurs is lower than in natural mating. Following implantation, embryonic mortality during pregnancy and parturition is abnormally high, so that the number of young born alive is no greater than normal.

On receiving privately from Drs Fowler and Edwards an account of their work, we made a preliminary study* of the ages at which superpregnancy could be induced. In the strains of mice used, super-ovulation and mating at 30 days of age was regularly followed by pregnancy, although spontaneous sexual activity, and hence the possibility of natural pregnancy, does not appear until some 5–10 days later. We shall refer to this stage as *adolescence*. It is preceded by the *juvenile* stage, studied by Runner & Gates (1954) and by Smithberg & Runner (1956), in which induced ovulation is followed by mating and conception but not by implantation, and is succeeded by the *adult* stage in which oestrus and ovulation occur spontaneously.

It is clear from the foregoing facts that before we can hope to increase the reproductive yield, or decrease the reproductive age, by artificial means, many questions still require answers. The following are among the questions to which the present work is addressed:

(1) When does adolescence begin?

(2) How do adolescent females compare with adults in their capacity to initiate and maintain super-pregnancy?

(3) What is the pattern of embryonic mortality in adolescent and in adult super-pregnant females?

(4) Are the large prenatal losses in super-pregnancy due to the excessive number of embryos carried or to some other attribute of the experimental treatment?

The experiment to be described also provided information on embryonic growth. The presentation of this material will be deferred to a later paper...

---

* This experiment, described by Michie in the *Journal of the Animal Technicians Association*, 8, no. 1 (1957) suffered from a number of defects and should be regarded as superseded by the present work.

DISCUSSION

At the outset of this paper the possibility was mentioned of artificially increasing the reproductive output of mice and other mammals. The question is not entirely academic The suggestion has been made (Adams, 1954) that the induction of pregnancy in sexually immature animals might be used in livestock farming to diminish the interval between generations. Not only an increase in productivity but also an acceleration of progress in selective breeding could in principle be thereby achieved. Studies have already been made (e.g. Robinson, 1951) of induced super-ovulation in sheep and other farm animals as a possible means of increasing productivity; these studies have not been extended, so far as we know, to sexually immature females.

In mice we at first thought that the adolescent phase of sexual immaturity, in which induced super-ovulation and mating is followed by implantation and pregnancy, would prove too early a stage to obtain good yields of live young. It seemed likely that embryonic mortality would prove heavier than in super-pregnant adults, and so offset the time gained in using younger females. Our results have shown that this is not the case. Partial loss of pregnancies through the death of individual embryos is in fact somewhat heavier in adult than in adolescent super-pregnancies, owing to the greater (unexplained) incidence of early embryonic death. The loss of entire pregnancies is commoner in the younger adolescent groups (24 and 26 days old at pairing) than in the adults, but not in the older adolescents (28 and 30 days). Hence 28–30 days would be the age of choice if we were set the task of extracting the greatest number of live full-term embryos in the shortest possible time out of a given number of TO strain female mice supplied to us, say, at weaning. This choice is reinforced by considering the proportion of treated females which mate and the proportion of mated females which become pregnant. The mating rate is near to 100 per cent at 28–30 days and falls to below 60 per cent in both the younger and older groups. The pregnancy rate among mated females falls steeply as we reduce the age of pairing below 28 days, but is high in the 28-day, 30-day, and adult groups.

A further disadvantage of adult females relative to adolescents is the enormous variation which they show in respect of the number of implants. This may reflect heterogeneity either in the number of eggs ovulated, or in the proportion of embryos which implant, or in both. In either case the greater variation in number of implants is undesirable from the practical standpoint.

Even in adolescent females, the death rate at all embryonic stages is very much higher following super-ovulation than in normal pregnancies. Deficiency of progesterone has been shown experimentally (Smithberg & Runner, 1956; Hall, 1957) to be capable of causing embryonic death at some stages of pregnancy. But in our material progesterone therapy was not effective either against early death or against the catastrophe of placentation which occurs during the middle period when the number of implants in a single uterine horn rises above 8. There is no reason, of course, why progesterone should not alleviate the ill-effects of intra-uterine crowding when these are due to sheer compression of the embryo, since the hormone's effect in relaxing the wall of the gravid uterus is well known. For this reason a progesterone supplement might avert *late* deaths in super-pregnancy. These resemble middle deaths in being mainly dependent upon the degree of crowding of the single uterine horn. But the existence of a sharply demarcated threshold at eight implants per horn, above which the middle death rate increases abruptly, suggests that the limiting factor may be the amount of uterine surface available for the placentation of a linear series of implants, rather than the overall distension of the uterine horn. In the extreme case the interference between neighbouring sites of placentation is such that placental fusion occurs. The occurrence of this phenomenon in artificially crowded uteri has been made the subject of a separate paper (McLaren & Michie, 1959c).

An additional cause of embryonic death during the middle period which remains to be discussed is the double crowding effect displayed by super-pregnant adolescents but not by super-pregnant adults. Uterine horns in which more than eight implants enter the middle period alive suffer, as we have seen, an increased incidence of deaths in the middle period. But in the treated adolescents this incidence was further greatly increased when the opposite horn also contained more than eight implants surviving into the middle period.

A systemic factor must be sought with effects upon young mice only. An obvious candidate is the nutritional stress involved in supporting the growth of large numbers of embryos while the mother is herself still in the growing period. In support of this idea is the fact that the pregnant adolescent females were invariably found at 18.5-day autopsy to have exhausted their reserves of intra-abdominal fat. This was never observed in adult females. On the other hand it is difficult to see why nutritional stress should make itself felt so early in pregnancy. It is here, perhaps, that we may ascribe a role to progesterone insufficiency, arising from a partial failure of adolescent females to form luteal tissue. Such failure is total in pre-adolescent females after induced ovulation and mating (Smithberg & Runner, 1956).

Returning to our imagined task of obtaining the greatest number of live 18.5-day embryos from a given number of weanling female mice in the shortest time, we can say that the induced super-ovulation and mating of 30-day-old adolescents will give yields of about thirteen live embryos per treated female within 3 weeks of weaning the females, as compared with about nine in normal pregnancies within 5–6 weeks. It is worth noting that, despite the effects which we have described of intra-horn crowding upon embryonic mortality in the middle and late periods of pregnancy, we have found no signs of a ceiling to the number of embryos which a female mouse can maintain alive to term. This is brought out in a graph plotting the average number of live embryos against the average number of implants. The slight tendency shown by the adolescents for the curve to flatten out at the upper end of the range is not statistically significant. In an attempt to find a ceiling using another method, namely the transfer of fertilized eggs, we obtained a similar result (McLaren & Michie, 1959). Robinson (1951), in a study of super-ovulation in sheep, found that, with increasing numbers of implants, number of surviving embryos at autopsy reached a ceiling at a level somewhat under four per pregnancy. This is nearly four times the normal litter size of sheep, and so does not necessarily conflict with our findings in mice.

We have as yet said nothing of the greatest hazard of all, namely birth. Our evidence suggests that the greater the number of implants *the fewer* the number of young born alive. The cause of the heavy parturitional losses is unknown. But even were these losses overcome the survival chances of newborn mice in the large experimental litters might be poor, since such mice are extremely small, see Healy et al. (1959). In the pig, increased litter sizes have in the past not been wholly desirable, since the small size and heavy mortality of sucklings in the largest litters more than cancels out the initial gain in numbers. But methods of bottle-feeding piglings from birth have recently been developed, so that it might one day become possible to bring a litter of, say, 20 or more live-born piglings from an induced super-pregnancy to marketable age without undue losses...

REFERENCES

Adams, C. E. (1954). The experimental shortening of the generation interval. *Proc. Brit. Soc. Anim. Product*, pp. 97–108.

Bateman, A. J. (1958). Mutagenic sensitivity of maturing germ cells in the male mouse. *Heredity*, 13, 213–32.

Bowman, J. C. & Roberts, R. C. (1958). Embryonic mortality in relation to ovulation rate in the house mouse. *J. Exp. Biol.* 35, 138–43.

Engle, E. T. (1927). Pregnancy following superovulation in the mouse. *Proc. Soc. Exp. Biol., N. Y.*, as. 84–5.

Fowler, R. E. & Edwards, R. G. (1957). Induction of superovulation and pregnancy in mature mice by gonadotrophins. *J. Endocrin.* 15, 374–84.

Gates, A. (1956). Viability and developmental capacity of eggs from immature mice treated with gonadotrophins. *Nature, Land.,* 177, 754–5.

Gronebhrg, H. (1952). *The Genetics of the Mouse*, 2nd ed. Hague: Nijhoff.

Hall, K. (1957). The effect of relaxin extracts, progesterone and oestradiol on maintenance of pregnancy, parturition and rearing of young after ovariectomy in mice. *J. Endocrin.* 15, 108–17.

Healy, M. J. R., McLaren, A. & Michie, D. (1959). Superpregnancy in the mouse. 3. Foetal growth. (In preparation.)

Holt, S. B. (1948). The effect of maternal age on the manifestation of a polydactyl gene in mice. *Ann. Eugen., Lond.,* 14, 144–57.

McLaren, A. & Michie, D. (1956). Studies on the transfer of fertilized mouse eggs to uterine foster-mothers. I. Factors affecting the implantation and survival of native and transferred eggs. *J. Exp. Biol.* 33, 394–416.

McLaren, A. & Michie, D. (1959a). The spacing of implantations in the mouse uterus. *Mem. Soc. Endocrinol.* 6, 65–74.

McLaren, A. & Michie, D. (1959b). Studies on the transfer of fertilized mouse eggs to uterine foster-mothers. 2. The effect of transferring large numbers of eggs. *J. Exp. Biol.* 36, 40–50.

McLaren, A. & Michie, D. (1959c). Experimental studies on placental fusion in mice. (In preparation.)

Parkes, A. S. (1943). Induction of superovulation and superfecundation in rabbits. *J. Endocrin.* 3, 268–79.

Robinson, T. J. (1951). The control of fertility in sheep. Part II. The augmentation of fertility by gonadotrophin treatment of the ewe in the normal breeding season. *J. Agric. Set.* 41, 6–63.

Runner, M. N. (1950). Induced ovulations in immature mice as a source of material for studies on mammalian eggs. *Anat. Rec.* 106, 313–14 (Abstr.).

Runner, M. N. & Gates, A. (1954). Conception in prepuberal mice following artificially induced ovulation and mating. *Nature, Lond.,* 174, 222.

Runner, M. N. & Palm, J. (1953). Transplantation and survival of unfertilized ova of the mouse in relation to postovulatory age. *J. Exp. Zool.* 134, 303–16.

Russell, W. L., Russell, L. B. & Kimball, A. W. (1954). The relative effectiveness of neutrons from a nuclear detonation and from a cyclotron in inducing dominant lethals in the mouse. *Amer. Nat.* 88, 269–286.

Smithberg, M. & Runner, M. N. (1956). The induction and maintenance of pregnancy in prepuberal mice. *J. Exp. Zool.* 133, 441–57.

Snell, G. D. (1941). 'Reproduction', Chap. 2 in *Biology of the Laboratory Mouse*. New York. Dover Publications.

Snell, G. D. & Picken, D. I. (1935). Abnormal development in the mouse caused by chromosome unbalance. *J. Genet.* 31, 213–35.

The Transfer of Fertilized Mouse Eggs (1956)

INTRODUCTION

In 1890 Walter Heape performed a classical experiment which he described as follows:

> On the 27th April, 1890, two ova were obtained from an Angora doe rabbit which had been fertilised by an Angora buck thirty-two hours previously.... These ova were immediately transferred into the upper end of the fallopian tube of a Belgian hare doe rabbit which had been fertilised three hours before by a buck of the same breed as herself.... In due course this Belgian hare doe gave birth to six young—four of these resembled herself and her mate, while two of them were undoubted Angoras.

Heape thus demonstrated that a pregnancy could be artificially induced differing in two respects from a normal pregnancy. First, the Angora young had no blood relationship to their uterine foster-mother or to their foster-siblings. Secondly, their post-conception age differed by over a day from their foster-mother's post-coital phase, and hence from the post-conception age of their foster-siblings.

'The experiment...,' wrote Heape, 'was undertaken to determine in the first place what effect, if any, a uterine foster-mother would have upon her foster-children, and whether or not the presence and development of foreign ova in the uterus of a mother would affect the offspring of that mother born at the same time.'

To this may be added another main category of inquiry opened up by Heape's achievement: the effect of the presence and development of foreign ova upon the uterine foster-mother herself. As a single example: was the duration of pregnancy in Heape's recipient rabbit influenced by her precocious fosterlings? For it is certain that either the fosterlings were born prematurely or their foster-siblings were born belatedly.

These three broad categories do not exhaust the range of problems in genetics embryology, reproductive physiology, immunology, and cancer research which can be attacked by the technique of egg transfer. A further reason for interest in the subject is the possibility of practical application to livestock farming. It has been shown that a sexually immature female can be induced by hormone treatment to ovulate an abnormally large number of eggs. These can be fertilized *in situ* and then transferred to a battery of sexually mature recipients. It therefore becomes possible in theory (1) to shorten the generation interval and thus to accelerate the improvement of livestock by selective breeding (see Adams, 1954), and (2) to multiply the genetic contribution to the breed made by outstanding females, just as artificial insemination can be used to propagate the good qualities of outstanding males. Improvement of methods of storing mammalian eggs also holds out the possibility of transporting an entire herd or flock about the world within the confines of a vacuum flask.

In all the uses to which egg transfer has been put in a variety of mammalian species, the yield of living young obtained has been low. For its full exploitation as a research tool the technique will require to be brought to a high level of reliability in a cheap, fecund, and rapidly maturing laboratory animal. As a step towards this end we have made a study of some of the factors affecting the implantation and survival of fertilized mouse eggs after transfer to uterine foster mothers…

SUMMARY

1. The origin and potential uses of the method of egg transfer in mammals are briefly surveyed.

2. An experiment is described in which genetically labelled fertilized mouse eggs were transferred to the left uterine horns of recipient female mice. Eggs were obtained both by induced ovulation of sexually

immature donors and by spontaneous ovulation of adult donors. Both pregnant and pseudo-pregnant recipients were used. The post-coital stages of donors and recipients were independently varied. At 16½ or 17½ days post-coitum the recipients were killed and their uterine contents recorded.

3. The operation had no effect upon the recipients' chances of becoming pregnant, nor did it have substantial effects upon the implantation and subsequent survival of eggs in the *uninjected* horn of the uterus.

4. In the injected horn, the implantation rate was reduced by about one-third in recipients both at 2½ and 3½ days post-coitum. Post-implantational mortality in the injected horn was increased in 3½-day recipients, but not in 2½-day recipients, except when the operation was accompanied by gross surgical trauma.

5. The yield of live embryos from eggs transferred to recipients which had themselves been mated to fertile males was highest in the 3½ → 2½ days combination, lowest in the 2½ → 3½ days combination, and intermediate in the two synchronous combinations. These differences may in part be attributable to competition between native and transferred eggs. Such competition was shown mainly to occur before, during, or shortly after implantation, and to be a property of non-synchronous rather than synchronous donor–recipient combinations. But the differences were in part independent of the presence of competing native eggs, as shown by transfers to recipients mated to sterile males; the yield from the 3½ → 2½ combination was still very much greater than that obtained from the 2½ → 3½ combination.

6. Transfers of eggs artificially ovulated from sexually immature donors gave results in all respects similar to those obtained with eggs spontaneously ovulated by sexually mature donors.

7. The distribution of alien embryos among the recipients suggested that apart from the random loss of parts of inocula through escape or death of individual eggs, there was another and distinct process at work causing the loss of whole inocula as units.

8. Over the range tested (0–18 eggs) the number of alien embryos and the number of implantations of all sorts in the injected horn rose linearly with increasing numbers of eggs injected. The number of native embryos in the injected horn declined with increasing numbers of eggs injected.

9. When the number of implantations, with increasing numbers of eggs injected, began to exceed the normal quota for one horn, the number of live embryos in the injected horn (alien + native) increased less steeply and the proportion of dead and resorbing embryos began to rise.

10. The 3½-day → 2½-day series gave some evidence that when the number of implantations in the injected horn was raised above the normal level, successful implantation in the *uninjected* horn was reduced, so that the total number in the two horns combined never exceeded an average of about 8½.

11. The experimental results are discussed in the light of previous work and of future application. We conclude that with reasonable control of natural and technical hazards a yield of about 50 per cent of fertilized mouse eggs recovered as live young should be attainable.

REFERENCES

Adams, C. E. (1954). The experimental shortening of the generation interval. *Proc. Brit. Soc. Aram. Product*, pp. 97–108.

Beatty, R. A. (1951). Transplantation of mouse eggs. *Nature, Lond.*, 168, 99s.

Bittner, J. J. & Little, C. C. (1937). Transmission of breast and lung cancer in mice. *J. Hered.* 38, 117–21.

Boot, L. M. & Mühlbock, O. (1953). Transplantations of ova in mice. *Actaphytiol. pharm. neerl.* 3.

Chang, M. C. (1950). Development and fate of transferred rabbit ova or blastocysts in relation to the ovulation time of recipients. *J. Exp. Zool.* 114, 197–226.

Danfokth, C. H. & De Aberle, S. B. (1928). The functional interrelation of the ovaries as indicated by the distribution of foetuses in mouse uteri. *Amtr. J. Anat.* 41, 65–74.

Enole, E. T. (1927). Pregnancy following super-ovulation in the mouse. *PTOC. SOC. Exp. Biol., N.Y.*, 25, 84–5.

Evans, H. M. & Simpson, M. E. (1940). Experimental superfecundity with pituitary gonadotrophins. *Endocrinology*, 37, 305–8.

Fawcett, D. W., Wislocki, G. B., & Waldo, C. M. (1947). The development of mouse ova in
the anterior chamber of the eye and in the abdominal cavity. *Amer. J. Anat.* 81, 413–32.

Fekete, E. (1947). Differences in the effect of uterine environment in the *dba* and C57 Black
strains of mice. *Anat. Rec.* 98, 409–15.

Fekete, E. & Little, C. C. (1042). Observations on the mammary tumour incidence of mice
born from transferred ova. *Cancer Res.* a, 525–30.

Fisher, R. A. (1925–50). *Statistical Methods for Research Workers*, § 32. Edinburgh: Oliver and
Boyd.

Gates, A. (1956). *Nature, Lond.* (In the Press).

Heape, W. (1890). Preliminary note on the transplantation and growth of mammalian ova
within a uterine foster-mother. *Proc. Roy. Soc.* 48, 457–8.

Hollander, W. F. & Strong, L. C. (1950). Intra-uterine mortality and placental fusions in the
mouse. *J. Exp. Zool.* 115, 131–47.

McLaren, A. & Michie, D. (1954). Transmigration of unborn mice. *Nature, Lond.*, 174, 844.

Michie, D. (1955). Towards uniformity in experimental animals. *Lab. Anim. Bur. Coll. Pap.*,
3, 37–47.

Pannett, C. A. & Compton, A. (1924). The cultivation of tissues in saline embryonic juice.
Lancet, 1, 381–4.

Parkes, A. S. (1942). Induction of superovulation and superfecundation in rabbits.
J. Endocrin. 3, 268–79.

Runner, M. N. (1951). Differentiation of intrinsic and maternal factors governing intra-
uterine survival of mammalian young. *J. Exp. Zool.* 116, 1–20.

Runner, M. N. & Palm, J. (1953). Transplantation and survival of unfertilized ova of the
mouse in relation to postovulatory age. *J. Exp. Zool.* 134, 303–16.

Snell, G. D., Fekete, E., Hummel, K. P., & Law, L. W. (1940). The relation of mating, ovulation and the estrous smear in the house mouse to time of day. *Anat. Rec.* 90, 343–53.

The Importance of Being Cross-Bred (1955)

A PRACTICAL PROBLEM

If you want a lot of mice (or rabbits or pigs or plants) all resembling each other as much as possible, how do you set about it?

For the experimental biologist this is often a very real problem. The more his animals vary among themselves, the more of them he must use in each experiment if he wants the significance of his measurements to stand out clearly. His results must, as it were, speak louder than the background noise which is made by uncontrolled variability in the responses of his animals.

More animals mean more money, not to mention more space, time, and hard work. The amounts of money may be considerable, especially in the use of animals on a mass scale to assay the potency of drugs, hormones, food factors, poisons, bacterial and virus suspensions, and so forth.

A recent survey showed that the number of mice used in Britain's laboratories in one year was 1,180,000. The cost of producing one mouse ranges between 1s and 1s 6d, so that the national expenditure on mice alone must be somewhere between £60,000 and £90,000 per annum.

BIOLOGICAL VARIATION: ITS DUAL CAUSATION

A large proportion of the variability between animals and plants of the same species is due to small differences in the environmental circumstances in which they have grown up. But there is another component of variation, due to genetic differences between different individuals. Biological variation is in fact the resultant of the forces of nature and nurture acting jointly. Penrose has defined nature as comprising all causes acting before fertilization, and nurture as all cases acting after fertilization.

As an example of the dual causation of biological differences, mice of the DBA/1 strain have thirteen pairs of ribs, while those of the BULB/c Scott strain have fourteen. Here is a difference due to nature. But Ingalls, Avis, Curley, and Temin found that the DBA/1 rib number, stable under ordinary conditions, reacted violently to a change in early nurture. On the ninth day of pregnancy DBA/1 females were subjected for five hours to an atmosphere deficient in oxygen, similar to that encountered by Tensing and Hillary during the last 2,000 feet of their Everest climb. In response to the transient oxygen shortage over half the embryos departed in their subsequent development from the rib number normally standard for their strain.

Another strain, however, with the same standard rib number as DBA/1 gave very little response when subjected to the same treatment. Here again is a genetic difference, but one that requires an environmental factor (prenatal oxygen shortage) to bring it to light.

The dual causation of variability is even more obvious with a character which varies on a continuous scale such as human height, where both nutrition and inherited effects are plainly recognizable.

THE BASIC BALANCE-SHEET OF VARIATION

Mathematically-minded biologists have been led to express this dual causation by drawing up a balance-sheet of biological variation, as follows:

$$\text{environmental variation} + \text{genetic variation*} = \text{total measurable (phenotypic) variation*}$$

If, then, we want a uniform group of organisms, how should we set about reducing these two components of variation?

* Measured in statistical terms as the 'variance'.

ENVIRONMENTAL VARIATION

First consider environmentally caused variation. It has become part of the ABC of experimentation to standardize as far as possible the conditions of diet, temperature, etc., in which the animals are raised, and for a given experiment to use them at a standard age. It may sometimes be desirable to go further. Some characteristics have been shown to vary according to the age interval separating them from their elder brothers and sisters.

But even when we have minimized such environmental causes of variation, we still have to reckon with the other, genetic, component.

GENETIC VARIATION

A method for reducing genetic variation in sexually reproducing organisms was demonstrated as early as 1903 by Johanssen. He bred a number of lines of beans by matting each plant to itself for several generations. He then practised selection for bean size within each line and showed that it was without effect. The plants grown from the largest beans bore beans which were no bigger in average size than those borne by the plants from the smallest beans. He concluded that inbreeding had purged all the genetic variation from his lines, which he accordingly termed 'pure lines'.

It is in fact doubtful whether complete 'purity' (absence of genetic variation) can be attained by inbreeding. The design of Johanssen's experiment has been criticized by Llysenko on the ground that in each generation he selected the biggest and smallest beans, instead of the plants with the biggest and smallest average bean size. He was thus to a large extent selecting from the variation between different beans of the same plant, which in any event we should not expect to be genetically caused. But in general terms Johanssen was right. It is a simple consequence of the fact that inheritance is particulate that genetic variation decreases towards a limit the longer a line is inbred; if inheritance were blending there would be no variation after the first generation.

Here seemed the answer to the rest of the experimenter's problem. You cannot self-mate most animals, but you can brother–sister mate them in each generation and thus evolve genetically highly uniform strains. In one branch of scientific work after another the use of highly inbred strains came to be adopted.

TWO PLUS TWO NOT EQUAL TO FOUR?

Inbred strains seemed to so obviously be an answer to a prayer that they were gladly adopted without an experimental check. It seems logical enough. Turning back to the basic balance-sheet we see an equation of the form $A + B = C$. By minimizing both A and B we must minimize their sum, C.

Where is the fallacy? The balance-sheet in its simplest traditional form rests on an unproved assumption: that A and B can each be varied while the other stays put. But suppose that A and B interact in some way? Suppose in particular that some methods of decreasing B (e.g. inbreeding) bring about an associated increase in A: reducing B may then leave C unaffected, or worse still actually increase it.

In terms of the balance-sheet of variation this would mean an increase of environmental variation in response to a decrease in genetic variation. For instance, one of the effects of intense inbreeding may be to make the organisms more susceptible to the small differences between the different environments in which they develop and grow up. By inbreeding we could then lose as much (or more) on the developmental swings as we gained on the genetical roundabouts.

WHAT IS THE EVIDENCE?

The earliest hint of such a possibility was given in 1930, when Livesay found that inbred strains of rats were more variable in body weight than the offspring of a cross between the strains. Such offspring are known as first-generation, or 'F1', hybrids.

Since, as we have seen, members of an inbred line resemble one another genetically very closely, they will be alike in the kind of sex cells which they produce. Moreover, members of such a line are genetically very 'pure', or in the geneticist's term 'homozygous'; so that any one member of the line produces sex cells like all the others. Hence effectively only one genetic kind of sex cell can be got from any one inbred line. It follows that only one genetic kind of F1 offspring can be got from crossing animals from any two such lines.

We can see then that Livesay's interstrain F1 hybrids should be genetically uniform, like the parent inbred strains. Their lower total variability suggests that during their development and growth they were for some reason less affected than the inbreds by unavoidable small differences, which must exist in any colony of animals, between the environments to which different individuals were expressed.

Nine years later Emmens made a direct test of the suitability of an inbred strain of mice for the bio-assay of oestrongens. He compared the variability of their response with that shown by a random-bred mouse. Neither Livesay nor Emmens offered a feasible interpretation, and their result—perhaps for this reason—did not attract attention.

Although Hagedoorn has already in 1939 noted and discussed the phenomenon of hybrid uniformity in connexion with animal breeding, the first explicit alarm to reach the ears of experimental biologists was sounded by Mather in 1946. He mentioned the possibility that, for some characters measured in bio-assay, inbred strains might prove to be more variable than interstrain hybrids.

This has recently been experimentally tested and the effect found to be surprisingly large. McLaren and Michie measured the duration of narcosis induced by a standard dose of the anaesthetic 'Nembutal' (pentobarbitone sodium) in mice, and found that an inbred strain was 3–5 times more variable than the F1 offspring of an interstrain cross. Claringbold and Biggers in a larger and better-designed experiment found a four fold superiority of F1 hybrids in the uniformity of their response to oestrogens.

These results well illustrate the magnitude of the saving of money and effort that may become possible through correct choice of experimental material—namely a reduction of the number of animals needed by something in the region of 70 to 75 per cent. The basis of the calculation is that an n-fold increase in variability (measured as the 'variance' in statistical language) requires an n-fold increase in the number of animals which must be used to obtain a result of a given accuracy.

THE PROPER USE OF INBRED STRAINS

We are here comparing inbred strains with F_1 hybrids between inbred strains. Although we have cited cases where random-bred animals proved to be more uniform than inbreds, this cannot by any means always be expected. Random-bred animals have the disadvantage that they differ from one another genetically, for which they may or may not compensate, by greater indifference to environmental causes of variation when compared with inbreds. F_1 hybrids on the other hand combine the advantages of both the other types: they have the genetic uniformity of inbreds, but since they are not themselves inbred they possess, as do random-breds, a high degree of developmental stability in the face of environmental disturbances.

The use of inbred strains has therefore not been eclipsed in bio-assay. On the contrary we are now for the first time in a position to put them to their proper use—the production of interstrain F_1 hybrids...

FURTHER READING

Hagedoorn, A. L (1939). *Animal Breeding*. Crosby Lockwood, London.

Lerner, I. M. (1954). *Genetic Homeostasis*. Oliver and Boyd, Edinburgh.

Mather, K. (1953). Genetic control of stability in development. *Heredity*, 7, 297.

Michurin, I. V. (1950). *Selected Works*. Foreign Languages Publishing House, Moscow.

Waddington, C. H. (1948). The concept of equilibrium in embryology. *Folia Biotheoretica*, ser. B, 3, 127.

Immunogical Tolerance
and Chimaeras
(1961)

INTRODUCTION

The classical test for the specificity of transplantation tolerance consists in challenging the tolerant animal with grafts of skin and other tissues from the original cell donor (or a member of the same inbred strain) and from a third party. If, as typically happens, the donor-strain graft survives indefinitely but the third-party graft is rejected, the recipient is said to be specifically tolerant of donor-strain tissue, and this condition is attributed by Billingham, Brent, and Medawar (1956) to 'an induced specific central failure of the mechanism of immunological response'. This explanation, however, is not the only one possible when, as is usually the case, the injected cells include many which are immunologically competent. In this event the tolerant animal might be a stable lymphoid cell chimaera, harbouring throughout its life a quota of functional cells derived from the original donor, and rejection of third-party grafts might be mediated partly or even exclusively through the activity of those cells. Such rejection would be 'adoptive' by analogy with the way in which a tolerant mouse carrying a skin homograft will reject the graft after being re-equipped with isologous lymphoid tissue (Billingham et al., 1956).

The possibility is thus left open that the host component of the 'tolerance chimaera' is immunologically inert rather than specifically tolerant, and that the host is only able to muster an immunological reaction by proxy. We have sought to dispose of this possibility by the use of Simonsen's discriminant spleen assay (see Simonsen 1960a, 1961), which distinguishes activity of the host component of a chimaera from that of the donor component. This is based on the principle that mice older than 3 days injected with homologous immunologically competent cells develop splenomegaly if, and only if, the injected cells are capable of reacting immunologically against the test animal, and the test animal is genetically disqualified from reacting against the injected cells.

Simonsen's test can be used in a roughly quantitative manner to analyse the spleens of tolerance chimaeras, according to principles which will be explained in more detail in the next section. The present investigation was designed not only to throw light on the main question outlined above, but also to detect any non-immunological causes which might conceivably contribute to the splenomegaly phenomenon. It is, for instance, within the bounds of possibility that spleen cells transplanted to genetically alien soil might proliferate unduly through disturbance of a balance held by gene-products other than antigens. Into this category might fall the substances responsible for regulating normal tissue growth and regeneration. It is essential to eliminate such a possibility if the splenomegaly test is to gain full reliance as a quantitative and unambiguous immunological assay. The appropriate procedure is to make a spleen assay in which the genetic requirements for the splenomegaly phenomenon are satisfied, but the immunological requirements are not. We accordingly included, in our analysis of tolerance chimaeras, assays of their spleen cells against newborns of the original donor strain. If the splenomegaly phenomenon is purely immunological, no enlargement should result...

DISCUSSION

The experiments reported above establish rigorously two conclusions about the constitution and status of animals made tolerant of homografts by injecting them at birth with homologous spleen cells.

PRESENCE AND STATUS OF DONOR CELLS

In the first place some of the immunologically competent cells in these animals are of donor type. In other words, the animals are chimaeras, and some at least of the persisting donor cells, or their direct descendants, have retained their immunological competence. This was not unexpected, but hitherto formal proof appears to have been lacking. In the case of animals rendered tolerant by neonatal injection of homologous cells, chimaerism was inferred by Billingham and Brent (1959) from their demonstration that donor-strain antigen persists in these animals. Their evidence, although highly suggestive, is not conclusive, since purified protein antigen can persist for many months in a tolerant recipient which is not a chimaera (Dixon and Maurer, 1955). The postulated chimaerism is, however, fully confirmed by the present study, and has been shown to extend to immunologically competent cells, presumably belonging to the lymphoid series.

Chimaerism has on the other hand been sufficiently demonstrated in certain dizygotic twins in cattle and humans, and in lethally irradiated animals resuscitated with homologous haemopoietic tissue (for review see Woodruff, 1960). Some of the evidence, based on the demonstration of donor-type antigens, is perhaps not quite decisive, but morphological evidence, based on female sex chromatin in the human male twin (Booth, Plaut, James, Ikin, Moores, Sanger, and Race, 1957), and an easily recognized somatic chromosome marker in the mouse (Ford, Hamerton, Barnes, and Loutit, 1956) is unimpeachable.

In the early stages of the chimaerism which we studied, the donor cells were shown to be actively engaged in a reaction against the host. In long-established chimaeras, however, this reaction had subsided, as judged by spleen weights and phagocytic indices. Since they nevertheless retained the competence to react against third-party antigens, it appears that the donor cell population, although initially derived from adult animals, itself became specifically tolerant of the host. The results thus support the claim to this effect advanced by Simonsen (1960b), and suggest that in our A(CBA) chimaeras a mutual accommodation was ultimately reached between donor and host components, each acquiring specific tolerance of the other.

PRESENCE AND STATUS OF HOST CELLS

Secondly, the great majority of immunologically competent cells in the chimaeras we have investigated are of host type. In other words the notion that rejection of third-party grafts by apparently tolerant animals might be due to cells of donor origin having 'taken over' completely the immunological defences of the animal, can now be rejected, and the original concept of tolerance as immunologically specific is confirmed.

A by-product of the investigation is the demonstration that specific tolerance is a property not only of whole animals but also of aggregations of cells, to wit the spleen-cell suspensions we have employed for the assay of the host component against donor-strain newborns. Whether or not specific tolerance is also a property of individual cells (see Woodruff, 1959) remains open to question, because if one accepts an elective interpretation of immunological specificity (Burnet, 1957; Lederberg, 1959) the phenomenon we have observed can be explained equally well by selective clonal elimination.

REFERENCES

Billingham, R. E. and Brent, L. (1959). Quantitative studies on tissue transplantation immunity. IV. Induction of tolerance in newborn mice and studies on the phenomenon of runt disease. *Phil. Trans.*, 242, 439–77.

Billingham, R. E., Brent, L., and Medawar, P. B. (1956). Quantitative studies on tissue transplantation immunity. III. Actively acquired tolerance. *Phil. Trans.*, 239, 357–414.

Billingham, R. E. and Medawar, P. B. (1951). The technique of free skin grafting in mammals. *Brit. J. Exp. Biol.*, 28, 385–402.

Booth, P. B., Plaut, G., James, J. D., Ikin, E. W., Moores, P., Sanger, R., and Race, R. R. (1957). Blood chimerism in a pair of twins. *Brit. Med. J.*, I, 1456–8.

Burnet, F. M. (1957). A modification of Jerne's theory of antibody production using the concept of clonal selection. *Aust. J. Sci.*, 20, 67–8.

Dixon, F. J. and Maurer, P. H. (1955). Immunologic unresponsiveness induced by protein antigens. 7. *Exp. Med.*, 101, 245–57.

Eichwald, E. J. and Silmser, C. R. (1956). The genetics of skin grafting. *Transplant. Bull.*, 3, 67.

Ford, C. E., Hamerton, J. L., Barnes, D. W. H., and Loutit, J. F. (1956). Cytological identification of radiation-chimaeras. *Nature, Lond.*, 177, 452–4.

Gorer, P. A. (1959). Some recent data on the H-2 system of mice. In: *Biological Problems of Grafting*. Les Congrès et Colloques de l'Université de Liège, 12, 25–33.

Gorer, P. A. and Mikulska, Z. B. (1959). Some further data on the H-2 system of antigens. *Proc. Roy. Soc.*, B, 151, 57–69.

Howard, J. G. (1961). Changes in the activity of the reticuloendothelial system following the injection of parental spleen cells into F1 hybrid mice. *Brit. J. Exp. Path.*, 42, 72–82.

Lederberg, J. (1959). Genes and antibodies. *Science*, 129, 1649–53.

Simonsen, M. (1960a). Identification of immunologically competent cells. In: *Ciba Symposium on Cellular Aspects of Immunity*. Churchill, London.

Simonsen, M. (1960b). On the acquisition of tolerance by adult cells. *Ann. W. Y. Acad. Sci.*, 87, 382–7.

Simonsen, M. (1961). Graft-versus-host reactions, their history and applicability as tools of research. *Progress in Allergy*. Basle, Karger.

Woodruff, M. F. A. (1959). Contribution to discussions. In: *Biological Problems of Grafting*. Les Congrès et Colloques de l'Université de Liège, 12, 237 and 258.

Woodruff, M. F. A. (1960). *The Transplantation of Tissues and Organs*. Charles C. Thomas, Springfield, U.S.A.

Science and Society

'From Our Science Correspondent'

Writing to advance the public's understanding of science is not easy. A great breadth of knowledge, a prodigious memory, a well-stocked library, a writing-style that can appeal across cultures, and a knack of getting to the heart of things all help, but, even as masters of the art like Isaac Asimov acknowledged, it takes time and effort. Donald Michie's writings in this category are extremely varied and span over half a century, starting with regular science columns for the *Daily Worker* in the 1950s, to occasional book reviews for the London *Spectator* in 2007. Given this choice, for every article I have picked, there was inevitably another that would have been just as appealing. Nevertheless, no doubt readers would still like some reasons for this particular selection, and here are some. 'Scientific Advice to Governments' and 'Song and Dance Story' are included here because these clearly bear the imprints of the Lighthill affair. In 'The Black Death of Our Times' I found a remarkably sympathetic view of the effect on society of the disappearance of the skilled worker. The remainder are book reviews. 'Keeping One Jump Ahead' gives some additional insight into the code-breaking days at Bletchley. 'What They Read and Why' is a review of the results of a survey conducted in 1956 by the UK Department of Scientific and Industrial Research on where scientists get their information. The main result—that very few actually sit down and read long prose—is probably more applicable to our age of limited patience and attention spans than it was 50 years ago. But the best of the lot, 'Sciencemanship', is left for last, in which the book being reviewed becomes quite incidental to a remarkable description of the day-to-day practice of science.

Scientific Advice to Governments (1981)

The Lords' Select Committee on Science and Technology is turning its attention to the ways in which the government gets its scientific advice. Ancient Greece and Victorian England knew something of how it should be done. Even before the onrush of technology governments always turned, in the last ditch, to technical advisers of one sort or another—in ancient times to oracles. The qualities looked for have varied. The Athenians approached the Delphic oracle in the fifth century BC when faced with the Persian threat. Its advice was ambiguous:

> Zeus grants the Triton-born a wooden fort
> To stand unharmed and be a last resort ...

Was the 'wooden fort' the city's Acropolis or the Athenian navy? Themistocles, who had already talked his colleagues into parting with the cash for 200 ships, argued ingeniously for the latter interpretation, and was conspicuously vindicated by the naval victory at Salamis.

In the fourth century BC Dionysius the Younger, ruler of Syracuse, had begun to supplement his sources with a new kind of adviser. Plato had commended abstract thinkers as the best of all possible influences on government. As a politically minded mathematician, he himself typified this new breed. Dionysius' father had known Plato, but after hearing him lecture decided not to listen to him further, and reverted to the traditional oracles. Legend has it that the older Dionysius was so affronted by the lecturer's tedious praise of abstract justice, for which as a tyrant he found little occasion, that he had Plato seized and sold as a galley-slave. While conceding the reality of the 'adviser nuisance', modern taste may discern here an element of over-reaction.

The circumstances of Dionysius the Elder's death are ironical in this connection. He was told by the oracle:

> You shall not die until you have defeated your betters.

Being in the middle of a war against Carthage he superstitiously held off from decisive military engagement. In 367 BC, however, a play of his own composition won first prize at the pan-Hellenic drama festival, the Lemzia. His death followed from excessive celebrations on receipt of the news.

Plato's idea was that such a man as himself, the first-ever 'academic', was especially valuable in government. If he would not, or could not, be a ruler then at least he could advise rulers. He exemplified that kind of intellectual excellence which sets mathematical abstraction on a higher spiritual plane than the concerns of workaday mankind, and is evidently well equipped to attract the admiration of administrators. In his seventh letter he writes:

> I came to the conclusion that the condition of all existing states is bad—nothing can cure their constitutions but a miraculous reform assisted by good luck—and I was driven to assert, in praise of true philosophy, that nothing else can enable one to see what is right for states and for individuals, and that the troubles of mankind will never cease until either true and genuine philosophers attain political power or the rulers of states by some dispensation of providence become genuine philosophers.

Unfortunately 'academic man' sometimes combines with his special gifts the generalized one of being conspicuously wrong on ordinary questions of the day. On such occasions it is as if his judgement were usurped not by random conjecture but by a cognitive demon able to construct reliably false conclusions, provided only that the matter lies outside the pencil-beam of his specialized training. N. Parkinson describes a committee adviser with this aptitude, and introduces the theme with the question—

> Failing a man who is always right, what if the organisation contains a man who is always wrong? ... Why not ask him and then do the opposite?

Whether or not the judgement of academic scientists is indeed capricious beyond the norm, although widely assumed, is not entirely clear. A counter-example can be cited in one of the greatest of all academics, Isaac Newton. While occupying the Lucasian Chair of Applied Mathematics in the University of Cambridge he proved himself a wise and capable public man, negotiating on behalf of his university to good effect, and subsequently overseeing the Mint. Against this stands the advisory career of a later holder of that chair, the nineteenth-century Astronomer Royal, Sir George Biddel Airy. His research achievements continued at a high standard into extreme old age. But his advice to the government was uniformly, and sometimes preposterously, wrong. He stated that if the Royal Salute were fired outside the Crystal Palace the building would collapse. His advice on public funding of research in advanced computation, i.e. of Charles Babbage's difference engine, was more subtly wrong and is now believed to have had a complex motivation. Babbage had applied for a copy of the astronomical observations kept at the Royal Observatory, then directed by Airy. His request was refused, and on investigation he discovered that Airy was in the habit of selling the newly printed Greenwich Tables in bulk as waste paper, and had already disposed of more than five tons to one purchaser. Babbage commented, undiplomatically, that this seemed an extravagant mechanism for giving supplementary remuneration to a public man. The extravagance was, however, probably less than the ultimate cost to the nation of Airy's counter-attack. On his advice, government support for Babbage's difference engine was withdrawn.

Babbage succeeded Airy to the Lucasian chair. Although he was usually right in his opinions over a seemingly unbounded range of topics, no one at government level would ever have dreamt of listening to him. Partly this was because of his social behaviour. There was nothing about him of that 'leisurely and dignified manner' Airy assumed when a colleague predicted the position of a new planet. Airy's search for it was in the event too leisurely and dignified. Neptune was eventually discovered by someone else.

In considering how governments should be advised, Plato gave due attention to conventional oracles, which he divided into two categories:

1) *sane*, based on established rules of divination and orderly assessment, and
2) *inspired*, based on the utterances of a seer or prophet.

An echo of this distinction is discernible in the practice of contemporary government science agencies, which tend to veer between footslogging advisory committees and the sudden inspirations of eminent individuals. We look in vain for consistent principles which might bind together different prophetic episodes, and the record of oracles in science policy, whether 'sane' or 'inspired', does not encourage generalizations.

We can of course give precedence where possible to the 'sane'. But we should not overlook a sprinkling of unsatisfactory outcomes from this more cautious procedure. The British decision in 1912 to abandon all work on heavier-than-air flight, re-deploying resources into balloons, was the outcome of much patient work by Lord Esher's Sub-Committee of the Imperial Defence Committee. Documentary evidence had been sifted and expert witnesses cross-examined. Mercifully Esher had the courage to reverse himself in the following year, telling the Cabinet that he and his advisors had made a serious mistake.

Perhaps in the end the only safeguard lies in fostering, among those who may be called on to advise, the rare gift which enables a man who has gone out on a limb to say plainly and publicy, 'I was wrong!'

Song and Dance Story
(1979)

A cry of pain has arrived on my desk—an article by an Australian university zoologist entitled 'Peer Review: A Case History from the Australian Research Grants Committee' (*Search*, vol. 10, p. 81). The author, Dr Clyde Manwell, relates a tale of unhappy outcomes, first of a series of applications he made to the ARGC for research support, and secondly a number of energetic subsequent attempts to discover why these particular applications had been rejected.

The quest for explanations eventually involved his head of department, a former vice-chancellor, another vice-chancellor, and a member of parliament, all of whom helped procure for him replies which he had otherwise been unable to obtain.

At one point in his article Dr Manwell quotes from my essay 'Peer Review and the Bureaucracy' (*Times Higher Education Supplement*, August, 1978). This essay discussed, among other things, a recent statistical survey by three American authors seeking to discover whether the peer review system of allocating research money suffers significant biases. The survey's authors concluded that there was 'no evidence to substantiate recent public criticism'. My *THES* article made the point that provided the proportion of such cases were small (say 5% or less of all applications) quite gross abuses could occur, and yet they would be swallowed from sight in the statistics. As Dr Manwell points out, other inadequacies of the American survey have also been noted. So the question of peer review—its purity, utility, accuracy, and effectiveness, not to mention its costs—remains open.

When I began to read Dr Manwell's article I was expecting him to analyse these more general aspects of peer review, and perhaps come up with proposals for improvement. As I continued, I realized that someone suffering from a sense of injustice, personal bruising, and bewildered despair cannot reasonably be expected to play the elder statesman. So what happened to Dr Manwell, exactly?

Almost anyone familiar with the ways of the world will conclude that details concerning the arbitrary termination of his grant in 1971, followed by unsuccessful proposals for renewed support in 1971, 1972, and 1976, are almost irrelevant compared with one solitary paragraph near the end which reveals that in 1971 Dr Manwell...criticized the SA Department of Agriculture's fruit-fly spraying programme. Within a few weeks of those criticisms (repeated in the following years by other scientists with ultimately some improvement in the programme) an attempt was made to dismiss the author from his position. It required a four-year fight to have the author's name cleared of charges laid by a very eminent Australian scientist, which are now officially recognized as 'a number of errors' (Vice-Chancellor's statement, 3 June 1975, available from the Registrar, University of Adelaide, SA, 5001). Manwell adds that it was shortly after the sacking attempt that his grant was terminated without stated reason.

Let us take the hypothesis that a combination of the matter and the manner of his criticisms had indeed displeased some powerful insider. On such a supposition, what should Dr Manwell then have done? Clearly something different from the 'valiant for truth' campaign on which he doggedly embarked. But what?

After some 30 years in the world of science (which is not as different from the rest of the world as is sometimes thought), I would say the following:

First, whatever you do, don't become more attached to your wrongs than to your rights.

Secondly, purge the mind of illusion. Peer review, and the rest of the apparatus of grant administration, is not a court of justice. It is an arena. Points can certainly be scored by demanding the appearance of equitableness. But that is not even half the battle.

Thirdly, ask yourself the question: 'Once an influential insider has been fundamentally antagonized, what remains for me?' Options are (a) tough it out (as Dr Manwell is doing) with or without litigious pinpricks to the persecuting body; (b) raise an army of even more influential insiders for a decisive counter-attack; (c) patch it up (without crawling); (d) crawl; (e) emigrate; (f) leave science and take up investigative journalism.

If the idea of being a plucky loser has an appeal, or if the possibility of achieving an ounce of institutional reform outweighs a ton of damage to your scientific work, plus loss of time, sleep, faith, hope, and charity, then by all means consider option (a). Having considered it, consider dropping it.

Option (b) is not, in normal circumstances, even remotely feasible. It takes an awful lot to beat City Hall.

Option (c) is of course ideal. But in most cases it requires both diplomatic flair and insider status. Dr Manwell in all probability lacks at least one of these.

Option (d) requires knowing the limits of your own crawl-capacities. These may be more elastic than you think.

If professional opportunities and personal constraints permit option (e), then take it, and don't ever look back.

As for (f), if Dr Clyde Manwell is half the scientist that I take him for this option will not even have crossed his mind. When the time comes, though, he might consider as a retirement project preparing a readable and well-documented monograph on officialdom in science. As the poet Mayakovsky wrote:

> The future is a place
> In which officials disappear
> And in which there is much
> Dancing and singing!

The Black Death of Our Times (1981)

PART I

Practitioners and scholars of information technology can reasonably be accused of wandering in a plague-struck world with undisclosed antidotes in their pockets.

The black death of our times is the world's escalating complexity. Outbursts of hysterical aggressions, the growth of crank religions, fantastical promotion of economic nostrums, superstitious trust in nihilism: these are the human mind's immune reactions to social panic, triggered by the monstrous growth of complexity—impenetrable, intractable, and with no meaning to us all. Bureaucratic complexity, economic complexity...they are everywhere on the march, and in the countries of advanced technology the march has lately been breaking into an ominous run.

Those paid to do our thinking for us round the globe tell simple tales to quieten children: after Milton Friedman, the promised land; after Marx, the millennium; after a just war, freedom. Yet one or two facts suggest something different from all this, namely a grave deterioration of our mental power to cope.

How can this be in Britain, where we are plainly not becoming less intelligent, nor in any absolute sense less educated? The catch is in the words 'any absolute sense'. Life does not test the power of mental coping in abstract, but only relative to the difficulty of some environment. The true determinant is the 'coping ratio', and it has both the numerator (comprehension) and a denominator which is a getting out of hand.

Fifty years ago H. G. Wells described our predicament as a race between education and catastrophe. Although we might re-define 'education' more broadly than was possible for Wells in his day, few will doubt that the force of his words has been multiplied over the intervening years.

Quarrelsome

Each life strikes a balance between a skilled mastery of problems as they come in and a sense of slopping and sliding in a welter of other people's purposes. That balance determines a large part of the difference between a resentful and demoralized workforce and a team; between a rigid and insensitive management and a leadership; between an obstructive and self-serving bureaucracy and an organ of transmission of the democratic will; between an island crammed with distractable and quarrelsome inmates and a creative and self-respecting nation.

Symptomatic of the disease is a passion for one-shot sweeping remedies. We may well prefer those which proceed a step at a time. Some of the needed steps can be facilitated by intelligent application of information technology, for example:

- Reduction of the organizational complexity of governmental and commercial bureaucracy by radical advances in office automation;
- Mass availability of expert advisory systems to enable the ordinary persons to re-establish mastery over his own affairs;
- Use of micro-based training aids, including intelligent teaching systems and data-type networks including telesoftware facilities. Schools, polytechnics, universities, professional courses, industrial training establishments, and retraining schemes could all benefit;
- Exploitation of the recently discovered phenomenon of 'knowledge refining', by setting up pilot refineries in selected subject areas, for example in association with the Open University;
- Use of advanced robotics to reverse 100 years' de-skilling of factory work, and in a particular to end the tyranny of the assembly line.

Advanced technology, while in some respects enhancing man's coping ratio, has progressively eroded it in other respects, in particular by de-skilling life inside the factory while adding to its complexity outside. Sub-division of tasks into idiot sub-tasks and their subordination to the assembly line has turned each job into one which can be learned in ten minutes by a moron. Most painful of all, the trained man sees the craft to which he devoted his life 'rationalized' out of existence.

Treat a man like a moron and you make a moron. Yet for a steadily growing proportion of the working week, each man so treated is confronted in his off hours with another job which gets harder all the time—the job of everyday life. This is not a job for morons.

Here then is the rub.

PART 2: RE-SKILLING THE WORKS

Several years ago, in an initiative towards restoring to the task of assembling automobiles some of the lost interest and dignity of work, Volvo tried an experiment in which the work-force was divided into teams, each of which assembled entire cars one at a time. Economically it proved to be marginal. But a case may one day exist for re-opening the question as the basis of a new move in computer-based robotics.

I refer to the possibility of developing programs for sensing and control, smart enough to enable robots to act as cooperative members of such teams as those of Volvo's experiment.

Gains

Programming methods of the required kind are quite general. Energetically developed they could in some cases enable the craftsman to retain and extend his skill while increasing his productivity. A home-bicycle maker under present conditions assembles for sale 10 machines per day. If investment in a suitably capable seeing and self-trainable device enabled him to raise output to 30 per day, economic gains could obviously accrue, but also something more: supervision of a new kind of teachable assistant would enlarge the scope and versatility of his aspirations, while still permitting him to work from home.

The general argument draws support from two considerations:

1. As Joseph Engelberger of Unimation among others has pointed out, experience has shown that the job of minding even today's blind and stupid robots is coveted on the shop floor and confers added status.
2. The trend of component costs for robots and associated micro-electronic gear indicates a favourable balance of profitability.

A worrying corollary of the second consideration is that enrichment of jobs will presumably be accompanied by a reduction in their number. The only apparent alternative is reduction in hours worked per employed person.

Starting from a level of 60 to 70 hours per weak, reduction of working hours has been urged by the trade unions throughout industrial history and resisted every inch of the way by the employers and managers.

Rather than dismiss this resistance as blind capitalist greed, we should acknowledge that managers are managers and have their reasons. These reasons can be seen operating alike to bolster working ours in socialist economies, which absorb the displaced labour into token jobs, and in capitalist economies which absorb it on to the dole. The reasons have to do with the competitive position of an enterprise or consortium relative to its foreign counterpart. They derive their force from the simple arithmetic which relates a resource's yield to its maintenance cost (including rental, amortization, etc.).

A factory worker is a resource costing full maintenance for 168 hours of each week, round the year. His yield can be calculated by multiplying the number of working hours by his productivity per hour. The latter is largely determined by the degree and form of automation.

More Wealth

It would appear then that some improved form of automation, let us say intelligent robots, conferring a 30 per cent increase of productivity could be accompanied by a 15 per cent shortening of working hours and still come out ahead

(1.30 × .85 = 1.10, a 10 per cent gain in production). The worker gets paid the same for less work.

But he produces more wealth. Apparently everybody makes a bit.

Not so, says the manager, showing the scars of past export campaigns. What if the West Germans meanwhile introduce identical automation, but only reduce the work-week by 5 per cent, or not at all? It is easy to point out that West Germany Ltd is not particularly helped as a whole, since the additional unemployment has to be subsidized out of taxes. But this consideration lies outside the terms of competition between the individual German company or consortium and its British opposite number.

Compromise

Acting and choosing within this narrow frame, whichever has the tougher-minded management will be the one that unloads at the lower price on the world market.

Some flexible compromise between stiff import tariffs and the present downward slide to the scrap-heap must surely be possible. A friend who combines scientific distinction with impressive practical experience suggested in conversation a two-tier currency. An adjustable proportion of all state-financed wages, salaries, and benefits would be paid in domestic coin, good for buying a Mini-Metro but not a Toyota. Some mark-up of the remuneration paid in funny money would have to be permitted. But there is the germ of something here.

There may be also the germ of something in the re-skilling potential of self-trainable multi-purpose robots.

Keeping One Jump Ahead (2006)

Over half a century has passed since the Allied victory in Europe in the Second World War. In significant measure it was expedited by the interception and decryption at Bletchley Park of the 'Fish' cipher traffic over communication links between Hitler's Berlin headquarters and the army groups in North Africa, Italy, and Western Europe. The veil of secrecy over these operations has only recently been lifted, and *Colossus* by Paul Gannon is the first to have the full story.*

I joined BP in the early summer of 1942, and later worked with the high-speed electronic Colossus machines. These enabled our group to expand the daily breaking of enciphered traffic to round-the-clock mass production.

Upon the German surrender I was given the leaden job of condensing the work of many hands into two detailed volumes on how our various tricks were worked.

History-writing traditionally allows inferences, conjectures, stories, jokes, and even the occasional grinding of an axe. This was not history. It was an exercise in embalming—a necessary exercise but with no assurance that the embalmed specimen would ever be seen again.

In the mid-1970s small leaks began to occur, fertilizing a crop of popular and semi-popular books of varying remoteness from reality. After 20 years of this I paid a number of visits over a two-year period to the Government Communications

---

* *Colossus: Bletchley Park's Greatest Secret*, by Paul Gannon (London: Atlantic, 2007).

Headquarters (GCHQ), pleading for declassification. On 29 September 2000 the more significant of the two, the General Report on Tunny, was released to the Public Records Office. Gannon's new book is the first to take advantage of this 505-page report and of a wealth of other key materials that he has brought to light.

In refreshing contrast to many earlier publications, his account of wartime interception and decryption is deeply researched. It is also masterly in its breadth and sweep, with an interesting assessment of the role of the Colossus enterprise in Britain's post-war computing. But although Gannon makes a glancing reference, he has skimped the whole story.

To understand how, we need to grasp a fundamental distinction between 1) The patterns of the rotary wheels used by enemy machines to encipher traffic over given links, and 2) the starting-points, or settings, to which these wheels were set for enciphering each individual transmission.

In February 1944 when the first Colossus electronic code-breaking computer began operation, it was never imagined that it could do more than hugely speed up the finding of wheel settings, leaving it to the excruciatingly slow and chancy efforts of cryptographers to break the patterns by hand. Yet by this stage of the war the Germans were changing the patterns every day on every link as well as changing the settings for every new message. Gains in the speed of finding these latter were thus nullified. To find settings you must first have the patterns. Yet to break just one set of patterns by hand could take days.

In April 1944 I made to my co-worker Jack Good a suggestion simple enough for the two of us to validate in a couple of hours' experimentation. It was a way of rejigging Colossus for breaking wheel patterns, a role for the machine not previously entertained. We reported it at once to our section head Max Newman, and a 'crash programme' was authorized at War Cabinet level to have a working Colossus of the new design in time for D-day. At the end of hostilities nine new-design Colossi were operational and 63 million characters of high-grade German messages had been decrypted. Using precious Colossus time for the lowly task of wheel setting became something to be avoided wherever possible.

The three individuals who could have briefed Gannon on this are the three whom Max Newman first appointed when he founded the 'machine section', namely Jack Good, David Rees, and myself, all of whom are still alive. The author acknowledges that he did not consult any of us. It is puzzling that a writer of evident diligence and scholarship could commit such an oversight.

But I nevertheless commend the book to both the professional and the general reader.

What They Read and Why (1960)

Bernard Shaw once said, 'Reading rots the mind'. Surprising facts have now been unearthed which suggest that Britain's scientific and technological research workers may be in secret sympathy with this Shavian dictum.

A little while ago the Department of Scientific and Industrial Research asked the Social Survey Division of the Central Office of Information to conduct an inquiry into the reading habits of applied scientists and technologists. The findings are summarized in Nigel Calder's pamphlet.* The survey covered more than 1,000 industrial scientists, technologists, and other senior technical staff in the electrical and electronics industries. In so dynamically expanding a field one might think that the case for *improving* the mind by reading the scientific literature was unusually strong, and the risks of rotting it correspondingly small. However, the DSIR and COI felt that the first step towards coming to conclusions should be (in the words of Nigel Calder), 'to put aside angry preconceptions of what technologists ought to make of the literature, to step into their shoes and see what importance they really attach to it'.

In *What They Read and Why* the first surprise is as follows: 'Do technologists read to find something out? No.' The question was put, 'If you want information on a technical problem with you cannot solve from your memory or your usual standard references, what do you usually do first?' Only one in five replied that

---

* *What They Read and Why*: No. 4 in the series Problems of Progress in Industry, by Nigel Calder (London: HMSO, 1959).

they would go to the library or some other source of literature. The rest said that they would ask somebody else (usually somebody working in the same organization), either by picking up a telephone or walking down a corridor. The majority could not remember any occasion on which they had obtained useful knowledge from a scientific or trade journal.

The investigators thought that perhaps they were asking the question in the wrong form. So they tried to pin their victims down by asking those who were currently engaged on a problem, 'What steps did you take today/yesterday?' *Only 2 per cent of those that did anything about their problem in the twenty-four hours before the interview had referred to the literature.*

Why, then, do scientists and technologists read at all? The survey's answer is 'for ideas and stimulation'. Perhaps this throws light on the startling finding that 59 per cent of those questioned did most of their technical reading at home. Calder points out that 'children, television, domestic chores, and so on, must often be distracting to say the least'. Presumably, therefore, a scientist and technologist picks up a journal in much the same sprit as he picks up a newspaper or detective novel looking for topical news and relaxation, and certainly not regarding it as a natural part of his job. It comes perhaps as an additional shock for those who take the Shavian view, that the average technologist only sees about five journals regularly.

Does all this matter? For the non-Shavian who has managed to retain his preconceptions in the face of the facts so far cited, it presumably matters very much. His interpretation would, I suppose, be that the nation's scientists and technologists are misguided or lazy, that they not know what is good for them, and that they *ought* to read far more journals in a far more serious, sober spirit. Calder himself favours the conclusion that wide reading of the literature helps to make a good technologist. On the other hand, this is his one conclusion which is not buttressed by objective and unambiguous fact. It is true that the survey and that men with higher degrees see about twice as many journals as do the remainder. But this is in itself not good evidence, and may merely introduce a spurious correlation between merit at the job and the amount of reading. For various reasons, men with higher degrees are likely to be better technologists than others, and for various other reasons they are likely to do more reading. About the most striking feature of the report is the total lack of factual evidence that scientific and technological workers get any thing more out of reading the literature than plain fun.

This being the case, I am tempted to a suggestion. Why should not scientists, technologists, and scientific editors draw the moral when it comes to writing and publishing articles and papers? If the reader reads for fun, why not write in such a way as to give him as much fun as possible? This means that anything that can be said with a picture instead of with words should be deported from the text into a picture. By the same token, printed numbers whenever possible should be converted into histograms, curves, isotypes, and so forth. After all, why does television threaten the magazine circulations?

Language and style should be colloquial, short of irritating the small but possibly important literary section of the readership to the point where they actually stop reading. A striking feature of colloquial speech is that it is pictorial, rightly so, because most people think in pictures. This means, among other things, that passive constructions, so loved by science writers, should be shelved and replaced with the frank use of 'I' and 'We'. The reader can visualize a person and likes to feel that there is someone there talking to him. One of the reasons for the immense readability of Darwin, and many other early scientific writers, is the honest and disarming admission of personal existence, and, by implication, of all the personal weaknesses, passions, and predilections which make up a man as distinct from the discreet paragon which modern scientific opinion would have us pretend to be.

This means that much pride and prejudice will have to be jettisoned. I would even suggest, however outrageous it may sound, that the scientist and technologist must be prepared on occasion to seek the guidance of advertising experts when it comes to presenting his paper: for these are the people whose craft it is to use words and pictures to put information across in ways which can be readily understood and remembered. The fact that the advertiser's information is so often false or even pernicious is no argument against the utility of the same techniques when it comes to communicating genuine and valuable information.

Returning to the DSIR pamphlet *What They Read and Why*, a strong impression emerges from it that the overwhelming mass of scientific information is circulated and exchanged through talking—talking in pubs, talking in clubs, talking at departmental coffee, talking at home with scientific friends amid the clutter of 'children, television, and domestic chores'. If the DSIR maintains the objective and systematic approach which is so pleasantly and so readably exemplified in this pamphlet, we may, I hope, soon expect a follow-up entitled *What They Talk About and Where*.

Sciencemanship (1959)

Prof. C. Northcote Parkinson gave us the Law of Business Administration and Stephen Potter, the Law of Games. The research scientist will he grateful for Murphy's Law on how to make scientific experiments behave scientifically.

The latest book on How To Be a Good Scientist is by Prof. D. J. Ingle of Chicago, and has the title, *Principles of Biological and Medical Research*. At the end I found myself wondering why it had so little to add to the admirable earlier studies of Beveridge (*The Art of Scientific Investigation*) and of Wilson (*An Introduction to Scientific Research*). Perhaps it is not so easy to break fresh ground in this field. However, I am not entirely convinced of this.

MURPHY'S LAW

I think that the deepest and most durable impression which the research man's mind sooner or later receives is how unexpectedly, how unjustly, how distressingly difficult it seems to be to discover or prove anything at all. The research worker would be spared much early perplexity if his formal instruction included a sound treatise on Murphy's Law.

This important Law is described by H. B. Brous Jr. in the September number of *Astounding Science Fiction* as stating, 'If anything can go wrong, it will.' Research men among my readers will instantly recognize the truth and generality of this Law, even if they have not previously come across its verbal formulation. But having recognized it, what to do about it? Ingle's book, in common with those of Beveridge and of Wilson, has no definite proposals to make.

Here, then, is a suggestion, offered as a stimulus to others interested in this uncharted territory. The moment to take account of Murphy's Law is clearly when you are planning a new investigation. You have worked out how much material will theoretically give you the required amount of information. We will call this theoretical estimate x. x may be the number of rats to be treated, or of acres to be sown, or of soil samples to be collected, and so on. You then attempt to make rational allowance for all the things which might go wrong. While judging any specified mishap to be highly improbable, you might yet consider that the joint effect of all the improbable mishaps might amount to, say, a possible 30 per cent wastage. You therefore decide to budget for 1.43 times the theoretical estimate (after 30 per cent wastage, $1.43x$ becomes x), and the multiplier you use (in this case 1.43) I call the Rational Multiplier, R.

$$M = R^2$$

It is at this stage that we usually finalize our plans, and live to regret it. It turns out that although some of the possible hazards did not materialize, we had forgotten that a proportion of the rats might have fatal convulsions on hearing a whistling kettle, and that a colleague might mistake some of the clearly labelled organs stored in the refrigerator for goldfish food, and act accordingly. It is before any of this happens that Murphy should be consulted. Having quizzically surveyed the wreckage of many an experiment, I assert that the needed prophylactic lies in the use of the Murpheian multiplier, M, in place of R, to which it is related by the simple expression $M = R^2$. In our hypothetical case, supposing that the inexperienced (entirely theoretical) man would procure 100 rats from the dealer or animal house, the 'rational' man would procure 143, but Murphy would procure 204.

The expression $M = R^2$ rests on more than empiricism. It was derived, with the aid of my colleague, Anne McLaren, from certain theoretical considerations. These involve the idea that the Rational Multiplier depends on the number of discrete risk-bearing operations into which the total experiment can be broken down. If the rationally foreseeable risk attached to each of these is assumed to be accompanied by an independent, unforeseen, Murpheian risk of equal magnitude, then the above equation follows. Of course, the assumption is crudely approximate. But it is a beginning.

NECESSITY OF IDLENESS

Beveridge has emphasized the need of the research man to lie fallow for periods of time, and quotes J. Pierpont Morgan as saying, 'I can do a year's work in nine months, but not in twelve months.' Unfortunately, he offers no concrete suggestions. A former colleague at one time installed a camp bed in his lab so that he could lie down when he felt tired or lazy. His Departmental Head disapproved, but I think that the idea is interesting.

An allied problem is the Visitor Menace. I knew a famous man of science who, when a self-invited visitor was in the offing, would retire to the cloakroom. He took with him his papers and books, and emerged only when the 'all clear' was sounded. I find no reference to the cloakroom manoeuvre in Ingle's book, and Beveridge and Wilson are also without practical recommendations.

The visitor menace is an expression of a general, and truly paralysing, affliction which overtakes most research men in their mature years. This is the Earnestness of being Important. Ingle says, 'The early years in the laboratory are the golden years for many scientists. After he becomes known, the volume of mail, telephone calls, number of visitors, organizational activities, including committees by the dozens, and demands for lectures, reviews, and community activities grow insidiously and will destroy the creativity of the scientist if unopposed.' But how to oppose them? In a delightful essay on 'Heads of Research Laboratories' (translated in SCR *Soviet Science Bulletin*, 1957, vol. 4, pp. 1–6) the Soviet Academician A. L. Kursanov utters a similar warning: 'They come to us, these administrative commitments, of their own accord in the fullness of time, and the less we want them the sooner they come.' But he also fails to advance a concrete plan of self-defence for the research man.

FIVE PRINCIPLES

If only to start the ball rolling, here are five principles of evasion, not yet tried and tested, but perhaps deserving of trial.

1. No committees.
2. No refereeing.
3. No editing.
4. No book-reviewing.
5. No invited papers.

Special dispensation can possibly be granted for anything for which the hard-up research man can get sufficiently well paid (for example, reviewing Ingle for Discovery). The fifth item is the least obvious, but rather interesting. I added it recently when I had been going through my collection of reprints of the scientific papers of others, to discard those which I felt I could do without. At the end, I found to my surprise that my reject pile contained a high propotion of papers which had been delivered by invitation to some conference or symposium. I looked at them again. Many were by highly gifted authors on subjects of great interest to me. I still did not want them. The proportion of invited papers in my non-reject pile was small.

The clue probably lies in the recipe which one tends to follow for putting together an invited paper for a special occasion. The recipe is hash and waffle. By 'hash' I really mean re-hash of results which have in the main already been published somewhere else. The concoction can be diverting and informative for one's listeners. But it seems that hash and waffle is a dish that does not keep.

This is not to suggest that published symposia and colloquia are not of immense value for the advance of science. Quite the contrary: the explosive expansion today of almost every sector of the scientific front makes a vital necessity of any and every means of keeping scientific workers in touch with each other, and with the latest advances in their own and neighbouring fields. The scientist who helps to perform this service richly deserves the gratitude and admiration of his fellows. But let him not think that he thereby necessarily makes an original and lasting contribution to knowledge. If this happens to be his ambition, there can be no compromise. He must be prepared ruthlessly to disembarrass his thoughts and his time-tables from every preoccupation other than his central quest.

CHAP ROTATION

I once worked in an applied research outfit which, among other peculiar practices, operated a sort of rotation of crops, or, rather, rotation of chaps. Once in every while—I do not now recall whether it was once in six or seven or eight weeks—each man was banished to a small room for a week, in which his only duty was to sit and muse. No one asked at the end of the week, 'Did you have any bright ideas?' for this in itself might damp the muse. He was only asked to abstain from all routine work during that week. In exchange, the exile had arbitrary powers to commandeer any of the outfit's equipment or labour force if he wished to test his latest bright idea.

Some heads of research teams may look askance at this scheme. To those who are tempted to try it in their lab, I should emphasize the following. It must be made very clear that the exile who spends an apparently barren week with his feet on the table reading the comics gains the same merit in the eyes of the team and its leader as the one who emerges to suggest six new experiments and a modification of the Second Law of Thermodynamics. Otherwise the whole point is lost.

BROWSING

The rotation of chaps is only one of many possible devices for recharging the research man's mental batteries. The necessity of recharging is eloquently stated by Kursanov, employing a different metaphor: 'A scientist is not a balloon, to reach a certain height and remain there for a long while on account of the material it was once filled with. He is "heavier than air", more like an aeroplane, which has to keep going to maintain height or climb.' It is well known that height is on average not maintained. Beveridge cites Lehman's figures for output at different ages. Taking the decade of life 30–39 as 100, the output for the years 20–29 was 30–40%; for 40–49, 75%; for 50–59, about 30%. Assuming that the slow start is due to lack of knowledge experience, is the later decline entirely due to biological ageing? I think not. Two features of a young scientist's life at once occur to me which tend to disappear with time and which may be important. One is browsing and the other is fairly frequent change of work and surroundings.

What senior scientist can be found sitting all day in the library looking through research periodicals because he has nothing else particular to do? And what research student does not from time to time do just this? As for change of work, Beveridge mentions the case of Ostwald, who successfully rejuvenated his mind by this means when he was over fifty years of age. In this connection a proposal made by Kursanov's countryman, the nuclear physicist Peter Kapitsa, deserves attention. Kapitsa intends his suggestion for adoption in Russia, but there seems no obvious reason why it should not be applied more widely.

COMBAT FORCES

His idea is the setting up of *ad hoc* 'mobile combat forces', each to be regarded 'not as a permanent institution but as one set up to tackle a given problem over a period of months or years'. Such a force would consist of scientists drawn from a number of different specialities, each with some special angle on the problem to be solved. After the successful solution of the problem, the combat force would be dissolved and its members would return to the permanent department or institutes from which they had been recruited, or some of them might join new combat forces.

Something like this in fact occurred in Britain during the war, but with a measure of compulsion inadmissible in peacetime. Apart from the gain in efficiency, I see a valuable psychological advantage in such a scheme. It would enable even the senior research man to reverse his trend towards stagnation, for the scientific mind is more like medicine than a wine: it should be well shaken before use.

Many readers will have other, better suggestions than those which have been aired here. But enough I think has been said to show how many and how inviting are the paths in which Ingle has failed to tread.

Peace and Goodwill

In a letter dated 11 July 2007 to the *Guardian*, Andrew Murray writes:

> Your obituaries of my parents-in-law Donald Michie and Anne McLaren (July 10) do ample justice to their great scientific achievements. However, they also shared a lifelong commitment to socialism: both joined the Communist party during the cold war, and from the world peace congresses of the 1950s to the recent anti-war demonstrations they were always there, often together. Donald was for years the *Daily Worker*'s science correspondent, drawing on his broad-based understanding of the sciences, as well as the Marxism that was always his intellectual template. The politics of solidarity were central to Anne, from helping postwar Yugoslavia build a railway to actively supporting trade union struggles nearer home. They integrated scientific inquiry with the struggle for social justice—one without the other would have made no sense to them. As they sought to enlarge scientific knowledge, so also they worked to change society to allow that science to flower for the universal good.

It would be an important failing of this book if it did not capture some of these aspects of Donald's character. But to do this just through his writing is a bit harder, and will inevitably fall short. The first essay relates to a rather remarkable journey that he and a fellow scientist undertook in 1957. Armed with what they called their 'tramp's charter', they undertook a journey from London to Moscow—the Iron Curtain was now firmly in place—without official documents, accommodation, and, quite often, even money. With peace and goodwill, they reasoned, all these difficulties can be overcome. It is hard to imagine, even in these days of relative free movement within Europe, a pair such as this even getting past Dover. Nevertheless, they did make it all the way, and the essay here is a record from that time.

The second article is from a more recent time. As indicated by Andrew Murray, Donald actively protested against British involvement in the Iraq conflict. 'Descent into Unreason' is long, but I have elected not to edit it. It captures the deeply-felt convictions of a scientist and a man of peace.

The Tramp's Charter (1957)

From the Introduction to the original article:

> *Below we record the impressions of two young scientists, Donald Michie and John Matheson, who succeeded in driving an elderly Standard drop-head coupe from London to Moscow and back without benefit of interpreter, hotels, restaurants or formality other than what they term 'tramp's charter.'*

CAMPING THROUGH THE CURTAIN

East Germany was a bore. There were moments, though, such as when the two motorcycle People's Police, who came to persecute us for erecting a tent beside the Berlin corridor road, remained to push our venerable car. I remember, too, the note furtively passed to us by the waiter in a down-at-heel café near the Polish border: 'Long live your Königin Elisabeth!'

Across in Poland my co-driver and I found real trouble, however. The frontier office would not change travellers' cheques; we had no other money, and no petrol.

Micawber-like, we trailed to the nearest filling station hoping for something to turn up. Something did, in the shape of a very fat man.

'You English?' he began, waving enormous arms, 'I'm French. Poles all crazy! Pay anything for watches. Bigger the watch, more they pay. You go around with big alarm clock on wrist, friends all say "Big man, very important!" I'm off home, This country, it's fantastic! You got a watch?' Yes, we had.

'Polish automobilist here, very good fellow. Wants a lift towards Poznan.'

'We'll take him.' The Pole was brought over and introduced. Just one small thing, we added. We had no petrol and no money.

The tank was filled without further question, and we set off. The sale to our passenger of our £2 17s 6d watch (it was quite a large one) took us in comfort through Warsaw to Brest Litovsk.

The Russian frontier officials seemed a little taken aback by our arrival. To be fair, I must admit that not only did we look like tramps, but insisted that we were tramps, with no tourist documents or bookings and no intention of acquiring any.

The tramps' charter that they eventually extended to us will, I fancy, go down in history as a second treaty of Brest Litovsk, equal in importance to the first. From Brest Litovsk to Moscow we cooked our meals in the open and slept by the road side, unaccompanied and unmolested.

Did I say unmolested?—the first night it was the continuous blare of a motor horn which brought me from my sleeping bag out into the dews. Two motorized police confronted me. From their efforts in fragmentary German (they soon gave up testing my Russian) I jumped to the conclusion that the tramps' charter had been revoked. 'Schlafen verboten?' I queried, with an attempt at icy scorn. 'Nicht verboten! Schlafen Nicht verboten!' they repeated excitedly.

It turned out that the car was parked the wrong way round for their road safety rules. This was a pity, since the car formed an essential part of the tent. As we trudged round in bare feet, holding up trousers with one hand while wrestling with tent-pegs, guy ropes, ground sheets, and tent poles, my companion let loose a steady stream of bitter wrath unequalled in those parts, I should guess, since the liquidation of the kulaks. Our second dose of the 4 o'clock treatment was in the suburbs of Moscow itself. Made wary by previous experience, I passed the entire episode at the bottom of my sleeping bag. I never got a clear story from my wild-eyed and pallid companion at breakfast. It seemed to be a matter of cows, and a Mongolian herdsman who had insisted on driving them through the tent to the nearby agricultural exhibition. I pressed cups of tea into his shaking hands and let him ramble on.

The last dawn knock was on the door of our car. We were breakfasting inside it preparatory to starting the long trek home. Curiously, it was not a Russian this time. It was an English man who knew a Russian. The Russians wanted to buy our car. Jubilation! After a few days' driving in Moscow one comes to loathe one's car.

This is because the traffic regulations of Moscow have been drawn up with one object only in mind: to ensure that in six easy moves all motorists become stranded in the outskirts. It is not permitted to turn left. Except under special circumstances, it is not permitted to turn right. Sometimes the special circumstance is that the lights are red, sometimes that they are green. It is not permitted to do a U-turn except at special points. These are so placed that by the time you reach one you have forgotten (a) where you came from and (b) where you want to go.

And inevitably, as you search frantically for a place to turn right, or to turn round, or even to park while you collect your thoughts, the houses begin to thin out, green fields appear, and you realize that once more you are exiled in the tractless Russian countryside. No: when in Moscow, take a taxi.

At the Lenin Film Studio Mr Rogovoi, the Russian film director, explained with great charm why he wanted to buy our car. He was making a film about an English airman who was shot down by the Germans and rescued by a Russian girl in the Resistance. For one sequence he had rigged up a Moscow street to look like one in London. All he wanted was an authentic-looking car to go with the street.

The negotiations came to nothing. Russian cars are cheap and the price we wanted (plus air tickets home) was more than he could run to. But he went on to speak of his ambition of reviving through his film some of the Anglo-Russian understanding that has been lost since wartime days. I look forward to seeing the film if it comes to this country. And meanwhile good luck, Mr Rogovoi!

Descent into Unreason
(How Jack Straw Ruined My Book)
(2003)

To occupy Iraq would instantly shatter our coalition, turning the whole Arab world against us, and make a broken tyrant into a latter-day Arab hero. It could only plunge that part of the world into even greater instability.

George Bush 1st, in his 1998 book A World Transformed

We meet here during a crucial period in the history of our nation and of the civilized world. Part of that history was written by others. The rest will be written by us.

George Bush 2nd, cited in New Statesman, p. 14, 10.03.03

Charlene Barshevsky, from 1999 to 2001 director of Resources, Plans, and Policy at the US State Department, has pointed to some salient features of the Middle East. Its population, she says,

is young and growing, having nearly doubled to 300 million from 170 million since 1980. Meanwhile its place in the world economy has shrunk...In 1980, Muslim countries in the Middle East controlled 13 per cent of world exports and received almost 5 per cent of direct investment. Today the figures are barely 3 per cent of world exports and 1.5 per cent of investment. Last year, the entire Muslim world received barely more foreign investment than Sweden.

Int. NY Herald Tribune, 25/02/03

Of all the countries in that stricken region, one of the poorest is Iraq. Created in a map-redrawing exercise between the two world wars, Iraq suffered devastation during the first Gulf War, and was crippled by sanctions in its aftermath. The country has today sunk to such destitution that its people must think it impossible that things could get worse. In the light of present Anglo-American prescriptions, they may have to think again.

> Bush's spokesman Ari Fleischer said Iraq could pay for its own reconstruction, even though experts warn that it may be years before the country's oil fields are producing at potential.
>
> *Paul Krugman*, Int. NY Herald Tribune, 25/02/03

The context is the US launch of a new military invasion of Iraq, then still a plan, now a reality. Bush's solution entails a diversion of resources following invasion, from the 'food-for-oil' arrangement, on which some 60 per cent of the Iraqi populace have been dependent, to 'reconstruction-for-oil' to finance the rebuilding of roads, bridges, reservoirs, pumping stations, hospitals, schools, and the like.

Such a diversion of resources from food supply sounds like a recipe for increased starvation. It is noteworthy that our own Prime Minister, Tony Blair, would apparently promote the USA's general course of action even if America had not itself adopted it:

> I am truly committed to dealing with this, irrespective of the position of America. If the Americans were not doing this, I would be pressing for them to be doing so.
>
> Guardian *interview*, 01/03/03

I decided to see if I could infer Britain's independent thinking on these matters from the public statements of our Foreign Minister, Jack Straw. The documentary trail since the turn of the year should be sufficient. On points of special difficulty I consulted the Foreign Office (I will use this abbreviation for the Foreign and Commonwealth Office).

My assumption was that political leaders mostly have a clear idea of the thinking behind a policy, regardless of whether they derived it for themselves, or alternatively have understood the reasoning by which their officials evolved it. Either way a government minister is able then to justify his actions on different occasions in the confidence that his statements will be consistent with each other.

So what was the thinking that underlay the proposition that Britain should help the USA to invade Iraq? My probings led me to replace the above assumption by a revised model, the 'Rationally Assisted Minister'. A Minister, perhaps short of background knowledge, may sometimes have the time only to read an intricate rationale prepared by his specialist assistants, but not necessarily to understand it in context. A lapse in the coherence of his successive utterances could then resemble an actor's lapse on stage. Recovery by ad libbing requires that he should have had time not only to memorize his lines but also to understand the plot.

FIVE HYPOTHESES

I had my book mapped out. Topic: the reasons underlying the UK Foreign Secretary Jack Straw's pronouncements on attacking Iraq. He has given different grounds. The question is: which of them is the real one? Soon I began to worry. Did the various grounds cohere?

The book was planned as an experiment in applying scientific method, starting with the earlier-described 'simplistic' background assumption, that is, assuming logical consistency among different public utterances.

Five hypotheses were on the table about Mr Straw's primary concern:

    (1) to re-establish and defend human rights inside rogue states;

    (2) to prevent proliferation of weapons of mass destruction (WMD));

    (3) to reverse the rising tide of world terrorism;

    (4) to secure dependable oil supplies for Britain;

    (5) to go with America right or wrong.

Mr. Straw has at different times announced (1), (2), and (3) as justification for attacking Iraq. That they are three rather than one sufficiently demonstrates that his own grounds are not the only ones he has on offer. Other grounds could legitimately move others. His motivating grounds might even correspond to (4) or (5), and thus be unrelated to those publicly expressed.

Item (1) has immediate popular appeal and is free of commitment to consider current human rights practices inside allied states such as the USA or Turkey, as opposed to rogue states. The point is worth emphasizing in the light of detailed accounts (e.g. *Int. NY Herald Tribune*, 10 March, p. 1) of US methods for extracting of information from prisoners suspected of terrorism. It is the practice of rogue states that should dominate the immediate agenda. For the reader's convenience I list these states below:

- Iraq
- Iran
- N. Korea
- Libya
- Somalia
- Syria

The first three constitute George W. Bush's 'axis of evil'.

As grounds for helping to invade another country hypothesis (2) offers better prospects than (1) for legitimacy under international law. Under the British system, omitting to share with the electorate the true reason for an act of state is not ruled out. The duty of the Foreign.Secretary is first to promote our own country's vital interests and second to respect international law. If the two clash, then it is considered mannerly to offer the public conscience a more formally legitimate substitute reason. For this purpose (2) is well positioned, especially if UN authorization can be claimed.

Item (3) gains powerful salience from the horrific events of 9/11. But for it to acquire relevance to the case for attacking Iraq, a leap of faith is required that Saddam Hussein is directly linked to the terrorist organization of fundamentalist Muslims responsible for 9/ 11, generally referred to as Al Qaeda...

As remarked, (4) is not suitable for public mention. On the other hand (5) could be judged an effective argument. On 18 February in a context consistent with (5), the UK Prime Minister Tony Blair warned that 'people who want to pull Europe and America apart are playing the most dangerous game of international politics I know.'

These words of danger appear to contradict Blair's earlier-cited disavowal of US influence. Yet for reasons not necessarily to the forefront of his own Foreign Minister's mind they could actually be true. British abrogation of certain wartime and immediately post-war Anglo-US treaties could precipitate, in the interests of security, immediate US seizure of control over British military signals intelligence and other nerve centres. However, this particular peril may not be what he had in mind, nor may it be the only way to explain Jack Straw's fixation on Iraq.

Of the above five, only (1) of necessity involves invasion and regime change. Given Iraqi cooperation, destruction of WMD under (2) could arguably be secured by a sufficiently resourced and effective UN inspectorate. For countries that feel threatened there are many ways to pursue (3), the campaign against terror. Pursuit of (4) could continue along existing lines as far as Britain's oil requirements are concerned, without need of invasion. The last item, no. (5), only involves invasion of Iraq in the case that the USA invades.

Under international law only (2) can be legitimate grounds for invasion, and then only in one of two specific circumstances, namely:

- as necessary self-defence in response to an act of aggression;
- as an action specifically authorized by the Security Council.

I aimed to work down the list. So which, if any, of the five corresponded to Mr Straw's actual reason?

STARTER SET: (1) HUMAN RIGHTS WITHIN IRAQ

Use of force to improve the domestic practices of other countries has not historically been a part of British foreign policy. Such enforcement (in the aftermath of invasions) was once the concern of the old-time Colonial Office. To give effect to (1) as an added responsibility the Foreign Office would need first to place the world's countries in some priority order in respect of disregard of human rights. Among those countries judged to be in need of remedial intervention, that is to say rogue states, an assessment would then be required of relative immediacies. On an accountancy that includes comparative costs of intervention, Iraq might be found to head the list. But in the absence of any overt signs of such an exercise, I dropped (1) for the time being.

Note, however, that after further enquiries had eliminated other listed items, human rights made a late come-back. It figured as a key component of an extended case made by Tony Blair at the Labour Party's spring conference in Glasgow on 15 February. The new goal was compounded of a moral case (human rights) for invading Iraq and a political goal (Iraq's disarmament) that might be achievable without invasion. Note though that to hold back from invasion could mean forgetting Blair's moral case. I shall return to (1) after considering (2), (3), (4), and (5).

STARTER SET: (2) WEAPONS OF MASS DESTRUCTION (WMD)

The publicly promoted urgency of Iraq's assisting the UN inspectors to locate and destroy its WMD arose from conjectured Iraqi plans to pass secret supplies of biological and chemical weapons to world terrorists, and more specifically to the movement known as Al Qaeda. The latter could then transform (2) into an immediate and deadly threat to the homelands of the USA and Britain, nations that by reason of geographical remoteness could not otherwise be attacked from Iraq. A policy of treating (2) as a serious menace was thus logically dependent on Jack Straw's belief that close links exist between Al Qaeda and the Iraqi government. The chosen method was initially to disarm Iraq via UN renewal of inspections, replacing the UNSCOM team withdrawn in 1998 by a new and larger team known as UNMOVIC.

STARTER SET: (3) WAR ON WORLD TERRORISM

Jack Straw for many months kept the spectre of Al Qaeda to himself, not releasing the first hints until 20 January. From these it became apparent that he saw an invasion of Iraq as having the potential to reduce the future incidence of world-wide terrorist outbreaks through two main mechanisms. First, conspicuous brutal and violent internal repression by rogue states encourages potential terrorists everywhere to plan and enact their brutal and violent behaviours. Second, rogue states possessing WMD may leak them to terrorists.

> we have to expose the connection between the terrorists who respect no rules, and the states which respect no rules. It is the leaders of rogue states who set the example: brutalise their people; celebrate violence; provide a haven for terrorists to operate; and, worse than that, through their chemical, biological and nuclear weapons, again in defiance of all rules, provide a tempting arsenal for terrorists to use.

Evidence consistent with Jack Straw's conviction that Iraq was developing WMD for passing to Al Qaeda was subsequently presented to the UN Security Council by the US Secretary of State, Colin Powell. Investigation on the ground by the inspectors then failed to validate it. Yet the notion of a secret compact between Saddam Hussein's government and the Al Qaeda terrorist network continued to cast a powerful spell not only over Straw's mind but also over Prime Minister Blair's, President Bush's, and beyond. A *New York Times*/CBS News survey has found that 42 per cent of the US populace believe that Saddam Hussein was personally responsible for the 9/11 attack on the World Trade Center and the Pentagon. In fact the atrocity was executed by Saudi-based Islamic fundamentalists inspired by the wealthy Saudi Arabian renegade Osama bin Laden. A senior American member of the UNSCOM inspectorate in Iraq, Scott Ritter, when asked in 2002 about a possible Al Qaeda connection, had this to say:

> This one is patently absurd. Saddam is a secular dictator. He has spent the last thirty years declaring war against Islamic fundamentalism, crushing it...Osama bin Laden has a history of hating Saddam Hussein.

He's called him an apostate, somebody who needs to be killed ... It would
be ludicrous for Iraq to support Al Qaeda, either conventionally, as many
have claimed, or even worse, to give it weapons of mass destruction ...

S. Bitter and W. R. Pitt (2002), War on Iraq, London: Profile Books, p. 45.

At this point the interviewer, William Pitt, interjected the suggestion that in that
case Al Qaeda might turn around and use the weapons against Hussein. Ritter
responded: 'Not might. Would! Saddam is the apostate, the devil incarnate. He's
evil in the eyes of these people.'

STARTER SET: (4) DEPENDABLE UK OIL SUPPLIES

Item (4) of the above list was first implicated in my mind by David Frum, speech-
writer to Bush during 2001 and author of the phrase 'axis of evil'. In *The Right
Man* he writes of the USA's Middle Eastern mission:

If successful, this campaign will bring new freedom and new stability to
the most vicious and violent quadrant of the earth—and new prosperity
to us all, by securing the world's largest pool of oil.

Presumably for the UK the terms for acquiring Iraq-sourced oil from US-secured
vendors would be more favourable than its present direct purchase from Iraq
under the UN's 'oil-for-food' programme. Supplies might also be seen as more
dependable in the long term if obtained in the aftermath of a military victory. But
for war on this account to be in the British and US national interests we have to
assume a post-war imposed replacement of the present Anglo-US supply of food
by a new oil-for-food exchange rate, or even (as we saw earlier) by decreased attention to the country's food requirement in the interests of broader reconstruction.

I parked 'oil' as a possible supporting factor rather than a determinant of
policy, together with an even more far-reaching variant developed by the
American writer Norman Mailer. He adds control over water supplies as a lever
of domination over the region:

Iraq is the excuse for moving in an imperial direction. War with Iraq, as
they [the 'Bushites'] originally conceived it, would be a quick, dramatic

step that would enable them to to control the Near East as a powerful base—not least because of the oil there, as well as the water supplies from the Tigris and Euphrates rivers—to build a world empire.

Int. NY Herald Tribune, 25/02/03, p. 8.

It is not obvious that Britain's vital interests coincide here with those of the USA. To find a probable basis for Britain's joining in such military action we may have to look to item (5) below, in which we set aside Blair's claim concerning a wholly independent evolution of UK policy.

We should comment as a footnote to the above quotation, that water is indeed set to replace oil as a primary bone of international contention. Any doubt about this can be dispelled from readily accessible geostatistical sources such as Nares Craig's *World Rescue—Climate Facts* (London: Houseman's Bookshop Publications, 2003), or summaries such as Peter Woicke's 'Safe to Drink', *Int. NY Herald Tribune*, 18/03/03, p. 9.

STARTER SET: (5) AMERICA RIGHT OR WRONG

Item (5) is the argument from *force majeure*. Three treaties concluded between Britain and the USA during the period 1943–7 spelled out the somewhat one-sided terms that should govern the two countries' future military partnership. The treaties were declassified a few years ago but retain their force. I have reason to know this. One of the three turned out to be why a couple of years ago, the Foreign Office had to seek clearance from the US National Security Agency before a document of my own wartime authorship could be released into my possession.

Jack Straw himself has never mentioned them. So I decided simply to hold (5) in mind as a theory of last resort. Jack Straw picked human rights for starters. But in contrast to Bush, he can't sit still.

First the goal was regime change to protect human rights in Iraq. But for such purposes military action is not sanctioned by the UN Charter. 'Oops!' says Straw in effect, 'OK then. It's really about weapons of mass destruction. The Iraqis hide them. We have to find them.' Prompted at Camp David by Tony Blair, the USA became the leading drafter of UN Resolution 1441.

In the longish lucid interval that followed, a hypothesis seemed to lie on the table for serious investigation: namely that after the 1998 withdrawal of UN inspectors, Iraq had renewed earlier efforts to develop WMD.

Under Resolution 1441 in late 2002 the UN Security Council sent in new inspectors, headed by Hans Blix (chemical and biological) and Mohamed El-Baradei (nuclear), equipped and manned on a scale not seen before. Wherever they went, they were accompanied not only by Iraqi officials but by the world's press. Their energetic programme passed its third month and had found large shortfalls in Iraq's submitted documentation of their alleged destruction of their own WMD, and also some dozens of missiles which arguably exceeded the terms of the earlier post-war agreements. It has not yet uncovered evidence of substantive WMD development programmes. At this relatively early stage, Jack Straw burst in parallel into public expression of a train of less analysable ideas. Some of these seemed to border on delusion, possibly acquired by trans-Atlantic contagion from George Bush and aides. Certainly the virus of fear is there to be acquired. 'He's worried about another attack every morning that he walks into the Oval Office', says Bush's chief of staff, Andrew Card (*Int. NY Herald Tribune*, 10 March, p. 13).

DELUSIONAL BELIEFS: INDIVIDUAL AND COLLECTIVE

Delusion is a strong word. It labels the state of a mentally disturbed person whose beliefs grossly conflict with those of others and seem impossible to reconcile with reality.

Yet under pressure of their prevalence in some immediate peer group, such beliefs can be embraced by a sane person. In the Europe of an earlier age, belief in witchcraft was prevalent. What if a person were found from a parish record to have accused a neighbour of causing his illness by casting a malign spell? Should we say that the accuser must have been mad? Not at all. If anything was crazy it was the system of social belief, not the individual. So it seems today with Jack Straw He is plainly sane. At first the grounds he gave for backing Bush's war on Iraq seemed solid enough. Then they began to wander. He may have been influenced by the vivid mental images that had meanwhile taken hold of the US President.

Today a majority of British people, in line with those of continental Europe, have been shown by the polls to reject reasons offered them for joining a US go-it-alone war and to be particularly dismissive of the supposed Al Qaeda/ Saddam link. But, as remarked, around the end of January 2003 Straw confessed to having all along been nursing a state of considerable apprehension concerning such a link. If this state of mind cannot be traced to any coherent framework of evidence, this is not to say that he is mad. He could be swept along in a collective delusion shared by a small group of sane but consequential people. Such involvement of the mentally normal in transient crazes may be commoner than we think. We have to entertain the idea of beliefs held by deluded groups whose members cannot be regarded as individually deluded.

Here is Bush, as reported in the London *Evening Standard* of 29 January 2003.

> 'Before 11 September many in the world believed that Saddam Hussein could be contained,' he warned. 'But chemical agents, lethal viruses and shadowy terrorist networks are not easily contained. Imagine those 19 hijackers with other weapons and other plans, this time armed by Saddam Hussein. It would take one vial, one canister, one crate slipped into this country to bring a day of horror like none we have ever known. We will do everything in our power to make sure that day never comes... Secretly, and without fingerprints, he could provide one of his hidden weapons to terrorists, or help them develop their own,' he said, insisting the threat was facing every American family.

Mr Bush dismissed calls to wait for firm proof that Saddam still possessed weapons of mass destruction. 'Since when have terrorists and tyrants announced their intentions, politely putting us on notice before they strike?'

Note the emphasis on deceit and concealment, placing the originators of the feared dark deeds in an undetectable category, penetrable only by the seeing eye—'shadowy networks', 'without fingerprints'. Admittedly this is reminiscent of paranoia. But given the restricted and uniform nature of Bush's social environment, this much freedom from fact and reason is certainly within the bounds of sanity.

BUSH PROBABLY SANE

Further consider this. Before Bush's speech a major part of his overt anxieties focused not on chemical agents and lethal viruses but on a hypothesized revival of Iraq's nuclear weapons programme. This was spelled out in his speech of October last year.

> The evidence indicates that Iraq is reconstituting its nuclear weapons program. Saddam Hussein has held numerous meetings with Iraqi nuclear scientists, a group he calls his 'nuclear mujahidin'—his nuclear holy warriors. Satellite photographs reveal that Iraq is rebuilding facilities at sites that have been part of its nuclear program in the past. Iraq has attempted to purchase high-strength aluminum tubes and other equipment needed for gas centrifuges, which are used to enrich uranium for nuclear weapons.

But on the day before Bush's January speech, Mohamed El-Baradei, Head of the International Atomic Energy Agency and the ranking member of Dr Blix's UN Security Council inspectorate, reported after two months' work inside Iraq: 'We have to date found no evidence that Iraq has revived its nuclear weapon program since the elimination of the program in the 1990s'. There were no indications that Iraq could produce weapons-grade nuclear material when its inspectors left in 1998. After El-Baradei's team returned last year they took samples from rivers, canals, and lakes, testing for tell-tale isotopes. The inspectors also visited all of the buildings that had been identified through satellite photos as possible sites for working on nuclear arms.

'No prohibited nuclear activities have been identified during these inspections', El-Baradei summed up, adding that his agency had also looked into Iraq's attempts to purchase aluminium tubes. While the agency's investigation is still proceeding, he said Iraq had made a plausible claim that the tubes were for making non-nuclear rockets.

In his State of the Union speech on the following day Bush avoided specific mention of the nuclear component of WMD. He confined his expression of fear to chemical and biological agents. However overwrought he may feel about the perceived threats, if he were psychotically deluded he could not so readily withdraw a core belief in face of contrary evidence. In spite of its manifest intent to suggest otherwise concerning Bush, a spoof letter to the *Observer* newspaper carried a meticulous portrayal of typical paranoid psychosis. I say 'portrayal' rather than 'caricature'. Anyone who has ever seen the condition will instantly recognize the letter as no caricature. While realizing that George Bush has a way to go before his mind could reach that point of no return, I have not been able to resist reproducing the letter's opening paragraphs.

Sunday January 26, 2003 the *Observer*:

> I'm really excited by George Bush's latest reason for bombing Iraq: he's running out of patience. And so am I. For some time now I've been really pissed off with Mr Johnson, who lives a couple of doors down the street.
>
> Well, him and Mr. Patel, who runs the health food shop. They both give me queer looks, and I'm sure Mr Johnson is planning something nasty for me, but so far I haven't been able to discover what.
>
> I've been round to his place a few times to see what he's up to, but he's got everything well hidden. That's how devious he is. As for Mr. Patel, don't ask me how I know, I just know—from very good sources—that he is, in reality, a Mass Murderer. I have leafleted the street telling them that if we don't act first, he'll pick us off one by one.
>
> Some of my neighbours say, if I've got proof, why don't I go to the police? But that's simply ridiculous. The police will say that they need evidence of a crime with which to charge my neighbours. They'll come up with endless red tape and quibbling about the rights and wrongs of a pre-emptive strike and all the while Mr Johnson will be finalising his plans to do terrible things to me, while Mr. Patel will be secretly murdering people.
>
> Since I'm the only one in the street with a decent range of automatic firearms, I reckon it's up to me to keep the peace.

THE FORRESTAL CASE

But it seems anyway unlikely that any holder of high office could long escape detection by his peers if he or she were clinically deluded. The sole counterexample known to me is that of James Forrestal, the US Defense Secretary in 1947–9. He was found wandering in the Washington street seeking to warn passers-by of an imminent Soviet attack. He was taken into care, and his occupancy of high office ceased.

Unlike Forrestal, Bush re-adjusts his beliefs. In the light of the El-Baradei report, he switched emphasis from atoms to chemicals and viruses. All this points to sanity. However, it has to be admitted that later in the same speech he briefly forgot himself. According to the *Herald Tribune* of 30 January, 'he also repeated an American allegation that has been called into question by UN inspectors, that Iraq's attempts to import aluminum tubes were meant to restart its nuclear programs.' The possibility has to be entertained that Bush's grip on reality, although generally firm, suffers occasional lapses.

ACTIVE COOPERATION

Following Bush, Straw now declared that the Iraqis must proactively lead the inspectors to the sites where they have hidden their WMD stocks and/or WMD development factories. If Iraq cannot or will not do this, says Straw, they will be in 'material breach' and should be invaded, so that we can dismantle what they say they no longer have.

It is at this point that reason begins to falter. Start by assuming that the Iraqis haven't got WMD. Then they are obliged to fail the test through non-compliance. From this non-compliance we'll then conclude that they have something to hide, i.e. that they *have* WMD. Alternatively start by assuming that they have WMD. Either way they stand convicted.

But the inspectors' remit was to find any WMD that exist, or alternatively to continue investigating so thoroughly as to be able eventually to certify that they do not. At this point reason seems to say, along lines proposed by France, Germany, Russia, and China, that the investigators, having so far found nothing substantive, should continue the job and their numbers and facilities should be strengthened.

The test came later, when a different but equally prohibited category of weapon surfaced, namely Iraq's Al Samoud 2 missiles. Test firings of missiles without their on-board guidance systems or payloads found them to exceed the 93-mile range permitted under the Gulf War 1 settlement. The Iraqi side argued that if tested when fully loaded their performance would be found to be in compliance. Although this argument was never answered, the Iraqi's bowed to the UN Inspectorate's demand and on 1 March set about destroying the missiles as part of a range of activities aimed at compliance. These included taking the inspectors back to Al Aziziya, 60 miles southeast of Baghdad, where Iraq says that in 1991 it destroyed 157 R-400 bombs containing aflotoxin, anthrax, and botulin. They claimed that in recent excavation of the site they had so far uncovered eight intact bombs, and that they had also destroyed 1.5 tons of VX gas as they hoped to show to the inspectors' satisfaction.

Jack Straw's comment was:

> It's a very familiar pattern. Iraq first declares a total 'zero', saying that they have nothing illegal to declare. Then, under pressure, they cynically trickle out concessions to divide the Security Council, buy time and avert military action while continuing concealment.
>
> Observer, 2 March 2003, p. 4.

This proved to be an extraordinarily difficult statement to analyse. If our side demands specified concessions and the concessions are then made, they are at once denounced as 'cynical'. Is it perhaps that the Iraqis were wearing cynical expressions? In the British Army there was, and perhaps still is, a certain air that a subordinate might adopt while complying with an order. It was termed 'dumb insolence' and was of course diagnosed somewhat subjectively. But it was punished objectively enough. Distortions of perception commonly fortify delusional beliefs to the point that the subject 'knows' that others have this or that maleficent attitude. This may conceivably include cynicism. I decided to leave it at that.

LAST ATTEMPT AT SALVAGE

How about the idea, though, that Mr Straw only backed UN Resolution 1441 commissioning the new UNMOVIC inspecting team on the basis of a mental reservation concerning the limits on what inspections can accomplish without extremely active cooperation? In spite of the apparent ongoing successes of the inspectorate's nuclear arm, Straw could come to feel that chemical and biological problems are so tricky that the decision to inspect was a mistake. With only about half of the site visits done and an equal number still planned, what should he do?

Jack Straw's sense of the dignity of his position may preclude him from saying 'I was wrong!' So I redirected my attention to modern weapons inspection and its limitations. What can it hope to accomplish? The Pitt–Ritter book, in which Ritter looks back in some detail on his work as a senior UN weapons inspector during 1991–8, makes clear that their exercise had been able to accomplish destruction of some 90% of Iraq' chemical, biological, and nuclear capabilities. So Mr Straw's problem seemed hard to understand. But a different line of probing proved fruitful.

The picture radiating from Mr Straw was of the mighty nations of the earth seized by fear of imminent attack from this particular small, remote, impoverished, and recently devastated country. This sat oddly with his treatment of a concurrent outburst of nuclear sabre-rattling from the more formidable-looking North Korea. Following Bush, he at once announced that a diplomatic rather than military response was appropriate. Had I fundamentally misread the reasoning? How sure was I that Bush really saw Iraq as the most dangerous of today's rogue states?

HORSE'S MOUTH SPEAKS AT LAST

In the USA others had been asking just this question. In a statement reported 6 February (*Int. NY Herald Tribune* p. 3), Deputy Secretary of State Richard Armitage was responding to a group of senators on Capitol Hill. Senator Chuck Hagel, a Nebraska Republican, asked whether North Korea's potential capacity to sell raw materials for nuclear bombs to terrorists made it 'far more dangerous' than Iraq.

Armitage replied that 'it's quite a different situation in Iraq' because whether or not Saddam Hussein is more dangerous in terms of WMD, the Iraqi president wants to 'intimidate, dominate and attack' his neighbours.

But did Armitage have an alternative to mind-reading Saddam's intentions as a basis for picking on Iraq? Unknown to him he had, from Bush himself. Bush, like Chuck Hagel, regards North Korea as militarily far more dangerous. Simon Chesterfield, author of *Just Peace? Humanitarian Intervention and International Law*, summarizes the relevant passage of President Bush's 28 January State of the Union address, as expressing the following pragmatism:

> Nuclear-armed North Korea must be dealt with diplomatically precisely because it poses a greater threat than Iraq. In the meantime, the United States must defeat Iraq while it can.

Simple, concise, and to practically minded US patriots compelling. No wonder if in his endeavours to prove the wrong premise, Jack Straw had been making such heavy weather!

Just how heavy is revealed by a dossier supplied by Straw's Department (*Guardian*, 7 February, p. 1) to support Tony Blair's rehearsal of earlier reasons for going to war. Presented as late-breaking intelligence, four of the report's nineteen pages turn out to have been copied (with minor editing and a few insertions) from an internet version of an article published by a graduate student, Ibrahim al Marashi, last September in the *Middle East Review of International Affairs*. Six more pages rely heavily on articles by Sean Boyne and Ken Cause in *Jane's Intelligence Review* in 1997 and 2002. None of these sources are acknowledged, still less that al Marashi's primary materials were documents captured in Iraq in 1991, over a decade ago.

Two government departments were involved in this fiasco, namely the Foreign Office and the Prime Minister's Office. It seemed best to let it float downstream, taking note meanwhile of the advisability of double-checking even seemingly unimpeachable documentary evidence.

FOREIGN OFFICE TO THE RESCUE

Back to Square 1, I decided to forget about past motivations and mishaps. A new anxiety of Jack Straw's confirmed my earlier suspicion that he had lost his nerve about inspections. He now revealed a fear that no amount of inspection would be adequate to find concealed WMD. This led me to phone the Foreign Office and to follow up as follows:

> Subj: Current FO Iraq policy
> Date: 12/02/2003
>
> We spoke this afternoon, Wednesday, and you kindly offered to let me have an explanatory comment on a particular point of current policy. The question is this:
> According to recent statements by the Minister, Jack Straw, war can still be averted if the Iraqis admit their possession of weapons of mass destruction (WMD) and supply a complete list of locations. But this fails fully to specify the criteria to be applied for verifying completeness of the list.

Suppose that Iraq were to make such a disclosure, claiming it (possibly falsely) to be complete. The only means of checking completeness would presumably be to seek and find the omitted WMD items. By how many fold would the present number of inspectors have to be increased to check the disclosure for completeness? On the face of it, the numbers required could be of a similar order of magnitude to those required in the case of zero disclosure, already described by Mr Straw as more than a 'thousandfold', meaning I think 'no increase however large'.

Put in these bald terms there would appear to be no way in which the Iraq authorities can satisfy the condition as stated (i.e. admit possession and supply complete location list). It may then be misleading to state that Iraqi options still exist for avoiding war.

Time passed. After one or two phone reminders, I re-transmitted my query on 25 February and received renewed assurances of imminent attention. After further phone discussions and emails in early March, my contact at the Foreign Office told me that the delay in sending me a reply was because there was some confusion whether my enquiry should be handled by the relevant policy department or by the Foreign Office's Press Office. I then supplied him with the following clarification of the point I wanted to elucidate:

- Mr Straw has stated that without proactive cooperation from the Iraqi side no amount of strengthening of the UN inspecting team could suffice to locate the hypothesized hidden WMD.
- Suppose that, thanks to a sudden access of proactive cooperation, Iraqi WMD's are located and destroyed. The Iraqis then say 'OK, that's all there is.' What verification measures would then suffice to show that full and active cooperation had not reverted to deceit and concealment before all hidden WMD had in fact been found and destroyed?
- On the face of it, this new problem would be no different from the initial one, for which the Minister had said that no amount ot strengthening of the inspectorate would be enough.
- In that case, is it not misleading for him repeatedly to state that the Iraqi side has had a feasible option for averting war? Whatever the Iraqi response, are we not obliged to act on the worst-case assumption that WMD disclosure is still incomplete and to throw the switch to military action?

He duly forwarded this to the officials of the FO's Non-Proliferation Department, who now had my original query under review. Their reply proved to have been worth the wait.

The most directly relevant part is reproduced below

> UNSCR1441 confirms, in its very first operative paragraph, that '…Iraq has been and remains in material breach of its obligations under relevant resolutions, including resolution 687 (1991), in particular through Iraq's failure to cooperate with United Nations inspectors and the IAEA, and to complete the actions required under paragraphs 8 to 13 of resolution 687 (1991).'

The onus is therefore on Iraq to prove its innocence, and to come up with an adequate explanation about what happened to its 1.5 tonnes of VX nerve agent, the biological growth media (enough to produce over 3 times the amount of anthrax Iraq claimed to have produced, etc. etc.), not on the international community to prove its guilt.

How can Iraq prove its innocence?—By offering full and active cooperation by volunteering information, documents, personnel, by actively showing what has been done. By not waiting to be asked, but by offering. And, as a first step, by answering the outstanding questions. They can do this through:

- volunteering information (preferably backed by documentary evidence, orders, invoices, etc.) on what they had, and when/how they destroyed it. In some instances, UNMOVIC can carry out tests to see if there are any traces left, and thereby verify some of the claims.
- full and unconditional access to the sites/remains. For example, Iraq has still not accounted for 50 missile warheads, which included CBW warheads. Where are the remains?
- full and unconditional access to the people who made the stuff, and who allegedly destroyed it, so UNMOVIC can interview them and see if their stories are credible.

The bottom line is that none of the questions identified by UNSCOM, or by Amorim, have so far been answered. In fact, we now have more questions, such as:

- Iraq declared that it produced 8,500 litres of anthrax, which it unilaterally destroyed in 1991. But Iraq has still not provided the evidence that it destroyed its anthrax.
- According to Dr Blix on 27 January, 'There are strong indications that Iraq produced more anthrax than it declared, and that at least some of this was retained after the declared destruction date. It might still exist.'
- Iraq admitted to the Amorim Panel in February 1999 that it imported a significant quantity, some 650 kgs, of bacterial growth media. The quantity of media involved would be enough to produce about 5,000 litres of

concentrated anthrax. Dr Blix, 27 January: 'As part of its 7 December 2002 declaration, Iraq resubmitted the Amorim panel document, but the table showing this particular import of media was not included. The absence of this table would appear to be deliberate as the pages of the resubmitted document were renumbered.' What happened to the growth media? Why was this not reflected in the Declaration?

- According to Dr Blix, documents handed over by the Iraqis show that 6,500 fewer bombs were used by Iraq in the Iran–Iraq war than Iraq had previously declared—the amount of chemical agent in these bombs would be in the order of about 1,000 tonnes. Why has this only just come to light? What happened to these bombs, and the chemical weapons they contained?

While missing the point which I had laboured so long to formulate, namely by how much the inspection team would need strengthening, this reply conveyed valuable background statistics.

An updated assessment concerning these was delivered by Dr Blix to the UN Security Council meeting of Friday 7 March, and will be discussed later. Meanwhile it is worth drawing attention to an overlooked suggestion that at this late stage the Iraqi authorities may have been hoist by their own petard, so as now to be unable fully to document the missing materials. In the earlier-cited interview Scott Ritter remarks:

> Iraq was supposed to turn everything over to the United Nations, which would supervise its destruction and removal. Iraq instead chose to destroy unilaterally, without UN supervision—a great deal of equipment. We were later able to verify this. But the problem is that this destruction took place without documentation, which means the question of verification gets messy very quickly.

In response to a query concerning their reasons for destroying the weapons instead of turning them over, Ritter continues the interview:

> In many cases the Iraqis were trying to conceal the weapons' existence. And the unilateral destruction could have been a ruse to maintain

a cache of weapons of mass destruction by claiming they'd been destroyed.

Pitt and Rivers (2002)

If they were now to make a clean breast of these long-past, and as it turns out counter-productive, acts of concealment, then the Iraq government could yet save itself and its people from annihilation. Those who know the Arab temperament better than I do will be able to judge whether even this fate might seem preferable to so humiliating a climb-down.

BLAIR SPEAKS: ARITHMETIC OF MORALITY

Three days after I had sent the FO my original query, two things happened.

1) Over a million people marched to Hyde Park in London as a protest against a war, the largest protest rally in the country's history.

2) In Tony Blair's address to the Labour Party's spring conference in Glasgow he introduced a new concept. It has been an error to look for a single-level policy predicated on the simplistic basis of British national interest. Britain's foreign policy is, or at least will henceforth be, a double-decker. On the upper level the question is: 'what is the moral decision?' On the lower level the question is: 'what is the nationally expedient decision?' Implicitly the complete decision rule is formed as a weighted combination of the scores for the two principles of morality and legality are not always identical.

A relevant excerpt from his speech is the following;

> But the moral case against war has a moral answer, it is the moral case for removing Saddam. It is not the reason we act. That must be according to the UN mandate on weapons of mass destruction. But it is the reason, frankly, why if we do have to act, we should do so with a clear conscience.

If there are 500,000 on the march, that is still less than the number of people whose deaths Saddam has been responsible for. If there are one million, that is still less than the number of people who died in the wars he started.

Blair's utilitarian definition of morality (essentially 'the greatest good of the greatest number') invites numerical treatment. Suitable facts were indeed available.

THE NUMBERS GAME: FOOD AND WATER

The radio station Go Pacific, operating under the aegis of the US-based ABC agency, broadcast the following in its 'World Today' programme of 12 February 2003. Eleanor Hall is the 'anchor'.

Humanitarian disaster looms in Iraq: UN

Transcript (unedited):

ELEANOR HALL: Well, as the divisions continue, the United Nations is warning it's not even close to being prepared for the humanitarian crisis that will inevitably follow war in Iraq. It's just released revised predictions on the impact of a war which put the number of Iraqi people who will be in need of immediate food assistance once the fighting starts at 10,000,000. At the moment the UN has food stocks for only 250,000 people. And then there's the problem of access to water. Twelve years of sanctions have already seen at least 5,000,000 Iraqis denied access to safe water and sanitation. And the UN predicts those figures will double if critical infrastructure is damaged again.

[David Laughlin-Carr is a senior humanitarian officer at the United Nations headquarters in New York and he's been speaking to Tanya Nolan.]

DAVID LAUGHLIN-CARR: It's almost incredible that 60 per cent of the population rely solely on the food basket provided by the, the Oil for Food program. So if it was disrupted, there could be an expectation that 60 per cent of the population, that's definitely more than 10,000,000 people could in fact be, be rendered vulnerable. And basically we would have to provide the food assistance for them, during and immediately after a conflict...

TANYA NOLAN: The water supply, the supply of fresh water to Iraqis, is already very precarious. How much worse do you envisage that situation to be if there is a war?

DAVID LAUGHLIN-CARR: The water sector is considered absolutely critical, particularly in a case like Iraq with two river systems running down the middle where people are basically dependent on that. And destruction of power stations themselves would in fact place the, the purification, treatment plants in jeopardy making people basically in need for immediate provision of food, of, of water assistance. This is, this'll be very critical because as you know water is not easy to transport. It's extremely heavy. And it's a, it's a big cost item on, on any agency's budget.

> ['The World Today' is created by an independent transcription service.
> The ABC does not warrant the accuracy of the transcripts.]

> 14/02/2003 16:34:35 *The World Today*

Using the above roadmap we need to compare

(1) the expected human cost of continuing the present inspections for WMD, and

(2) the expected human cost of achieving the WMD goal by a military invasion.

Continuation of sanctions is in all scenarios currently on the table. So where do we place the 5 million people denied access to safe water and sanitation as a result of sanctions? Seemingly on both sides of the balance sheet: no motion to the UN for conditional suspension of sanctions is in preparation at the time of writing. So those 5 million people go short of drinkable water either way.

HUMANITARIAN EMERGENCY

On the 'continued inspection' side is the police-state regime of terror, torture, and executions to which Mr Blair refers. On the 'war' side of the balance are the added humanitarian costs cited in the above-quoted 'World Today' broadcast, involving at least a further five million victims and perhaps as many as ten million in the event that war leads to abandonment of the present flow of UN food aid, plus terror, torture, and executions of Northern Iraq Kurds at the hands of a US-sanctioned irruption of Turkish troops (see later).

We should add to this the possibility of the numbers escalating out of control, not for getting unplanned and unforeseen knock-on effects. For example in Gulf War 1, smoke from the burning Kuwaiti oil fields in 1991 was the cause of crop failures in the Middle East and southern Asia and a typhoon in Bangladesh killing over 100,000 people. A UN planning document, reported by BBC1 news on 21 February, envisages from a new Gulf war a possible 'humanitarian emergency beyond the UN's bounds' to address. All in all, the moral balance seemed to favour the continued inspection option—one might almost say overwhelmingly. It is the alternative that begins to look immoral. The same unequal balance was doubtless in the minds of the Archbishop of Canterbury and the Roman Catholic Archbishop of Westminster on 20 February. They took the step of issuing a joint statement expressing their deep disquiet about the 'unpredictable humanitarian and political consequences' of an attack. Charities and aid agencies, to whom one would normally look for moral evaluations, agree with them. In a letter to Blair the director of Christian Aid stated

> Your moral argument for war asserts that the long-term benefits for the people of Iraq will outweigh the short-term costs of war, but this is far from certain. War is always unpredictable—our experience in post-conflict Afghanistan teaches us that there will be significant chaos and suffering in Iraq long after military strikes have ended.

Indeed, Christian Aid's reference to the precedent of Afghanistan suggests that the moral shortfall may be a lot greater. Paul Krugman had this to say in the *Herald Tribune* of 22 February, p. 4:

> In the beginning [of the war in Afghanistan] money was no object: victory over the Taliban was as much a matter of bribes to warlords as it was of special forces and smart bombs. But Bush promised that America's interest wouldn't end once the war was won; this time we [the USA] wouldn't forget about Afghanistan, we would stay to help rebuild the country and secure the peace. So how much money for Afghan reconstruction did the administration put in its 2004 budget?
> None. The Bush team forgot about it. Embarrassed congressional staff members had to write in $300 million to cover the lapse.

TURKEY AND THE MORAL EQUATION

It gets worse. Continuing with Paul Krugman:

> Turkey has reportedly been offered the right to occupy much of Iraqi
> Kurdistan. Yes, that's right: as we move to liberate the Iraqis, our first
> step may be to deliver people who have been effectively independent
> since 1991 into the hands of a hated foreign overlord.

Indications that Krugman had it about right came in news reported in the *Herald Tribune* of 25 February, p. 4, of a plan that would allow thousands [about 60,000] of American troops to use Turkey as a base to attack Iraq, while at the same time cushion the Turkish economy from any potential shocks that a war might bring. The agreement also envisions the intervention of thousands of Turkish troops [about 40,000] into northern Iraq.

The Kurds are an ancient nomadic and mountain people, settled for some 3,000 years, including in what is now Northern Iraq. Turkey annexed this Kurdish group in 1514 and savagely put down successive rebellions, culminating in an uprising in 1925 whose 48 rebel leaders were publicly executed. During most of the time since then the Turks have fought a guerrilla war with the Kurds, with associated torture of captives and wholesale destruction of homes. The end of the Second World War saw a substantial minority of this far-flung Kurdish people included in territories contained within the state of Iraq.

In 1970 the Baath party which had come to power in Iraq in 1968, conceded the creation of an autonomous Kurdish region and gave it certain rights. 1988 saw repression against the Kurds following the Iraq–Iran war. In March Baghdad used chemical weapons against the village of Halabja. 100,000 Kurds fled to Turkey. On 5 April 1991 the United Nations adopted Resolution 688 demanding an end to repression of the Kurds and asking Baghdad to facilitate the passage of humanitarian aid.

In 1992 free elections took place in Iraqi Kurdistan, but no stable authority followed. The Democratic Party of Kurdistan (KDP) controlled the north of the region up to the Turkish border, and the Patriotic Union of Kurdistan (PUK) the south up to the Iranian border.

In 1998 the Washington Accord was concluded between the KDP and PUK on the formation of an interim parliament and government in Iraqi Kurdistan and in 2002 the leaders of the KDP and PUK signed a peace agreement, reactivating the unified parliament. This unification occurred around the time that Iraq invaded Kuwait, precipitating the first Gulf War and more miseries for the Kurds, some at the hands of the Turks.

One can conclude that anxieties felt today by Northern Iraq Kurds at the prospect of a fresh incursion of Turks are not without historical roots.

REVULSION AND RATIONALITY

In the event, the Turkish Parliament voted narrowly to defeat their leaders' motion to let the USA launch part of their invasion of Iraq from Turkish territory. A reshuffle of the Turkish cabinet is now set to reverse this outcome.

It was at just about this point at which my elastic snapped. Patient elimination of candidate reasons seemed to have come full circle. To paraphrase Maureen Dowd of the *Herald Tribune* (12.03.03, p. 7), Mr Straw wants the US to bomb a country that isn't a world record-holder for genocide and torture (like Turkey is); that didn't mastermind 9/11 (like Osama bin Laden did); that isn't resuming banned nuclear developments (like N. Korea); that isn't financing Al Qaeda (like Saudi Arabia); that isn't home to Osama and his lieutenants (like Pakistan); that isn't a host body for terrorists (like Algeria, Iran, Lebanon, and Syria). A long-growing sense of strain turned to revulsion. Had my efforts to understand Jack Straw's reasoning processes and moral evaluations been misdirected?

All the Minister's seeming contradictions would in a flash be resolved by an opposite assumption to that of informed and principled rationality. What if Jack Straw were nothing but a fawning hypocrite and liar? What if he were animated throughout by mere career advancement and the currying of favour?

Rather than rush to such an extreme, I settled for the earlier-mentioned model of the 'Rationally Assisted Minister'. It seemed to accommodate the reality of Straw's shifting positions, whereas informed rational choice did not. I decided to consider a separation between acts of choice exercised by a Minister and the prior informed reasoning carried out by his civil servants.

Thus, the back-room team reasons its way to selected options, each with its own ready-made justification consistent with the chain of past choices. If the Minister happens to know and to understand the underlying thinking, well and good. If he does not, then he'll still he OK. But his risk is greater. For suppose he only partially recalls the justifications for some of the actions taken? He may then drift into contradictions.

On Friday 7 March Hans Blix submitted his further report on the work of the UN Inspectorate to the Security Council. Its salient conclusion was that thanks to significant improvement of active cooperation from the Iraqi side since early Janurary, the systematic work of locating and destroying prohibited weapons and materials had been proceeding at a faster pace. Many large gaps remained in the record, but some had been at least partially closed. Completion would require months rather than weeks or years.

The earlier inspecting team of 1991–8 had destroyed more weapons than had been accomplished militarily by the Gulf War allies. So the Blix target did not seem unrealistic. But meanwhile a radically new foreign policy stance for Britain had been revealed on the previous day by Tony Blair during a televised debate for the music channel MTV. Even if a resolution authorizing imminent war failed to be passed by the Security Council, Britain would still join with the USA in launching a pre-emptive attack.

At the Security Council the next day Jack Straw made the threat more concrete. To avert such a consequence Iraq would have to accomplish within a further ten days the complete disarmament that the inspectorate had estimated to require months. And President Bush came on television with a terse statement that confirmed the strictly lawless goal of deposing Iraq's ruler and regime by military force.

END OF THE LINE

With such words as these was coherence finally thrown to the winds, and the United Nations Charter rubbished. As for Jack Straw's true grounds, these stood revealed as being (5) of my original list—America right or wrong. His successive utterances had all the time been no more than a knowingly crafted knitwear of misdirection and deceit. History is not kind to duplicitous toadies. What is the best, then, that Jack Straw's friends can now hope? Surely that history will draw a veil over this most inglorious of British Foreign Ministers.

Meanwhile my probings of the puppet had thrown light on the goals of the puppet-master, as perceived at least by President Assad of Syria on 10 March. Hitherto I have quoted solely from the rogue states' detractors, and in that respect could be faulted for failure to maintain a level playing field. By borrowing the words of the Syrian leader I here make some redress.

> No matter how much Iraq co-operates, the response will be, 'This is not enough,' because the goal is clear...The United States wants to secure Iraq's oil, destroy its infrastructure and redraw the regional map, not to topple a dictatorial regime in Baghdad.
>
> Int. NY Herald Tribune, 15 March, p. 4.

But the saga had one last twist to come. On Monday 17 March George Bush announced on national television an explicit abandonment of the UN route, together with a new, final, and sufficient condition for averting war. Saddam Hussein and his sons must leave Iraq within 24 hours.

In the case that Saddam does this, then the clear implication is that there's no need to disarm Iraq by military force. Additionally, by brushing past Hans Blix's pending report to the Security Council on the UN inspectorate's work due the next day, he placed a question-mark against its relevance to the USA's thinking. Perhaps Iraq's disarmament had not ever been the operative goal. Perhaps it was regime-change all along.

The apparent mismatch with President Assad's conjecture, quoted above, is not absolute.

His diagnosis can be fixed to accommodate Bush's final revelation and the possible relevance of WMD as follows:

The United States wants

- to secure Iraq's oil,
- to destroy its infrastructure,

- to destroy its presumed WMD stocks,
- to redraw the regional map,
- and, to these ends, to install a more submissive regime in Baghdad.

THE BUSH TEAM: ARE THEY MONSTERS?

The power of modern aerial weaponry is now set to reduce this Mesopotamian cradle of Western civilization to rubble, triggering levels of population displacement, thirst, disease, and malnutrition that are certain to blight the lives of millions. Are they monsters, Bush and the people around him, that can plan in cold blood so Satanic an act?

To avert a superpower atrocity will require more forceful and sustained dissent than the world's ordinary people have ever mustered before. These notes are offered in the hope of contributing to a speedy return to national sanity.

Publications

Selected Publications in Biology

1952 A new linkage in the house mouse: vestigial and Rex. *Nature*, 170, 585–586.

1953 Affinity: a new genetic phenomenon in the house mouse: evidence from distant crosses. *Nature*, 171, 26–27.

1954 Are inbred strains suitable for bio-assay? *Nature*, 173, 686–687 (with Anne McLaren).

1954 Transmigration of unborn mice. *Nature*, 174, 844 (with Anne McLaren).

1954 Factors affecting vertebral variation in mice. I. Variation within an inbred strain. *J. Embryol. Exp. Morph.*, 2, 149–160 (with Anne McLaren).

1955 Genetic and environmental influences on the secondary sex ratio in mice. *J. Genet.*, 53, 200–214 (with Alma Howard, Anne McLaren, and G. Sander).

1955 Genetical studies with "vestigial tail" mice. I. The sex difference between vestigial and Rex. *J. Genet.*, 53, 270–279.

1955 Genetical studies with "vestigial tail" mice. II. The position of vestigial in the seventh linkage group. *J. Genet.*, 53, 280–284.

1955 Genetical studies with "vestigial tail" mice. III. New independence data. *J. Genet.*, 53, 285–294.

1955 Affinity. *Proc. Roy. Soc.*, 144, 241–259.

1955 The importance of being cross-bred. In *New Biology*, No. 19, 8–69. Harmondsworth: Penguin (with Anne McLaren).

1955 Factors affecting vertebral variation in mice. II. Further evidence on intra-strain variation. *J. Embryol. Exp. Morph.*, 3, 366–375 (with Anne McLaren).

1955 Ovary grafting into the uterus. *Transpl. Bull.*, 2, 5–6 (with Anne McLaren).

1955 Factors affecting vertebral variation in mice. III. Maternal effects in reciprocal crosses. *J. Embryol. Exp. Morph.*, 4, 161–166 (with Anne McLaren).

1956 Studies on the transfer of fertilized mouse eggs to uterine foster mothers. I. Factors affecting the implantation and survival of and transferred eggs. *J. Exp. Biol.*, 33, 394–416 (with Anne McLaren).

1956 Genetical studies with "vestigial tail" mice. IV. The interaction of vestigial with brachyury. *J. Genet.*, 54, 49–53.

1956 Variability of response in experimental animals. A comparison of reactions of inbred F1 hybrid and random bred mice to a narcotic drug. *J. Genet.*, 54, 440–455 (with Anne McLaren).

1957 An experiment on "telepathy" using television. *Nature*, 180, 1402–1403 (with D. J. West).

1958 A proposed genetic analysis of the Eichwald–Silmser effect. *Transpl. Bull.*, 5, 17–18 (with Anne McLaren).

1958 Variance control in the animal house. *Nature*, 182, 77–80 (with J. D. Biggers and Anne McLaren).

1958 The third stage in genetics. In *A Century of Darwin* (ed. S. A. Barnett), London: Heinemann.

1958 The growth and development of mice in three climatic environments. *J. Exp. Biol.*, 35, 144–155 (with J. D. Biggers, M. R. Ashoub, and Anne McLaren).

1958 An effect of the uterine environment upon skeletal morphology in the mouse. *Nature*, 181, 1147–1148 (with Anne McLaren).

1958 The effect of the environment on phenotypic variability. *Proc. Roy. Soc. B*, 148, 192–203 (with M. R. Ashoub, J. D. Biggers, and Anne McLaren).

1958 Factors affecting vertebral variation in mice. IV. Experimental analysis of the uterine basis of a maternal effect. *J. Embryol. Exp. Morph.*, 6, 645–659 (with Anne McLaren).

1959 Studies on the transfer of fertilized mouse eggs to uterine foster-mothers. II. The effect of transferring large numbers of eggs. *J. Exp. Biol.*, 36, 40–50 (with Anne McLaren).

1959 The spacing of implantations in the mouse uterus. *Mem. Soc. Endocrin.*, 6, 65–75 (with Anne McLaren).

1959 Experiments with egg transfer in the mouse. *Proc. Soc. Study Fertil.*, 10, 141–149 (with Anne McLaren).

1959 Superpregnancy in the mouse. I. Implantation and foetal mortality after induced superovulation in females of various ages. *J. Exp. Biol.*, 36, 281–300 (with Anne McLaren).

1959 Superpregnancy in the mouse. II. Weight gain during pregnancy. *J. Exp. Biol.*, 36, 301–314 (with Anne McLaren).

1959 Experimental studies on placental fusion in mice. *J. Exp. Zool.*, 141, 47–73 (with Anne McLaren).

1960 Congenital runts. In *CIBA Foundation Symposium on Congenital Malformations*, pp. 178–194 (with Anne McLaren).

1960 Foetal growth in the mouse. *Proc. Roy. Soc. B*, 153, 367–379 (with M. J. R. Healy and Anne McLaren).

1960 Control of pre-natal growth in mammals. *Nature*, 187, 363–365 (with Anne McLaren).

1961 Experiments on the maternal–foetal barrier in the mouse. I. A test for the transmission of maternal erythrocytes across the mouse placenta following X-irradiation. *J. Embryol. Exp. Morph.*, 9, 618–622 (with M. Finegold).

1961 Tests on the tolerance-inducing power of lethally irradiated spleen cells. *Transpl. Bull.*, 27, 455–456 (with J. G. Howard).

1961 Splenomegaly as a host response in graft-versus-host disease. *Brit. J. Exp. Path.*, 42, 478–485 (with J. G. Howard and M. Simonsen).

1961 An investigation of immunological tolerance based on chimaera analysis. *Immunology*, 4, 413–424 (with M. F. A. Woodruff and I. M. Zeiss).

1961 Choice of animals for bio-assay. *Nature*, 190, 891–894 (with J. D. Biggers and Anne McLaren).

1961 Experiments on the maternal-foetal barrier in the mouse. II A test for the transmission of maternal serum albumin into the foetal circulation following X-irradiation. *J. Embryol. Exp. Morph.*, 9, 623–627 (with D. P. Knobel).

1962 Induction of transplantation immunity in the newborn mouse. *Transpl. Bull.*, 29, 1–6 (with J. G. Howard).

1962 Transplantation tolerance and immunity in relation to age. In *CIBA Foundation Symposium on Transplantation*, Churchill, pp. 138–153 (with J. G. Howard and M. F. A. Woodruff).

1962 Induction of specific immunological tolerance of homografts in adult mice by sublethal irradiation and injection of donor type spleen cells in high dosage. *Proc. Roy. Soc. B*, 156, 280–288. (with M. F. A. Woodruff).

1962 Transplantation tolerance and immunological immaturity. *Ann. N.Y. Acad. Sci.*, 99, 670–679 (with J. G. Howard).

1963 Specific and non-specific aspects of neonatal vaccination against graft-versus-host reaction. *Transplantation*, 1, 377–384 (with J. G. Howard).

1963 Nature of the systemic effect of litter size on gestation period. *J. Reprod. Fertil.*, 6, 139–141 (with Anne McLaren).

1963 Transplantation immunology. Chapter II of *Modern Trends in Immunology*. London: Butterworth. pp. 226–250 (with J. G. Howard).

1964 The behaviour of chromosomes during meiosis (ch. 7), 193–204. The chemical nature of the hereditary material (ch. 8), 205–215. The gene (ch.10), 245–279. In *An Introduction to Molecular Biology*, (ed. G. H. Haggis), London: Longman Green & Co.

1965 Comparison of the CAM and splenomegaly systems of graft-versus-host assay in the chick embryo. *Nature*, 208, 53–54 (with L. W. Coppleson).

1966 A quantitative study of the chorioallantoic membrane reaction in the chick embryo. *Proc. Roy. Soc. B*, 163, 555–563 (with L. W. Coppleson).

1966 A strong selective effect associated with a histocompatibility gene in the rat. *N.Y. Acad. Sci.*, 129, 88–93 (with N. F. Anderson).

1966 Party game model of biological replication. *Nature*, 212, 10–12 (with H. C. Longuet-Higgins).

1967 The biometrics of the spleen weight assay. In *Handbook of Experimental Immunology*, (ed. D. M. Weir), sec. 4, ch. 29. Oxford: Blackwell, pp. 969–987.

1968 BOXES as a model of pattern formation. In *Towards a Theoretical Biology* (ed. C. H. Waddington), Vol. 1, Edinburgh: Edinburgh University Press, pp. 206–215.

1998 Relationships between the developmental potential of human in-vitro fertilization embryos and features describing the embryo, oocyte and follicle. *Human Reproduction Update*, 4, (2), 121–134 (with R. R. Saith, A. Srinivasan, and I. L. Sargent).

Selected Publications in Computer Science

1961 Trial and error. *Science Survey*, part 2, Harmondsworth: Penguin, pp. 129–145.

1962 Puzzle learning versus game-learning in studies of behaviour. In *The Scientist Speculates* (ed. I. J. Good), London: Heinemann, pp. 90–100.

1963 Experiments on the mechanization of game learning. 1. Characterization of the model and its parameters. *Computer Journal*, 6, 232–236.

1964 High speed computing: its role in medical research. *Lancet*, 1, 33–35.

1964 Computers in medicine. *Brit. Med. J.*, 1, 203–204.

1965 Report to the Royal Society on a visit to the USSR in December 1964. *Exchange visits of Scientists between the Academy of Sciences of the USSR and the Royal Society*, London: Royal Society.

1965 *Computing Science in 1964: A Pilot Study of the State of University-based Research in the United Kingdom.* London: Science Research Council.

1966 Game-playing and game-learning automata. In *Advances in Programming and Non-numerical Computation* (ed. L. Fox), ch. 8, pp. 183–196.

1966 Experiments with the Graph Traverser program. *Proc. Roy. Soc. A*, 294, 235–259. (with J. E. Doran).

1967 Postgraduate training in machine intelligence. *Computer Bulletin*, 11, 228–234 (with J. S. Collins).

1967 Strategy-building with the Graph Traverser. In *Machine Intelligence 1* (eds. N. L. Collins and D. Michie) Edinburgh: Oliver & Boyd, pp. 135–152.

1967 Memo functions: a language feature with "rote-learning" properties. *Research Memorandum MIP-R-29*, Edinburgh: Department of Machine Intelligence & Perception.

1967 The two-armed bandit. *Research Memorandum MIP-R-31*. Edinburgh: Department of Machine Intelligence & Perception.

1968 Are game-playing heuristics useful? *ACM Sicart Newsletter*, 9, 22–23.

1968 BOXES; an experiment in adaptive control. In *Machine Intelligence* 2 (eds. E. Dale and D. Michie), Edinburgh: Oliver & Boyd, pp. 137–152 (with R. A. Chambers).

1968 A note on the measurement of heuristic power. *ACM Sicart Newsletter*, 8, 18–20.

1968 A comparison of heuristic, interactive and unaided methods of solving a shortest-route problem. In *Machine Intelligence* 3 (ed. D. Michie), Edinburgh: Edinburgh University Press, pp. 245–255 (with J. G. Fleming and J. V. Oldfield).

1968 Memo functions and machine learning. *Nature*, 218, 19–22.

1968 Application of Burstall's control routine to conversational statistics. *Research Memorandum MIP-R-39* Edinburgh: Department of Machine Intelligence and Perception (with S. Weir).

1968 Multi-POP/4120: a cheap on-line system for numerical and non-numerical computing. *Computer Bulletin*, 12, 186–189 (with J. S. Collins, A. P. Ambler, R. M. Burstall, R. D. Dunn, D. J. S. Pullin, and R. J. Popplestone).

1969 Man–machine co-operation on a learning task. In *Computer Graphics: Techniques and Applications* (eds. R. Parslow, R. Prowse, and R. Elliott Green), London: Plenum Publishing Co., pp 79–186 (with R. A. Chambers).

1969 'Local smoothing' in heuristic search. *Research Memorandum MIP-R-68*, Edinburgh: Department of Machine Intelligence and Perception.

1969 A comparison of Powell's general-purpose function optimizing algorithm with that of Hooke and Jeeves, using a real-time criterion. *Research Memorandum MIP-R-36* (revised), Edinburgh: Department of Machine Intelligence and Perception (with R. Ross).

1969 An introduction to conversational computing. *Mathematical Spectrum*, 2, 7–14.

1970 Experiments with the adaptive Graph Traverser. In *Machine Intelligence* 5 (eds. B. Meltzer and D. Michie), Edinburgh: Edinburgh University Press, pp. 301–318 (with R. Ross).

1970 Future for integrated cognitive systems. *Nature*, 228, 717–722.

1971 Tokyo–Edinburgh dialogue on robots in Artificial Intelligence research (with H. G. Barrow, R. J. Popplestone, and S. H. Salter), *Computer Journal*, 14, 91–95.

1971 Heuristic search. *Computer Journal*, 14 (1), 96.

1971 Formation and execution of plans by machine. In *Artificial Intelligence and Heuristic Programming* (eds. N. V. Findler and B. Meltzer), Edinburgh: Edinburgh University Press, pp. 101–124.

1972 G-Deduction. In *Machine Intelligence* 7 (eds. B. Meltzer and D. Michie), Edinburgh: Edinburgh University Press, pp. 141–165 (with R. Ross and G. J. Shannan).

1973 Machines and the theory of intelligence. *Nature*, 241, 507–512.

1973 Vision and manipulation as a programming problem. In *Proceedings of the First Conference on Industrial Robot Technology* (eds. T. E. Brock and H. S. Stephens), Bedford: International Fluidics Services Ltd., pp. 185–190 (with A. P. Ambler, H. G. Barrow, R. M. Burstall, R. J. Popplestone, and K. G. Turner).

1973 The Bletchley machines. In *The Origins of Digital Computers: Selected Papers* (ed. B. Randell), New York: Springer-Verlag.

1974 Some binary derivation systems. *J. Assoc. for Computing Machinery*, 21, 175–190 (with E. Sibert).

1975 Memory mechanisms and machine learning. In *Simple Nervous Systems* (eds. R. Newth and P. N. R. Usherwood), London: Edward Arnold, pp. 475–485 (with A. P. Ambler and R. Ross).

1975 Artificial intelligence in mass spectroscopy: a review of the Heuristic Dendral program. In *Computers for Spectroscopists*, (ed. R. A. G. Carrington), London: Adam Hilger, pp. 114–129 (with B. G. Buchanan).

1976 Life with intelligent machines. In *Proceedings of the Seminar on the Use of Models in the Social Sciences* (ed. L. Collins), London: Tavistock Press.

1976 Measuring the knowledge-content of programs. *Report No. UIU CD CS-R-76–786*, Urbana-Champaign: University of Illinois, Department of Computer Science.

1976 An advice-taking system for computer chess. *Computer Bull.*, ser.2, no. 10, 12–14.

1976 Bayes, Turing and the logic of corroboration. *AISB European Newsletter*, No. 23, 33–36.

1977 King and Rook against King: historical background and a problem on the infinite board. In *Advances in Computer Chess 1* (ed. M. Clarke), Edinburgh: Edinburgh University Press, pp. 30–59.

1977 A theory of advice. In *Machine Intelligence 8* (eds. E. W. Elcock and D. Michie), Chichester: Ellis Horwood; New York: John Wiley, pp 131–168.

1977 Improved resolution of a form of Mackie's paradox. *Firbush News 8*, (with I. J. Good).

1978 Pattern-based representation of chess end-game knowledge. *Computer Journal*, 21, (with I. Bratko and D. Kopec).

1979 Memory trick for infeasible computations. *Research Memorandum MIP-R-122*, Edinburgh: Department of Machine Intelligence.

1979 Machine models of perceptual and intellectual skills. In *Scientific Models and Man: the 1976 Herbert Spencer Lectures* (ed. H. Harris), Oxford: Oxford University Press, pp. 56–79.

1980 Expert Systems. *Computer Journal*, 23 (4), 369–376.

1980 Social aspects of artificial intelligence. In *Micro-electronics and Society* (ed. T. V. Jones), Milton Keynes: Open University.

1980 Chess with computers. *Interdisciplinary Science Reviews*, 5 (3), 215–227.

1980 A representation for pattern-knowledge in chess endgames. In *Advances in Computer Chess* 2 (ed. M. Clarke), Edinburgh: Edinburgh University Press, pp. 31–56 (with I. Bratko).

1980 An advice program for a complex chess programming task. *Computer Journal*, 23 (4), 353–359 (with I. Bratko).

1981 Oddities of complexity. *AISB Quarterly*, 40–41 Spring/Summer, pp. 23–25.

1981 A theory of evaluative comments in chess, with a note on minimaxing. *Computer Journal*, 24, 278–286.

1981 High-road and low-road programs. *AI Magazine*, 3 (1), 21–22.

1982 Experiments on the mechanization of game-learning. 2. Rule-based learning and the human window. *Computer Journal*, 25, 105–113.

1982 Computer chess and the humanisation of technology. *Nature*, 299, 391–394.

1982 Measuring the knowledge-content of expert programs. *Bull. of the Inst. of Mathematics and its Applicns*, 18 (11/12), 216–220.

1982 Information and complexity in chess. In *Computer Chess 3* (ed. M. R. B. Clarke), pp. 139–143, Oxford: Pergamon.

1982 'Mind-like' capabilities in computers: a note on computer induction. *Cognition*, 12(1), 97–108.

1983 Mismatch between machine representations and human concepts. Dangers and remedies. *FAST series Report No. 9.* (EUR 8426), Brussels: Commission of the European Communities (with D. Kopec).

1983 Game-playing programs and the conceptual interface. In *Computer Game-Playing*, (ed. M. Bramer), Chichester: Ellis Horwood.

1984 Automating the synthesis of expert knowledge. *ASLIB Proceedings*, 36 (9), 337–343.

1984 Towards learning plans and programs using computer induction. *Technical Report*, IBM Corporation Los Angeles Scientific Center, August 16 (with R. Dechter).

1985 Steps towards robot intelligence. *Proceedings of the Royal Institution*, 57, 151–165.

1985 Advances in knowledge engineering. In *Handbook of Information Technology and Office Systems*, New York: North-Holland.

1985 EX-TRAN 7: a different approach for an expert system generator. *Expert Systems and their Applications: 5th International Workshop*, Avignon, 1, pp. 153–170 (with T. Hassan, M. A. Razzak, and R. Pettipher).

1985 Expert systems and robotics. In *Handbook of Industrial Robotics* (ed. S.-Y. Nof), New York: M. A. Razzak, Wiley, pp. 419–436.

1986 Computer chess. In *Oxford Companion to the Mind* (ed. R. L. Gregory), Oxford: Oxford University Press, pp 155–157.

1986 Towards a knowledge accelerator. In *Advances in Computer Chess 4* (ed D. F. Beal), Oxford: Pergamon, pp. 1–7

1986 A self-commenting facility for inductively synthesised endgame expertise. In *Advances in Computer Chess 4* (ed D. F. Beal), Oxford: Pergamon, pp. 147–165 (with A. Shapiro).

1986 The superarticulacy phenomenon in the context of software manufacture. *Proc. Roy. Soc. A*, 405, 185–212.

1986 Case studies of building expert systems using Ex-Tran. In *Proc.Conf. Artificial Intelligence and Advanced Computer Technology*, Wiesbaden (with M. A. Razzak, T. Hassan, and A. Ahmad). Liphook: TCM Expositions.

1987 Ideas on knowledge synthesis stemming from the KBBKN endgame. *ICCA Journal*, 10 (1), 3–13 (with I. Bratko).

1987 Current developments in expert systems. In *Applications of Expert Systems*, Vol. 1 (ed J. R. Quinlan), New York: Addison-Wesley, pp. 137–156.

1988 Rulemaster: a second-generation knowledge engineering facility. In *Microcomputer-based Expert Systems*, pp. 182–188, IEEE Press (with S. Muggleton, C. Riese, and S. Zubrick).

1988 The Fifth Generation's unbridged gap. In *The Universal Turing Machine: A Half-Century Survey* (ed. R. Herken), Berlin: Kammerer & Unverzagt, also Oxford University Press, pp. 467–489.

1988 Generating expert rules from examples in Prolog. In *Machine Intelligence 11* (eds. J. E. Hayes, D. Michie, and J. Richards), Oxford: Oxford University Press, pp. 289–304, (with B. Arbab).

1988 Machine learning in the next five years. *Proc. Third European Working Session on Learning (EWSL)*, (ed. D. H. Sleeman), London: Pitman, pp. 107–122.

1989 Problems of computer-aided concept formation. In *Applications of Expert Systems*, Vol. 2 (ed. J. R. Quinlan), New York: Addison-Wesley, pp. 310–333.

1989 New commercial opportunities using information technology. *Knowledge-based Systems: Third Internat. Congr.*

1989 Brute force in chess and science. *ICCA Journal*, 12 (3), 127–143 (also in Marsland and Schaeffer (1990), see below).

1989 The Turing Institute: an experiment in co-operation. *Interdisciplinary Science Reviews*, 14 (2), 117–119.

1989 Application of machine learning to recognition and control. In *Science & Technology No. 5*, University of Wales, pp. 23–28.

1989 An experimental comparison of human and machine learning formalisms. In *Proc. Sixth Internat. Workshop on Machine Learning* (ed. A. Segre), San Mateo, CA Morgan Kaufmann, pp. 113–118, (with S. H. Muggleton, M. Bain, and J. E. Hayes Michie).

1989 Machines that learn and machines that teach. *Proc. Second Scand. Conf. on Art. Intell. (SCAI '89)*, Tampere, Finland, pp. 2–26 (with M. Bain).

1989 Learning by teaching. *Proc. Second Scand. Conf. on Art. Intell. (SCAI '89)*, Tampere, Finland, pp. 413–436 (with A. Paterson and J. E. Hayes).

1990 Personal models of rationality. *J. Statist. Planning and Inference*, Special Issue on Foundations and Philosophy of Probability and Statistics, 21, 381–399.

1990 Machine executable skills from "silent" brains. In *Research and Development in Expert Systems VII*, pp. 1–24, Cambridge: Cambridge University Press (for the British Computer Society).

1990 Human and machine learning of descriptive concepts. *ICOT Journal*, March, pp. 11–20.

1990 Brute force in chess and science. In *Computers Chess, and Cognition* (eds. T. A. Marsland and J. Schaeffer), New York: Springer, pp. 82–111.

1990 Cognitive models from subcognitive skills. In *Knowledge-based Systems in Industrial Control* (ed. M. Grimble, S. McGhee, and P. Mowforth), Stevenage: Peter Peregrinus, pp. 71–99, (with M. Bain and J. E. Hayes Michie).

1991 Use of sequential Bayes with class probability trees. In *Machine Intelligence* 12 (eds. J. E. Hayes, D. Michie, and E. Tyugu), Oxford: Oxford University Press, pp. 187–202 (with A. Al-Attar).

1991 Machine intelligence and the human window. *Applied Artificial Intell.*, 5, 1–10.

1991 Expert systems: the end of the beginning. *AI and Society* (Springer International), 5, 142–147.

1991 Experiments in rule-based control: beyond the neural paradigm for machine learning. In *Proc. Japan Soc. AI* (ed. K. Murakami), Tokyo.

1991 Controlling a "black box" simulation of a space craft. *AI Magazine*, 12, 56–63, (with C. Sammut).

1991 Methodologies for machine learning in data analysis and software. *Computer Journal*, 34, 559–565.

1992 Machine acquisition of concepts from sample data. In *Intelligent Tutoring Systems* (ed. D. Kopec), Chichester: Ellis Horwood, pp. 1–27 (with M. Bain).

1992 Learning to fly. In *Proc 9th Internat. Machine Learning Conf. (ML92)*, (ed. D.H. Sleeman), San Mateo, CA: Morgan Kaufmann (with C. Sammut, S. Hurst, and D. Kedzier).

1993 Turing's Test and conscious thought, *Artificial Intelligence*, 60 (10), 1–22. Reprinted as Chapter 2 of *Machines and Thought. Vol. 1* (eds. P. J. R. Millican and A. Clark), Oxford: Oxford University Press, pp. 27–51, 1996.

1993 Knowledge, learning and machine intelligence. In *Intelligent Systems Concepts and Applications* (ed. L. S. Sterling). New York: Plenum Publishing Corp., pp. 1–9.

1994 Building symbolic representations of intuitive real-time skills from performance data. In *Machine Intelligence 13* (eds. K. Furukawa, D. Michie, and S. Muggleton), Oxford: Oxford University Press, pp. 385–418 (with R. Camacho).

1994 Machine learning of rules and trees. In *Machine Learning, Neural and Statistical Classification* (eds. D. Michie, D. J. Spiegelhalter, and C. C. Taylor), Chichester: Ellis Horwood, pp. 50–83 (with C. Feng).

1994 Consciousness as an engineering issue, Part 1. *Journal of Consciousness Studies*, 1 (2), 182–95.

1995 Problem decomposition and the learning of skills. In *Machine Learning: ECML-95*, Lecture Notes in Artificial Intelligence, 912 (eds. N. Lavrac and S. Wrobel), Berlin, Heidelberg, New York: Springer Verlag, pp. 17–31.

1995 Consciousness as an engineering issue, Part 2. *Journal of Consciousness Studies*, 2 (1), 52–66.

1995 Game mastery and intelligence. In *Machine Intelligence 14* (eds. K. Furukawa, D. Michie, and S. Muggleton), Oxford: Oxford University Press, pp. 3–27.

1995 Behavioural clones and cognitive skill models. In *Machine Intelligence 14*, (eds K. Furukawa, D. Michie, and S. Muggleton), Oxford: Oxford University Press pp. 387–395, (with C. Sammut).

1995 "Strong AI": an adolescent disorder. *Informatica*, 19, 461–468. Reprinted as Chapter 1 of *Mind versus Computer* (eds. M. Gams, M. Paprzycki, and X. Wu) Amsterdam: IOS Press, 1997, pp. 1–8.

1997 AI and the information society. *Engin. Sci and Educ. Jour.*, February, pp. 4–8.

1997 Simulator-mediated acquisition of a dynamic control skill. *Proc. IFAC Conf. on Automated Systems Based on Human Skill* (with J. E. Hayes Michie) pp. 17–21.

1997 Machine intelligibility and the duality principle. *BT Technol. J.*, 14 (4) (with S. Muggleton). Reprinted in *Software Agents and Soft Computing, Lecture Notes in Artificial Intelligence* 1198 (eds. H. S. Nwana and N. Azarmi), New York: Springer, pp. 277–299.

1998 Learning concepts from data. In *Expert Systems with Applications*. London: Elsevier Science Ltd.

2000. It takes Two (at least) to Tango. *Electronic Transactions in Artificial Intelligence*, 4-B, pp. 1–19.

2001 Return of the imitation game. *Electronic Transactions in Artificial Intelligence*, 5-B, pp. 203–221.

2002 Colossus and the breaking of the wartime "Fish" codes. *Cryptologia*, 24 (1), 17–58.

Books

1964 *Introduction to Molecular Biology*, New York: John Wiley (with G. H. Haggis, A. R. Muir, K. M. Roberts, and P. M. B. Walker).

1967–2001 *Machine Intelligence* (editor, or co-editor), vols 1–18.

1968 *Computer Programming for Schools: First Steps in Algol*, Edinburgh: Oliver & Boyd (with A. Ortony and R. M. Burstall).

1974 *On Machine Intelligencem*, Edinburgh: Edinburgh University Press; New York: John Wiley.

1982 *Machine Intelligence and Related Topics*, London and New York: Gordon and Breach.

1984 *The Creative Computer*, Harmondsworth: Viking (with R. Johnston). Pelican edition released in 1985.

1986 *On Machine Intelligence* (2nd ed., revised and expanded), Chichester: Ellis Horwood.

Web Links

General Report on Tunny 1945 (with I. J Good and G. Timms). See: http://www.Alan-Turing.net/tunny_report

The Newman Digital Archive. See: http://www.cdpa.co.uk/Newman/

"The Lighthill Report". See: http://www.chilton-computing.org.uk/inf/literature/reports/lighthill_report/overview.htm

The BBC Lighthill Controversy Debate. See: http://www.aiai.ed.ac.uk/events/lighthill1973/

Recollections of early AI in Britain 1942–1965. See: http://www.aiai.ed.ac.uk/events/ccs2002/

Mechanization of Thought: Early Edinburgh Adventures. See: http://www.inf.ed.ac.uk/events/jamboree/2007/

Index